The death of a woman

Jane Hollister Wheelwright

in collaboration with Eleanor Haas,
Barbara McClintock, and Audrey Blodgett

ST. MARTIN'S PRESS, NEW YORK

The death of a woman *was edited and prepared for publication at*
The Yolla Bolly Press, Covelo, California, during the spring and fall
of 1980 under the supervision of James and Carolyn Robertson.
Staff: Diana Fairbanks and Barbara Youngblood.

LIBRARY OF CONGRESS CATALOGING IN PUBLICATION DATA

Wheelwright, Jane.
  The death of a woman.

1. Cancer — Patients — Biography. 2. Cancer —
Psychological aspects. 3. Death — Psychological aspects.
4. Women — Psychology. I. Title.
RC262.W47   155.9'37   80-24686
ISBN 0-312-18744-0

EXPLANATION OF DREAM SYMBOLS

Half-title page Adapted from a pre-Columbian seal. In some ancient
cultures people believed they were led to death by a dog. The Mayans
believed that yellow dogs were guides to death.

Title page The ancient lunar cat goddess, Bast, who was worshiped
as a symbol of consciousness, light, and healing, is a feminine symbol.

Page 275 Jung believed that the tree symbolized the regenerative,
unconscious life, which stands eternally when human consciousness is
snuffed out.

IN RECENT years public interest has increased concerning death and especially death from cancer. This book offers a new perspective on the subject: that of a Jungian analyst who recorded the dreams of a dying cancer patient and interpreted them in the light of the depth psychology of C. G. Jung. What seems to me the book's very special merit is its integrity; in no way does it claim spectacular success nor does it cover up the tragic facts. Moreover, it does not give death a falsely sentimental glory or hopeless horror. It is through and through honest — relying on the actual facts.

This work reveals, in a most impressive way, the slow, essential transformation which the soul, the unconscious psyche, experiences when death is imminent. The infinite devotion and patience of the analyst and the courageous truthfulness of the patient make it a most moving *document humain*. We can see here how slowly — and nearly imperceptibly — but surely the unconscious prepares us for death and helps us to make unbearable suffering bearable. Even the worst suffering, Jung said, becomes bearable if we can see its meaning.

In an age when death has been glorified, or more often shamefully "covered up," the dreams, such as those recorded in this work, bring us back to the basic truths of our instincts, to the realization that life and death are but two facets of *one* mystery, which Jung called the process of individuation. This process is still in large part unknown to us; it probably takes place in all of us but reveals its meaning only when we attend to it consciously.

This document will, in my opinion, not only help people who suffer from a similar condition and their friends, but "put right" in all of us some of our fears and wrong attitudes toward death.

Marie-Louise von Franz
June 1980

T HIS book is a factual and, as conscientiously as possible, a faithful account of my analytical work with a woman — whom I shall call Sally — who in her own heroine's way faced death by cancer.

Sally died in the early sixties; and the first draft of this book was written over ten years ago. Since then death and dying, once psychologically taboo subjects, have become popular concerns within the psychotherapeutic community specifically and among younger generations in general. The significant attitudinal changes toward death now impel me to expand for her and for the public my original account written in the late 1960s.

Only within the last decade has there been a widely recognized effort among psychotherapists to help terminally ill patients face death and to be psychically up to date when they die. When I began working with Sally, I proceeded on the assumption, however "unprofessional," that my guess was as good as anyone's. I worked with dying patients, and especially with Sally, in a way that seemed most comfortable to both of us. To do so, I discarded some of the stance and techniques of conventional psychotherapy. I felt that working with her would require an unusual commitment on my part. It would require personal concern and a willingness to give and take, to share interests as they touched on her life, and to give more theoretical explanations as she asked for them than I normally would.

As Jung's patient and student years ago, I was influenced by his idea of individuation and associated it not only with crises in our lifetimes but also as the key to death. Jung used the term, individuation, to describe the developmental process in adults by which an individual comes to recognize one's individuality in relation to the whole range of human life, learning to accept the paradox of uniqueness on the one hand and complete participation in the collective human experience on the other. Jung noted that those who are "stuck" developmentally are especially vulnerable to cancer. I learned in my old age to give my individuation precedence, and in this way to deal with the fear of death. This idea became the spearhead of my work with Sally.

To help her with the process of individuation, I worked in my own way with many of Jung's ideas as well as my own, making use of Sally's dreams, fantasies, and active imagination to interest her in the neglected, unexamined aspects of her psyche which are usually manifest in unconscious material. Jung conceived of the unconscious as including not only the personal contents of one's lifetime but primordial, archetypal images — those universal, collective motifs which we find in mythologies and religions of all cultures. Taking my clues from her unconscious material as it arose in our sessions together, I attempted to assume the voice of the disowned aspects of her personality so that Sally might begin to experience the tension of the opposites in her psyche. By doing so, Sally might come to accept her own transforming symbol for perennial life which could ease her struggle with death.

In the years since Sally's death I have become increasingly convinced that a woman therapist is of special value to the terminally ill patient. The need to go back to the mother, to solve the mother problem — if there is one — and the need to find the ideal inner woman in symbol and image are especially pressing for those who are dying and may be better served by a woman's help. During my work with Sally I did not take seriously enough the importance of the women in Sally's dreams nor her nocturnal cries for Mother, perhaps because I was not yet fully aware of my own importance as a *woman* in Sally's life. Death is in the province of the archetype of the female deity (great mother*), and a woman therapist may carry this projection better than a man. In mulling over my work with Sally, I am more and more inclined to believe that death needs a woman on the scene.

My work with Sally developed quickly into a kind of mutual research project. I needed to know about death for professional reasons and because I was already in my sixties and more consciously anticipating my own death. My client, desperately trying to find meaning in her sad plight and having had no one to consult, made up for my lack of experience by testing and querying me at every turn. No guidelines were available for either Sally or me, and we had to proceed in a trial-and-error fashion. From our very first visit I was convinced that our work together would be more helpful to her than her efforts in struggling alone. And certainly she would help me to face that greatest mystery of life, which is death.

I agreed to see Sally in her own home, and to charge a minimal fee or none at all, and I planned within myself to answer to her needs as fully as possible regardless of the time required. I was in a position to do this because I worked only part time professionally. I was more free to be available at odd times of the day than my colleagues who worked full time and had families to support. Also, it was important that Sally, so painfully aware of her financial burden to the family, not incur additional expenses.

I read extensively on the subject of cancer before and during my work with Sally. One theory I read was that bereavement — the loss of someone close or some necessary aspect of life — can cause cancer. I found this logical. Sally had suffered a sense of loss all her life. Although she was outwardly active, and her activity was in a way productive, it was mainly a desperate effort to escape living in a state of constant disappointment about the limitations she felt imposed upon her as a woman.

I read many medical reports and found little I could use. But one small book, *Living With Cancer* by Edna Kaehele, impressed me. The author, whose life situation was almost identical to Sally's, had been ill for many years. She had been given up as hopeless several times and finally was sent home from the hospital to die. She recounts the experience of looking at herself in the mirror and seeing the skeleton she had become. At the same time, however, she was aware of her self being very much there. She wrote, "If this divestiture of the flesh cannot alter the inner life — can anything? Can time? Can eternity? You know finally, simply, and irrefutably that you exist independent of this flesh; that you will continue to exist as an independent entity through aeons of changing matter." From that day on, she improved and six years later wrote her story. I suppose one could say that she was at last ready to let her body go because she had

experienced her spirit self. Apparently she had been too
dependent on or stuck in her body.

As my work with Sally began, I tried to find in myself an
awareness of my reactions, thoughts, and speculations, hoping to determine some new approaches to her terminal illness. To do this, I had to approach the problem in what I
felt to be my way, woman's way — one woman's way, at
least. I had to dare to trust my subjective feelings of what
transpired between Sally and me. I allowed a more personal
relationship to develop with Sally than is normal in analysis.
Professional critics might label this involvement "counter-
transference"* (the asterisk indicates a glossary definition).
I can only argue that our relationship worked well, possibly
because I relied on my own integrity and consciousness and
on the maturity that Sally had gained during seven years of
illness. Had I worked with Sally in more conventional ways,
problems might have arisen from suppression of my own
natural, female self in connection with her as a woman.
They, being denied under pressure of so serious a case,
could have sought an unconscious outlet via projection,*
creating a destructive counter-transference, which could
have been a burden to her. She might, for instance, have
felt that she must get well for my sake. Functioning as I did,
I could admit at times that I was prejudiced toward her
recovering.

Perhaps the most serious obstacle to a nearly ideal
arrangement for Sally and me was that I would be going
away on two trips with my husband during the six months
following our first meeting. In those days I had already
solved for myself the dilemma in which many professional
women find themselves — how to order one's professional
and family lives. I had made a clear decision that if a con-

flict arose between the two, I would put my family commitments first. For most patients in my practice my absences were invariably a benefit, enabling them to discover their independence. For Sally my absences, especially the first and longer one, were probably unfortunate, in spite of the attendance of a concerned and very sympathetic colleague, Sally's and my correspondence by mail, and her knowledge of my plans at the outset of the analysis. My being away did, in the end, seem to set her back, although I could not be sure that her regression was not because of the advanced stage of her disease.

In spite of her regression during my absences, there was a benefit in our separations. It was essential that she keep an intimate connection with her husband. Had I been with her throughout, he might have drifted away, unable to bear the enormous burden of her illness. Being a sensation type, Sally could not gain insight in an isolated vacuum on those days when we did not meet. She had to feel that her husband was available and had to relate to the family around her as a living, concerned, and concrete context of relationship. Finally, I felt better about our separations as I saw her marriage become a central motif in her unconscious material.

After Sally was gone, I discovered that her material had been left to me: she was reaffirming her wish that she had expressed to me many times that I transmit whatever I could of our work together to others, in the hopes that cancer victims and their families might not suffer as she and her family had. The letters I wrote to her were tied up with a pink ribbon. Her drawings were carefully dated and in order. The message was clear. I proceeded to put together the material I had gathered. For my own use, immediately after each interview and phone call, I had recorded everything I could remember that had transpired between us; I would pull off to the side of the road and write down whatever came to my mind about the interview. By the time I had reached my own house, some miles away, I had as complete a record as one could have without having taken notes during the interview or using a tape recorder.

Later, I persuaded Eleanor Haas to be the coauthor of this book. We composed the story from my records and amplified it with subjective reactions and conclusions, which for various reasons I had not communicated to Sally during the interviews. Eleanor wrote the story out of this mass of material.

Audrey Blodgett, a student of mine, researched the Jungian literature and formulated the definitions of words that appear in the glossary. These words, when they first appear in the text, will be indicated by an asterisk (*). These terms had come up in my interviews with Sally. They were important to her because of her intellectual bias and her need to understand the terms that came up in the books that she read on Jungian psychology. I hope the glossary performs a similar function for the reader.

The final editing, a major undertaking, was done by Barbara McClintock.

I want to warn the reader, before launching into the step-by-step account of Sally's last six months of life, not to expect this book to be an authoritative statement on Jungian analysis. It is one analyst's account of one person's analysis at a specific time and place and under specific circumstances. Should readers subscribe to my conclusions, I would hope they do so advisedly.

A note about Sally's family: I had the greatest respect and admiration for each member of the family. They, like Sally, were living in a desperately difficult situation. Jung makes the comment that dying is not hardest on the one dying but on those being left behind. I agree with him, and for this family it was more than true. The terminally ill often lose control; negative, destructive elements from the psyche get loose if the darkness has not been dealt with. At these times those closest to the one dying are sometimes under fire. Sally worked hard to keep from falling into such critical, dark moods but was not always successful. The family, therefore, underwent some harsh criticism from her that was not deserved; their forbearance touched me deeply.

Jane Hollister Wheelwright
February 1980

D RIVING slowly that hot July day, my car's first gear straining, I climbed upward along a narrow, steep road of a hill town above San Francisco Bay. I peered out of the car window at a corner street sign, half hidden by overgrown shrubs — still not the one I had written on a scrap of paper. I drove on.

I wondered what had prompted me to make another first visit to someone who might be dying. A psychoanalyst friend of my husband had called a few days before, saying that he had heard of my work with cancer patients. Could I possibly take on another one? This young woman, his friend, was now barely ambulatory and could not leave her house by herself. She was intelligent and artistic, he told me, and was articulately committed to life.

He described for me her physical good looks of four years before. Her body had been her best friend. Her hair was thick, chestnut colored, curling close to her face, which was broad from one cheekbone to the other, not pretty but arresting, especially the vibrant, intelligent eyes and the pleasurable mouth. Her friend sadly told me that her husband had loved her looks.

Now nothing mattered to her because her total reality had become suffering. Her screams of terror and pain during the night upset her anxious family. Except for frequent rages at her husband, she turned her despair inward and was now constantly depressed. She had never had any psychotherapy and in fact had always been skeptical of its value for anyone. She thought it foolish when she would probably die soon anyway to try to make a better adjustment to life—a waste of everyone's time and money. But she didn't know how she could bear living between now and the end, whenever that might be. Couldn't I help?

It was hard not to be drawn to answer this kind of plea. My recent experiences with dying people have shown me that I can maintain a close connection with someone who is terminally ill and perhaps even ease the way. But even one or two visits a week is an exhausting business. The issues surrounding death can be so powerful that to stay in contact with someone immediately faced with them can be nearly overwhelming. My stamina, never noteworthy, becomes more limited as I grow older; and lately, because of my increasing need for rest and reflection, I've found it necessary to turn prospective patients away. Besides, I have committed myself to my husband for several trips throughout the year, some of them to last as long as six weeks; separation would be an added source of pain for a dying person. On the other hand, few therapists are either able or willing to visit dying people at their homes on a regular basis. Still, considering my need to curtail my activity, why did I tell the psychoanalyst I would see this friend of his, whose street seems so difficult to find? I pulled over to the side of the road and stopped to think about it.

It is a well-established tenet of Jungian psychology that, in considering the analysis of a new patient, the analyst explore those personal experiences and biases or prejudices which will surely be brought to bear on the case in point. As I sat in the car under the shade of a tree, I found myself reflecting on those aspects of my own life which seemed to be drawing me to Sally. Death has been pushing painfully close to me in the past few years. It claimed my father and mother; Dr. Jung, who was my analyst; later a brother; and soon after a sister-in-law in whose dying process I participated. Those were difficult losses to sustain. My dreams have been full of narrow escapes from death — my own.

Whenever something touches me, I need to find out everything I can about it and to examine it most carefully. I have always chosen patients whose concerns especially resonate with my own at the time, because I've found that a mutual concern can be the medium in analysis for an opening up — a shedding of light — in both of us. So in this case I must still need to know much more about death.

I remembered my sister-in-law who had died of cancer. Our contact, once based on a familial social exchange, deepened when she shared with me her dreams and feelings about what was happening to her as she lay ill. Her situation saddened me and so did our having to say goodbye to each other. I'm sure she was aware of my feelings, but I also believe that my rational, dispassionate attitude made it easier for her to express her dark, fearful thoughts to me. She didn't have to worry that my feelings were too sensitive to bear them.

I looked at my watch. It was still early; unknowingly I had probably given myself time for these reflections. What had come next? My work with Jennifer, the young dental hygienist who eventually died of cancer. What complicated, impressive dreams and so many frightening nightmares had come from a young woman whose outer concerns seemed so

17

superficial! The dreams seemed to be compensating for her lack of education and experience, for her constricted attitude toward life. Sometimes they seemed bent on shocking her into accepting the inevitability of her situation. From her I learned much more about what people need when they are dying and how to help them, but her death evoked some speculations that were new for me. Surely in death the body goes, and the mind; but on another level, the level of dreams, there is the suggestion that death is a transitional phenomenon.

No orthodox religion offers me certainty about what happens in death and afterward. My own analytical work and my work with others have indicated a path, a line of inquiry to follow. I have lived a long life and as I help someone else, I continue to seek answers to questions that may never be answered.

Sally and I had made our first contact by telephone. Her voice then had sounded flat, with little affect. I told her immediately that before she decided to have me come out for the first interview, she must know that at times for family reasons I would be away traveling for perhaps as long as six weeks. She asked me to come anyway; she felt she had no choice and would have to take me in spite of that.

So be it. I started the car and continued up the hill. The next corner was clearly marked by a sign reading "Manzanita," Sally's street. I turned left as she had instructed and, five houses down on the right, I parked in front of her brown-shingled house.

CHAPTER TWO

I STEPPED over large, rough stones that became a path to the front door, a path edged by a cracked earth border of dying plants. Everything in the garden looked thirsty; even a cement form of an animal—on closer look, a dolphin—seemed bone dry. I knocked on the door and stood waiting for what seemed an unusually long time. Finally the door opened, and I saw Sally for the first time— her chalky, thin face; darkly encircled, lackluster eyes; a down-turned mouth; scrawny neck; a head of new, baby-fine, straight hair. I got a sense of her fragile body under her long, limp robe: one strangely anomalous breast, an old woman's abdomen, and skinny hips.

"You must be Mrs. Wheelwright. Come in, I've been expecting you."

I followed her as she made her way from the entry hall to the living room; it was a distance of only a few yards, but I could see how slowly she moved, with a limp that seemed to favor her right thigh. She sat down next to a telephone on the couch and rested a thin hand on the receiver.

"At least I can man the phone."

I sat in a comfortable chair opposite her, next to a stone fireplace. On its wooden mantel was a clay pot containing a variety of dried weeds and grasses, probably placed there long before. There were photographs and paintings on the walls (I recognized a Bufano serigraph of a cat), ceramic pots, ashtrays, paperbacks, and magazines on the tables. The room was large, shaded by redwood trees outside the narrow windows, and lined with dark redwood paneling that kept it cool. Low book-filled cases stretched across two walls; a worn and faded Oriental rug covered most of the hardwood floor. There was a vintage upright piano against the wall near the large wood-paneled dining room. My immediate impression was of a rambling old-fashioned home, spacious enough to assimilate neglect.

I sensed that Sally had been appraising me as I made my observations. I must have turned back to her expectantly because she leaned forward on the couch and in a slightly superficial tone began to tell me the history of her illness. Seven years before she had first detected cancer of the breast. The first operation occurred at that time. Three years later her ovaries were removed. Cancer of the bone was found, after that, followed by an operation from which her doctors didn't expect her to recover. Then, serially: chemotherapy, improvement, crippling, the need for a wheel chair, debilitation, hospitalization, more chemotherapy, baldness, depression, improvement, debilitation, hospitalization, chemotherapy that included prednisone, improvement. Now, although less crippled than she had been two years before, she had become inundated with negative feelings about everything. She existed in a state of continual distress and could do nothing about it; the constant pain in her head and her back and hips intensified these feelings; lately out of nowhere she was experiencing frightening premonitions of insanity.

With a sudden movement she reached for the box of

cigarettes lying on a stack of plastic-jacketed library books. She drew out a cigarette. lighted it, inhaled and exhaled the smoke with agitation. I was taken aback at her deliberate self-destructiveness but said nothing.

"My doctors have prolonged my life. Wonderful. Now they don't know what to do with the rest of it and neither do I. The mind is geared to a normal course of illness, not a prolongation of it. No wonder I'm nearly out of my mind! When I think of the end part, the nose tubes and all the rest, I get terrified. I'll kill myself if it comes to that."

Her voice was no longer superficial and disconnected from her feeling. When Sally and I first met, she must have thought that no one living outside her isolated world could possibly understand her serious state of mind. Perhaps she quickly sensed that I was someone who had seen enough grief to be able to understand hers, and she could be herself.

Sally continued, "Besides, the doctors tell you nothing. I want to know more about what's happening to me, and they ignore my questions as if I were incapable of understanding. They make me feel as though I were nothing more than a piece of broken-down machinery. If I were to tell them how I feel, they wouldn't even hear me."

She was angry—at her doctors for their evasive replies to her questions; at her husband for his separateness from her; at her friends with whom it was now difficult to connect; at C. S. Lewis, who recommended in one of his books that a person in pain set an example of courage and character for others; at her mother, "a zero"; and mother-in-law ("I hate Thelma"), who imprisoned and controlled her. Yet she knew her doctors were doing all they could; that Jim worked hard and was loyal and helpful to her in her illness; that her mother and mother-in-law, who took turns every few weeks

21

running the household, were good with the children and did their best.

"I know how insensitive some doctors can be. It must be awfully hard to take."

"Of course it's hard to take. It's infuriating!"

Until two months earlier Sally's inner resources had been intact, but now dark feelings plagued her incessantly and made her feel inferior. She wanted to die. She was no longer a religious person; she had lost most of her faith in God during her childhood. But occasionally she had experienced the feeling that life goes on eternally, beyond space and time. She was ambivalent about death.

"Sometimes I dream of a white boat gliding across the water. It's death coming for me. I want to get on that boat and at the same time I don't want to."

"Do you often dream, Sally?"

"Very rarely. When I do have dreams, I hardly ever remember them. Come to think of it, though, I did have a dream when I was in the hospital. It was about my childhood friend, Carla, who's been so helpful to me through all of this. She's my closest friend, but she's also very beautiful, and sometimes I'm jealous of her. In my dream she came to me when I was dying and frightened; she held me warmly in her arms."

She paused, looked away from me and seemed embarrassed. Her voice softened, "The embrace made me happy and brought me back to life."

I reflected for a moment on the fact that when she was totally desolate, a woman appeared in her dream.

"Perhaps together with your friend you became a whole person."

For the first time in the interview she relaxed and smiled,

although she obviously didn't understand my comment. I
had an intimation then of how attractive her face might
once have been. The bones were prominent; the hazel eyes
that regarded me steadily were set wide apart; the mouth
was generous and sensual. She leaned back and spoke more
slowly.

"But I was out of character in the dream because actually
I'm very reserved and not demonstrative like that."

I wanted to know more about her dark thoughts. I knew
they were probably intensified by the present circumstances
of her life, but I also suspected that they had been with her
at times before the illness. When I questioned her, her
response was immediate, definite.

"Oh, yes. I've been troubled with miserable spells of
depression ever since I can remember. And when I'm in
one, I feel totally worthless."

"I don't know anyone who doesn't feel that way at times,
Sally. It seems to be an inevitable part of living. But apparently you couldn't accept that feeling when you were well
either. How did you manage then?"

"By throwing myself into an absolute fury of activity.
More projects, more politics, more difficult music, more
friends over. And eventually the depression would pass."

"Well, that's certainly a way out, but did you ever stop to
think that depressions carry messages with them? If they're
worked off in the way you describe, those messages can't
come through."

"I wonder if that's true. I never stopped to think of anything during those times."

She went on to tell me that she had always been an
organized, energetic, excessively efficient person, active at
home and in the world. She had much preferred working to

taking care of her house and children and had held a job as an artist with an advertising agency until the birth of her older daughter.

"How that baby changed our lives! I just couldn't believe it. I was used to work, but housework—so much of it—was drudgery, and there was never a time when my mind was at ease. Besides, before she came on the scene my husband and I really were equal—equal pay, equal jobs, everything. Then our income was cut exactly in half and so was the quality of my life, it seemed. I missed the stimulation of work most of all."

Now, she told me, there wasn't much left she could do except read. She had even made a project of that earlier in her illness, reading classics she had not had time for during her active, healthy days. Recently she had reread the works of Dickens and the Bible. Somewhat sheepishly she glanced at the books on the table in front of her.

"I don't do that kind of reading anymore. Mostly I read mystery stories. Just trash, but that's about all I can concentrate on now."

I liked Sally from the start, even though her manner throughout most of the interview was formal and she didn't especially seem to like me. It was clear she had doubts about how helpful I could be to her, but I hoped we might work well enough together. Toward the end of our visit I asked her if she wanted me to come back.

"We could meet once or twice a week for a while and see what happens, Sally. But first I must repeat that I am committed to going away periodically, and you would have to see a colleague while I am gone."

"That's all right," she said hurriedly. "But what's your fee?"

It was clear she had no idea what a break in the analysis might mean. It was all too new to her. Besides, money was an immediate problem. She already knew how expensive therapy could be.

"It depends. I know what a burden the whole business of money must be for you at this point, and I also know you're not able to work to help pay for therapy. Frankly, I'd be willing to see you for nothing if it's not possible for you to pay."

"No, I wouldn't hear of that. I've a couple of friends in therapy now, and I think they pay twenty-five an hour. That's too much for us, but I would absolutely insist on paying something."

"Could you afford ten?"

"Yes, I think that will be all right."

"With Jim, too, do you think?"

"Yes, I believe so. He doesn't really approve of this kind of thing, but he'll go along with it for my sake. And he has a lot of respect for Ted, who told us about you. Ted said you were a Jungian. I don't know anything about Jungian analysis;* my friends see Freudian analysts. That doesn't matter because, to tell you the truth, I'm pretty skeptical about all of it. For me there are no authorities in that field because I don't believe there's proof of any of the theories. But I think I do need someone to help me get rid of my black thoughts."

"Or understand them?"

Paying no attention to my question she paused to light another cigarette and frowned as she exhaled smoke.

"But you must know that you could be wasting your time working with me. My chances of living through this aren't very good."

"Sally, please believe me, I need to know about what you are going through for my own sake. It couldn't possibly be a waste of time for me to help you live or perhaps die."

"All right then. Let's see what happens."

We arranged a time for our next interview, and I prepared to leave.

"Are you tired now?"

"Yes, I am. But it's all right; it's the kind of tired that will let me sleep well this afternoon."

When I opened the front door to leave, two young girls with long blond hair rushed past me and up the stairs. This was my first glimpse of Sally's children.

CHAPTER THREE

O N THE second visit I found the front door ajar. I
knocked and walked tentatively inside. I heard
children's voices coming from upstairs; then from
the living room, Sally's voice, stronger today.

"Come on in."

As I entered the room and took my same place across
from her, she said, "From now on I'll leave the door open a
little on the days you come. That way you won't have to
wait so long for me to answer."

"That's a good idea."

In thinking of Sally between these two visits, I remembered above all her strength of character, directness, and
intelligence. I had almost forgotten the pain expressed
around her eyes and her pathetic frailty; I was shocked
anew. I had also forgotten her surveillant look that had put
me more on guard than I usually was with a new patient.
But today the appraising glance was momentary. She
seemed eager to begin.

"I feel much more relaxed today. I have a new drug that
makes me sleep better, and that helps. But there's something else too. I feel as though I have some work to do now;
it's a little like starting a new project. And do you remember
I told you I rarely dreamed? Well, I've had three dreams

since you were here, and I remember all of them. The first once was especially vivid; it really got to me. But it's so difficult to understand. Maybe you can make some sense out of it."

I came upon a Sumerian tower with great ramps zigzagging to the top. It was also Southern California State College overlooking the University of Southern California. I had to climb to the top; it was a horrifying ordeal. When I got there I looked below, and throughout the city I saw buildings from the Sumerian, Romanesque, Gothic, and ancient Indian eras. There was a large, elegant book lying open before me. It was handsomely illustrated with architectural details of these buildings, of their friezes and sculptures. I awakened, terrorized by the height of the tower.

This first dream, a "big dream," is an all-inclusive, total statement. The Sumerian ziggurat, with its great ramps zigzagging to the top (like a mountain, a three-sided pyramid, a tower, a tree, Jacob's ladder), is an ancient, basic architectural symbol, of the deepest and most complex meaning. It is thought to have originated in the neolithic, possibly paleolithic, matriarchal era in Sumer. In ancient times religion was the heart and soul of society, and each individual was contained within it. The tower, common to many civilizations, was considered the center of the world, as it was known then. At the top of the ziggurat the connubial ritual of god and goddess was enacted. Earlier, in the neolithic period, the goddess, impersonated by a high priestess, dominated the ritual and took on a son or young man as her consort. Some authorities believe that he, as king, was ritually sacrificed each year.

I soon found out that Sally's relationship to her husband was a little along these lines—that she was, overtly at least, the "dominant" partner. The tower and the surrounding city in the dream represent the whole of Sally, both known and unknown. She is the total dream, a dream of the self.* It is a cosmic dream, a dream of ordered space, intimating the consummation of the sacred marriage—the Hieros-gamos,* which in our time is a psychological dramatization of a woman's need to experience herself totally. She ascends this highest,

28

centermost structure, which like the world tree or the center pillar connects heaven and hell with the earth. The effort surpasses ordinary experience, stretching her beyond the limits of human life and perhaps to a confrontation with death. Should she, through analysis, consciously strive to reach the ordered objective implied in the dream, she would of necessity embark upon an arduous, dizzying climb. Nothing would be more terrifying than the chaos that could come next. No wonder she is afraid.

The buildings around her symbolize the impersonal aspects of the psyche.* They are large and refer to her need to accept life in these cosmic terms. Possibly she has so far been consciously considering her plight from too pinched and narrow a point of view. She must begin to look upon the whole psyche as a grand, collective, religious, timeless edifice extending far beyond her personal life. The rewards of this broader attitude, symbolized by the comprehensive historical overview in the dream, could be enormous.

The large, elegant book, handsomely illustrated with architectural details of the many buildings, could serve as her guide. The book could mediate between her and the city-self within, showing her the way to integrate the meaning of the powerful symbols.

The dream is filled with dramatic opposites, side by side: the old and new, East and West, religious and secular. In my experience this juxtaposition of opposites, especially of such powerful symbols, demands a toll of suffering and depression from the patient. Indeed, this opposition of forces within her had already dangerously immobilized her, causing her to call for help.

First dreams in analysis, it has seemed to me, have a prophetic aspect. This one contains evidence of fear and depression, but she manages to hold her own in it, indicating that she will probably keep her balance to the end. Her remarkable breadth of potential is revealed in the dream and, most significantly, her potential to meet death in a conscious way. There is no other person in the dream. She, as a modern woman, has to go it alone.

Apparently Sally's unconscious* had needed to express itself for a long time. It was more than ready to speak up, and in powerful terms. The pressure from it seemed to have been building dangerously because there was no one who could listen to it before I came along. I welcomed its powerful statement in this dream because I felt we might have only a few months for our work, but her lack of background in analytical psychology allowed me to touch only lightly on the complicated, immense, and awesome meaning. Besides, I needed to think more about it.

Using the Jungian method of dream analysis, I asked Sally for one or two immediate reactions to the dream. "What's your association to this dream?"

"My fear of the tower's height is equal to my fear of analysis."

"What is it you fear in analysis?"

"I don't know exactly what it is. It's just scary for some reason. As I understand it, analysis means going below the surface and into the unconscious. I'm not really sure what's meant by the unconscious."

I began to respond, but I barely got started.

"No, wait, I really do know something about it. But to me the unconscious is a dark continent, and I prefer not to think about it. What I prefer doesn't make any difference though; it comes up to haunt me anyway, like just before losing consciousness under anesthesia — you know that awful place just before you go under? I'm afraid of that. And those dark thoughts I get at times terrify me. I guess it's because I've no control over any of that."

She shuddered, then braced herself.

"Altered states of consciousness, ESP, flying saucers — I'm not interested in any of that. I rarely have any notion of what my dreams are about. So tell me, what do you make of this one?"

Again I began to say something and was interrupted.

"I'm warning you, if you're going to tell me the tower I climbed in that dream is some kind of phallic symbol that shows my need—no, it's my wish, isn't it—for a penis . . ."

She left me no doubt that I was being put to the test. I felt a bit overwhelmed. How could I allay her skepticism? How could I translate the difficult concepts of her dream into ordinary language? For a moment I wondered how I could possibly succeed, especially since there might be so little time left for our work. If only I could communicate something to her about this first dream that would affirm the sense of awe in her words "it really got to me."

"Come on now, Sally. You can't really believe I'm going to tell you that. My God, not everyone dreams of climbing a ziggurat. How many people have even heard of one! And who gets up so high that the whole world is revealed? Reduce all that to nothing but penis envy? Oh, no! The tower's a symbol with much wider implications than that. It is a masculine symbol, yes, and a sexual symbol as well. But if that tower were concerned only with sex or penis envy, your dream would specifically have said so. That's our Jungian bias. I'm sure you know the tower is as old as humanity; it was a reality in ancient civilizations thousands of years before Christ. In mythology it stood for spiritual aspiration. Like the mountain, which was undoubtedly a forerunner of the man-made structure, it is a timeless, universal symbol, a configuration that's very much alive in us. For Noah it was an ark on a mountain peak above the deluge—beyond the reach of chaos; for the ancient Greeks it was Mount Olympus; for the Navajos it was the San Francisco peaks. A mountain climber will risk his life to reach the top. To be on a mountain is to be above the world and in the clear, with an objective view of everything."

She looked out of the window and was quiet for a time before speaking.

"Beyond the reach of chaos, yes. I used to feel that way when I'd go to the top of that mountain out there. I've walked over all its trails that bring you up high, and I've looked down on my world below. I haven't done that for a long time, but even now when Jim drives us up there, I still feel a sense of peace. I can look down on everything that functions so perfectly, cars never touching, houses neat and small, everything in order. I suppose there might be some connection; but the dream . . ."

"It's an impressive dream, Sally. Great rewards are promised, perhaps with religious overtones. Let's not get bogged down with all its complicated symbolism now. It's a statement from your center, from that part that is wiser than your conscious self. And through it you are connected with the substrata of humanity. You are sharing spiritual ideals and aspirations with peoples from the beginning of time. You are not alone. That is what I get from your dream; but there is much more, and I need time to study it."

She looked dubious but said nothing, so I went on to something I thought would interest her.

"Do you know that in those ancient civilizations people worshiped the female as well as the male god? We know from old manuscripts that long ago the female was considered equal to the male; not the same, but equal. And in earliest Chinese culture female and male principles of yin and yang were equal and opposite. That has not been true in our Western religions, as you know. In fact, only recently —about 1950, I think—the Catholic church proclaimed the Virgin's status equal to that of Christ. The Protestants, incidentally, have done nothing comparable. I was reminded of that because you spoke last time about your need to feel equal with Jim, especially after Sarah was born."

She regarded me thoughtfully.

"Mmm. Then the mother must have been as important as the father in those times. You know, I really know very little about the ancient religions."

"I think your dream is saying that knowledge of this kind might be helpful for you now. The great book and your view of the buildings representing so many periods of history may show that you hunger for a more comprehensive view of life, one that includes some knowledge of history, psychology, and religion. The book may suggest that you need to return to serious reading instead of what you've called just trash. Does that make any sense to you? I'm not trying to present myself as an authority on dreams, Sally. If whatever I say to you about this dream or any other doesn't sound right, just forget it."

"No, I think what you say might fit. But how can I find this knowledge now?"

"Why don't you try doing some reading? Perhaps Jim could bring you some books about ancient religion from the library. Jung goes into these subjects, too, and I'll bring you some books from home if you'd like."

"Yes, I think I'd like that. I'm not sure I'll be able to concentrate on anything so heavy now, but I'll give it a try."

I knew I was pushing her, and I hated to do that to someone already harassed and burdened, but I felt I had to help her begin to broaden her life as much as possible, as the book in her dream seemed to suggest. Study might help her to connect with her subjective life, from which she must have been cut off in early childhood. It would perhaps give her more to live for in the empty hours. Although learning would probably give her some satisfaction, it wasn't new knowledge that mattered so much. What mattered more was the effort she would have to give to the pursuit. I hoped this dedication might bring her some kind of religious sense, for dedication is what religion is about, especially for someone as skeptical as Sally seemed to be. I felt, as Jung did, that only when we satisfy our religious instinct are we whole.

Sally brightened a little and seemed eager to go on.

"Now let me tell you another dream that also seemed very strange to me."

> *I was driving a vivid blue Volkswagen. Mark and Susan, our neighbors, were with me. I drove somewhere to a party and parked the car. In a miraculous way I lifted off the chassis from its wheels and set it down on the curb. Indoors the party was going on, and music was being played on ceramic instruments. The music was beautiful and satisfying.*

Sally lifts off the chassis voluntarily, suggesting she has unconsciously accepted the idea of complete immobilization or possibly of death. This act is a miracle of strength; it is also somewhat ominous. She is potentially a heroine and must be prepared to exert herself beyond her endurance.

Music for a thinking person is an expression of feeling. Music also refers to harmony, order, and serenity. Music, serenity, and death may be symbolically connected. Since neolithic times, ceramics have been associated with death; to this day our ashes are kept in ceramic containers. These objects do not deteriorate like wooden ones; they last forever, so to speak, and can be shaped arbitrarily or restrictively to fit.

"Give me your quick reaction to this dream, Sally."

Asking for an immediate response often gets around an excessively rational mind and may draw out something from the unconscious.

"Mark and Susan are hippies; and I guess, to be truthful,

I was somewhat upset when they and their little son, Aaron, moved in so close to us."

"Why? Were they a bit lowbrow for you?"

"Yes, I suppose so, but I've grown very fond of them. The children love to go down to their house to play, and often Susan invites them there for supper. Jim is still kind of snobbish about them, though. Mark's a marvelous photographer; he took those pictures up there of Sarah and Beth."

She pointed to some framed studies of her daughters. In one set the girls seemed all sunshine; in the other both of them were serious and brooding.

"They're extraordinary photographs. I noticed them when I was here last time."

"And he's just as gifted in ceramics. I wonder why I should dream of them right now."

She was silent for a while, so I took the initiative.

"You say they're hippies. Well, you know, one might look at the hippie as a symbol of the future."

"How so?"

She shifted painfully on the couch, pressing on her right hip as she moved.

"You're uncomfortable, aren't you; do you want to stop?"

"No, go on with what you were saying. I want *you* to talk."

"The hippie is the character who breaks with tradition; he cuts across boundaries and opens the way to new attitudes. He's experimental and original; but because that originality can be used either positively or negatively, he's an ambivalent figure like the clown or jester. In Jungian jargon we call such a figure a symbol of the transcendent function.* But more on that later."

35

"Why not now?"

Her immediate curiosity, in spite of her pain, was impressive. But how to explain the transcendent function to someone with so logical a bias?

"Well, I lack the ordinary words to tell you, except to say that it means what it says. It transcends, goes beyond, rises above, resolves. Let me think about it some more, but meanwhile let's go back to the dream. It was your dream, Sally, not someone else's. You are the whole dream, and all the elements in it are parts of you: the Volkswagen—a car of the people, a "folk" car—and your hippie, lowbrow neighbors, who are exponents of change. The dream might be pointing out that you need to value those murky aspects of yourself, however lowly they seem to you, because they are the sources of the new vitality that you need right now."

"You find all that in this silly dream? It hardly seems possible. Yet there was also something new in my last dream —a kitten. Listen to this one."

Her eagerness to tell me the dream pleased me, for I sensed that the real work of analysis might already have begun. I felt we were in contact, and real contact was more important than theory now.

I was driving along the edge of the ocean in a station wagon. It was a beautiful scene at dusk. I heard a meow coming from the back seat, and when I turned around I saw a tiny kitten. It looked just like Cyrano, our cat; it was exactly the same type and color. I wondered if I could persuade Jim to let me keep it.

She had awakened from the tower dream in fear. The image of climbing to heights in dreams can signify a frightening descent into the deepest layers of the unconscious. In this dream the unconscious seems to be compensating for going so high by invoking the sea coast.

This dream also appears to compensate for so much masculine effort in the first dream and indicates her need for the feminine. The ocean, with its vast horizon, appears in contrast to the vertical tower and implies nature's all-inclusiveness. The kitten is the first indication of the female, instinctive, inner strength, and wisdom she will need for her battle for life or her confrontation with death. It represents the female aspect of the self. By her own account, Sally has concentrated heavily on the masculine side of life. Now she needs to give the female the same importance. She must strive for the equality of the sexes within as she had been yearning for their equality in her outer life. This is one of the tasks that modern woman does not always bargain for, and it seems to be a particularly difficult one. The kitten, just as important a symbol in the psyche as the tower, is young, hardly begun.

"It's just amazing. As I was telling you the dream, I could see it clearly in my mind, as if I were living through it once again. It was so comforting to be there by the ocean."

For a moment she seemed preoccupied. Then she said sadly, "But the ocean means death."

"I agree with you, Sally; it may be that we return to the ocean when we die. But the ocean is also the source of life. And don't forget the tiny kitten."

We sat quietly with each other until our reflections were interrupted by the sound of a heavy object being dragged across the floor upstairs. We heard a crash, some unintelligible conversation, a slap, and a yowl of outrage. Two children appeared on the uncarpeted stairway, the older one in pursuit of the other. Then all was quiet again. Sally relaxed and sighed. She looked very frail and tired, overwhelmed by what was obviously her two young daughters having it out with each other.

"They must be difficult for you now."

"It's harder now, yes; but then mothering has always been hard for me. I guess I just wasn't cut out for domesticity. I told you about how good it felt to work before the children came along. I could do anything well; I could help solve the most complicated problems that came up at the agency. Everything about work was easy and enjoyable for me. But taking care of children has been the hardest job I've ever had. Little children — anyone's — were never very interesting to me; and, to tell you the truth, my own babies bored me even more. I felt a lot of resentment toward them when they were little, then all kinds of guilt for my resentment."

She lit a cigarette, inhaled deeply, and watched the smoke come out as she spoke again. "And even now, in a way, I think my mother's better with them than I am, even though she's a total loss to me as a mother. She can play with the children and amuse them for hours, but when she's with me, she just sits in the room and stares. Of course, part of the trouble is her drinking; she starts around ten in the morning, so she's probably half-drunk most of the time."

"Has she always seemed a total loss as a mother for you?"

"Ever since I was twelve. That's when my father had an affair with another woman. He was a charmer, my father. Still is. He was handsome. He used to be a singer — first on the stage and later in movies. There was this woman . . . Well, I lost respect for my mother for not being able to hold him. I was just a kid — their only one — and they both came to me to ask for advice about whether to stay together. Naturally I told them to stick it out. I always felt I was taking care of my parents instead of the other way around. When I left home to marry Jim, I felt guilty about leaving them. It occurs to me only this minute that my present role as parent only duplicates my childhood responsibility."

"No wonder you resented having babies!"

I thought for a moment about what little childhood Sally had experienced and wondered how much that lack had caused the severe repression that cut her off and left her stuck. In the right circumstances so much early responsibility might have constellated* the potential modern woman that turned up in her dreams. If only she were not so frail, she might still have launched into that pioneering female role and legitimately lived out her rebellion and perhaps have even recovered.

"I can also imagine that you never openly expressed your feelings to them about their putting you in this role, or later to Jim about how taking care of the babies made you feel diminished; I mean, you never really misbehaved — never got nasty and let them know in strong terms."

"Not with my parents, no. It was too hard to do because, given their limitations, what else could they have done? And the babies were . . . Well, they were mine. Two healthy babies. How lucky can you be and all that. But with Jim it's always been easy to misbehave, even though he's really not responsible for everything that makes me angry."

"Maybe not, but I do think that now it's awfully important for you to face those negative feelings head-on when they come up, whether you feel they're justified or not. The option of working them off as you did before just isn't yours anymore. I may be wrong, but I really do feel this. It's a lesson I've learned myself, and I know it's true. Again, I say this not as an authority but as someone who has lived through that same kind of experience."

No one has the truth for everyone; one is always biased by one's own personal limitations. I thought that Sally needed to know this more than most patients because she was dying. At least, I thought so. If there had been more time, I might have waited for her to come to her own conclusions, but I had to hasten the process by telling her what I had learned. I felt that Sally's character and intelligence warranted it. I also sensed she would not be easily influenced. And sharing was important too. She had as genuine a curiosity about me as I had about her. It was part of our contract.

"Well, as I say, I do manage to let out a lot of my anger on Jim; in fact he takes the brunt of all of it now, I'm afraid. I know he hates it; he's told me so. Maybe I ought to tell him what you're saying."

Now she watched me closely, as if she were again putting me to a test — one she hoped I would pass. She continued, "I want to let you know I felt very negative about you when you came here for the first time. I can say that to you because I feel you're open enough to see all the way around my anger."

"If you mean I should be objective enough to do that, you're right. As you probably know, I've been trained to see people apart from their anger."

I felt Sally needed to accept herself in a positive way; she was already too much at home with the negative. I liked her and I could accept all of her, including her anger. I hoped she might unconsciously project her future self — her complete acceptance of herself — onto me until she could recover it for herself. I was twenty-four years older than Sally, and my own concern with death put us to some extent in a similar quandary. Naturally my concern was not as urgent as hers, but it was enough to give us a connecting bridge. Still, no amount of imagination can help one to realize what it is like to be faced with death at the age of thirty-seven.

Her hand pressed against her hip again, and the look of suffering I was to see so often came into her face. She had been alert and interested throughout this conversation, and I had forgotten that it might be time to end our session. For my part, I had been tired at the beginning of the visit,

40

fatigued from seeing too many patients that day, but the interview had refreshed me and I felt rested. That was proof to me that we were making contact on a basic level. The more basic our contact the better, because we were in what is usually considered to be the last stage of analysis, in which analyst and analysand relate to each other as equals. In the face of death we were equal. I hoped that our confrontation and exchange, as well as the sharing of ourselves, might bring about a creative acceptance of death in both of us.

I rose and went over to Sally. I had brought her a book by Edna Kaehele called *Living With Cancer,* and I offered it to her as I was leaving. She read the title and accepted it reluctantly.

CHAPTER FOUR

TODAY was the first time I had seen Sally dressed. Her conservative blue cotton dress and leather sandals surprised me; in spite of the illness I had expected her taste in dress to be more original, even flamboyant. As I entered the room, she put down the book she was reading and looked at me with eyes full of anger.

"I don't want to live with cancer! I don't like this book. This woman's story ends where mine begins. I want out! I hate to go on living when I'm ready to die. It's animal to live this way!"

With tense, staccato movements she reached over to the green glass pitcher on the table in front of her and managed to pour two tall glasses of iced tea. She offered me one; it was a warm July day and I accepted it gratefully. I sat down across from her couch in what was now my place.

"That book must have upset you, Sally, and I'm sorry. But you say all that with so much vitality, and you do look better today."

"I know; that's part of it. Listen, I would have killed myself if you hadn't agreed to see me when I first talked to you on the telephone. But since you've been coming, I've been feeling better and I resent it. Three times I was totally geared for death. I had accepted it completely. And three times it didn't happen, so I had to adjust myself to living longer. I hate the thought of going through that again. Oh, I wish I could kill myself."

"What prevents you, Sally?"

"Well, for one thing, I don't know how many pills it would take to do the job, and what a mess I'd make if I failed! I've got a stockpile of sleeping pills. Could you please find out how many it would take to kill myself?"

"Of course," I agreed, not wanting to put obstacles in her way at this early stage of our work.

"Besides, Jim, for some reason I can't figure out, doesn't want me to commit suicide. He just says it's wrong, period. No discussion. He simply doesn't understand how I can possibly see suicide as a solution to my predicament. Just a while ago he went camping for the weekend, and before he left he made a sort of joke about not knowing if he'd find me here when he got back. That really hurt."

It seemed to me at the time that if Jim had sympathized with Sally's suicidal feelings, she might have gone through with killing herself. Morality belongs to the feelings, an area in which she was unsure. She seemed to be allowing Jim to decide this issue for her.

"I guess we'll have to talk more about you and Jim. Now perhaps we had better get on to your dreams. Have you had any more since last time?"

"As a matter of fact, I have. But why do you pay so much attention to them?"

"Because they tell me what both you and I don't know about you. They're my authority. They could be yours. I wish you'd realize that your unconscious—that dark continent you spoke about with fear—can also be your best friend who sends you messages through dreams, who always

43

stays with you and levels with you, who never lets you down. You see, Sally, you're stuck. God knows that would be true for any of us in your situation. You can't be active in the world as you once were. But I feel there's something you can do that would help; in fact, you're doing it. You can focus your attention inward to the dreams and find a different movement in your life."

"You're right; I am stuck. All right then, let me tell you Sarah's dream first. She dreamed that Beth was coming through the bushes with a knife stuck in her back. But she was smiling and unconcerned. I think that knife was probably my cancer, don't you?"

"I think so too. You see, it looks as though this business of dreams is catching. The whole family's getting into the act."

"But that's just it, don't you see? I'm ruining everyone's life. They'd all be better off without me. If only my own problems in dreams were that clear! Listen to this one. I want to hear what you'll do with it.

It was six o'clock in the morning. I realized I was to be married at eight. A father figure appeared whom I didn't know. He approved of the marriage, but he also seemed worried about it. A deputy arrived with a subpoena to stop the marriage. I had to be in Sacramento by eight o'clock in the morning to answer charges.

Because this dream could be referring to marriage as either death (from cancer or by suicide) or perhaps as a spontaneous cure, it is one of Sally's most significant dreams. There are precedents for a connection between marriage and death. Some African tribes use the symbol* of the lioness for both love and death. People often slip and interchange the words "wedding" and "funeral," as if the meaning of the words were identical or implied two aspects of the same phenomenon — namely, the coming together of opposites.

The dream may be referring to her thoughts about killing herself. If it is, the imagery for suicide is positive because the father figure — who by patriarchal tradition is the authority for the daughter and who represents Sally's most considered, mature (although in this dream uncertain) opinion — approves of the marriage. Moreover, regardless of tradition, he stands for opinion reached through deliberative thought.

The deputy, who is the animus,* in its typical role of messenger, brings a second consideration to Sally, which arises from the possibility of analysis: she must not kill herself. And since the deputy represents the law, the thought is binding. This second thought, emanating from a deeper level than that from which personal thought or judgment comes, originates in the self — the center of her psyche. In this dream the center, or the self, is symbolized by Sacramento, the nucleus of the state, where the governor resides, just as in the first dream the self was symbolized by the tower, the nucleus of the multicultured city. The self, which can also be presented in dreams as a human figure of larger significance than the dreamer, as an object like a stone or tree, or as an animal (the kitten in the earlier dream), is often described as a governing agent that corrects psychic imbalances. To stop the suicide is the consensus of her own inner male authority. A female personification of her inner wisdom is this time conspicuously absent. The dream presents only the male aspect of the self. In analysis, along the way toward wholeness, she will have the opportunity to receive continuing messages from the self, male and female, for it is now apparent that her dreams emanate from an impersonal source and are rooted in her all-knowing center. This time the guiding male voice points out to her the way she must go. The growth that comes through analysis would be worthwhile to her in consciously meeting her three possibilities: cure, suicide, or death from cancer.

"What are your associations to this dream?"

"The father figure was middle-aged. About forty-five. Definitely not my father."

I waited for her to continue, but only silence followed. Considering the rich content of her dreams, I was impressed by how few associations she made to them. Perhaps it was because she was young and her dream themes were highly complex and abstract, with subjects that were foreign to her. Her dreams were coping with the subject of death in an archetypal way and would naturally invoke a language of the archetypes,* which was beyond her experience and comprehension. The drugs she took may have interfered with her ability to associate. Possibly she lived the experience of pain and of facing death too strenuously to talk much about it. Her fear of the unconscious, apparent in her first dream, and her general lack of imagination may have contributed to this paucity of association. Or it was because she was somehow psychically stuck deep down somewhere.

Under the circumstances I thought it best to draw out whatever association she might have.

"What about Sacramento?"

"Sacramento means Governor Edmund Brown. The subpoena was issued by him, so he was the one who was stopping the marriage. Jim must be the bridegroom. Jim also could be Brown. I'm disappointed in Brown because he's bungling and ineffectual. I'm particularly disappointed in Jim because he won't take me seriously when I say I want to kill myself. I'm disappointed in both of them because even though I'm on their side, they're not able to act the way I want them to act."

In spite of her negative associations to Jim and Governor Brown, I thought that Jim, Governor Brown, and the deputy were connected in the dream: all of them were holding out the goal of increased consciousness* and possibly the experience in life of what Jung called individuation.* After all, she had supported these two men by marrying one of them and voting for the other. With the help of analysis she might realize in her lifetime her uniqueness and importance. Also analysis might enlarge her horizon psychically to offset the degrading physical effects of her illness. The conscious effort might bring about the experience of regeneration, which could give her much-needed insight, objectivity, and detachment. I wanted her to give it a chance.

"In what way is Jim bungling, Sally? You told me that he worked hard and did well in his job. What do you mean when you say he's unable to act the way you'd have him act?"

"I don't know exactly, but he's bungling when it comes to me. He's unable to express himself about my situation, and he can't talk about the two of us truthfully and about what goes on in our relationship. What's happening to me is hard on him; I know that. Still, he's simply not responsive to my needs—physical or emotional. I just wish he could be; that's all."

"It does sound as if you two have lots of work to do with each other, but that would be natural. You're both young and that's the time for people to work on the rough parts of their marriage. For you and Jim, because of your special predicament, the need is even more pressing. And maybe as you make an effort to resolve these personal problems, some concerns of your own about marriage on a deeper level will become evident. I think your first dream of the tower spoke to this; it somehow brought to my mind the sacred marriage of the king, as god, with the goddess that was enacted on the ziggurat. In the early stages of patriarchal times just after the matriarchal era, when men came into their own, the god must have been on an equal footing with the goddess, if only for a short time. Equality in marriage seems to me to be the solution for modern times. I also like to think that there was a cultural flowering at those times when there was a balance between the sexes. Hopefully we might have it again."

Considering the level of her consciousness at the time, I felt it was important to follow Sally's association that the marriage was her marriage to Jim, even though her dream of the tower implied the impersonal theme of sacred marriage, or in Jungian terms, of individuation. The difficulties in their relationship would constellate this deeper-level issue for her. She, like most practical people, would reach the level of the archetypes and the self (the sacred marriage level) through the experience of everyday life. She could not solve the problems of her marriage through imagining their resolution; she would have to go step by step through the actual experience of the solution. Struggling with Jim every day on a personal level would not allow her to forget her main task, the purpose of her life—her individuation. It would also keep before her the need for the release of her personal female side that had roots in the kitten of her earlier dream. It would be an enormous task, especially because Jim was not convinced of the importance of this kind of development for himself. The kind of effort that could lead her to the experience of the self might possibly open the way to a spontaneous cure. To contact Jim she would have to bring up her positive feeling for him, stretch her imagination beyond a rational approach, and find within herself components of her female self that still lay in the unconscious. In other words, she would have to honor the unlived part of her life.

The unconscious seems to want people to round out their lives before they die. When death is the issue, the unconscious takes up in dreams whatever is unresolved. The marriage theme, personal and archetypal, in a dream would rightfully belong to Sally because she is young, and youth is the time when marriage is a problem. Marriage would represent for her the situation of greatest difficulty, and its deeper impersonal implications (the positive coming together of the opposites) could be the final resolution of her life. The dreams of an older person might not take up this theme, because at the time of a fully lived old age the ego* and the animus are no longer necessarily problematic.

I did not want Sally to kill herself. My wish that she see things through may have weakened her determination to commit suicide, may have kept her alive unnecessarily. It is difficult to know. Perhaps suicide, in instances of devastating illness, may be regarded as a positive act, especially if there is no one available whose help can give any meaning to the illness. For Sally, suicide might have brought about an involuntary experience of the self since, according to her dream, the decision to kill herself (i.e., to get married) would have been a serious one and not an impulsive expression of defeat. But because of my own irrational feelings and because this dream of stopping the marriage indicated to me the hope of a creative aspect of death, I was prejudiced against suicide and in favor of her struggling toward a conscious realization of her whole being. I hoped that individuation, and not death, would become her primary concern, as it was becoming mine.

Sally looked at me quizzically, remained silent for a moment. Whatever she may have been thinking, she neither expressed her thoughts nor stayed with them long.

"Jim really is unresponsive."

"Maybe you could help by asking him for what you want."

"That would be difficult because, in the first place, I've been so independent all my life that it's hard for me to ask anyone for anything. And, secondly, I'm afraid if I ask him

49

to express himself about us, he might not be able to respond."

"Perhaps verbal response is not his way. Suppose you begin by asking him for help only when you find yourself physically helpless. That way your psychic independence would remain intact, and that seems to be important for you now."

I felt that married couples do best when each one allows the other one to fill in where she or he is most able. It was not a question of her learning how *not* to be independent in order to appeal to his chauvinism. Besides, I saw her rebelliousness and negative struggle for independence as part of her inner modern woman's need to surface in any way that it could.

Sally seemed to cheer up. "Maybe I'll try that. You know, it does help to talk to you about my problems with Jim. Our conversations are like dress rehearsals for talks with him. We still have some pretty awful fights, but communication between us has improved since you've been coming, and that makes me feel good."

She got up and stretched, then groaned as she pushed at the small of her back with her left palm. She picked up the empty tea pitcher.

"Come on with me while I see if there's more tea in the kitchen. I get awfully nauseous lately and the tea helps a little. But please excuse the mess out there."

I followed her as she limped carefully through the dining room, one hand supporting her right hip. She pushed open the swinging door, held it for me, and we both walked through a pantry into the kitchen. The room smelled vaguely of cooked hamburger. A greasy cast iron frying pan was still on the stove; in the sink a piece of hamburger bun on an unwashed plate caught a drip from the faucet. Glass panes in the cabinet doors exposed china and glassware that had been carelessly shoved away. The linoleum floor, once perhaps orange and brown, had faded to a dreary non-descript color and had buckled at the sink. But it was sunny in the kitchen, and there were touches of optimism: apothecary jars of herbs and spices, two luxuriantly sprouted sweet potatoes in separate dishes, a shelf of cookbooks, a wicker basket filled with summer fruit, a poster of the cheeses of France, and an abstract pebbled mosaic, which served as the countertop on one side of the sink.

"That's a beautiful mosaic, Sally. Who made it?"

"I did, when we first moved to this house. I had planned to do the whole counter that way, but I never had the chance to finish it. It's made of pebbles from the California beaches where we've been over the years."

She opened the door of the refrigerator.

"Would you like a beer?"

"No, thanks."

She took one for herself, closed the door, opened the can, and turned to me.

"Come. I'll show you where I've done most of my living, if you can call it that, since stairs became impossible."

She led the way to a small room just off the kitchen. It was a bright cubicle, probably once a maid's room, which was just large enough for a bed, a small table, and a chest of drawers. A striped gray cat lay dozing at the foot of the unmade bed; it looked up at me with an arrogant sniff.

"That's Cyrano. I love him even though he's a fair-weather cat. Whenever I feel miserable, he disappears for days at a time. I never understand why, but I'm sure it means something."

51

I thought to myself that the cat, being close to the wild, would instinctively reject someone who was in conflict, and Sally was in conflict about death. One may speculate that if cats have psychic powers, her cat may also have left to avoid the danger of illness.

"Don't mind the look; it's just his way of letting you know he belongs wherever he happens to be. Do you like cats?"

I thought to myself how cats were sacred to the Egyptian matriarchal goddess, Bast, when she was the supreme deity. This goddess, in cat form or later as a human figure with the head of a cat, was thought of as sun, moon, and earth, day and night. She was later incorporated into the sun god, Ra, as his all-seeing eyes.

"Yes, but I like dogs better. They stay right by you even when you're in awful trouble. But I have to admit there is something I like in cats that reminds me of true female self-containment. It's probably their ability to go it alone. I think that female cats in the wild, like bears, raise their young alone without help from the males. Wasn't it a kitten like Cyrano that you dreamed about back in the beginning?"

"Yes, and there was another dream last week with kittens just like him in it. He's an important character."

Again we walked through the kitchen and back into the living room. It seemed that moving this much had been a painful effort for Sally. She sat down slowly and sighed.

"If you'd have come to visit before I was sick, you might have had something decent to eat with your tea — a slice of spice cake maybe, or a good piece of French apple pie. Now about all I can do in the kitchen is make popcorn for the children."

She took a sip from the can of beer and sighed again as she looked around the room.

"I love this old house. We had just begun to remodel it when I got sick again. I'd started back to school for an advanced degree in the humanities, too, just before my second operation. That was something else I couldn't finish."

"So much frustration. But tell me, how was it for you, returning to school after so many years?"

"Well, it was difficult coping with all the demands at once, but I managed, and I did well. But why, I wonder, did I get ill just at that moment?"

"I suppose the way you studied didn't help. My impression is that you weren't fulfilling an instinctive need — that you were only finding a distraction from the home life that was making you unhappy. You may have been going back to the excitement of using your efficient brain without considering how your studies might have helped you personally. An animus jag is another way to describe it. And studying against the grain like that would only wear you out."

I realized that it may not have been coincidence that cancer recurred when Sally began her work for an advanced degree. Such an effort to achieve, rather than to obtain subjective nourishment, would have driven her further away than ever from her female nature. She already lived too much on her male side, or animus. A woman must engage her whole being in her pursuits in the world. She cannot deviate too far from her subjective needs without risking a takeover from the animus. An animus invasion produces an accompanying feeling of emptiness, which the woman, unaware of her need for female expression and development, usually tries to fill with further animus achievement. Thus the invasion is self-perpetuating.

Sally continued, "Well, anyway, I enjoy reading books on religion now. Not that I'm at all religious, the subject just interests me, that's all. And by the way, thanks for dropping off Nancy Wilson Ross's collection of Zen writings. I liked them very much. The thoughts give me a feeling of calm, and I could easily float away on them. But I think they take me too far from my family, and I don't like drifting away; the family needs me, and I want to stay with them."

"But what about you, Sally; what do you need?"

"Oh, that doesn't matter now. I've begun reading Jung as well. Jim brought me *Memories, Dreams, Reflections* and *Modern Man in Search of a Soul* from the library. I like his writings. They're comprehensive like Thomas Mann's and Mann is a favorite of mine. Jung talks so much about how you have to know yourself. I have trouble with that although this whole thing about dreams is getting very interesting. I get a lot of new ideas about myself from them. Sometimes I feel as though you and I are engaged in a kind of creative work together, almost as if we were writing a play, the two of us. I like that. You'll probably be interested to hear a dream I had last week.

I was in a lovely, spacious new flat. It had gold and turquoise carpeting and white walls. Beth, who was only three or four years old, but who was behaving as if she were nine, was helping me prepare for a large, grownup party. Just before the guests arrived she brought in five tiger kittens resembling Cyrano. I was delighted to be in that flat.

Moving into a new place usually means moving into a new attitude, but it can also be a premonition of death. I wondered at the time if such a dream may have been constellated by an acceptance of death, or if indeed it indicated that she might recover.

"Give me your quick reaction to it."

"The flat was modern, not full of old and secondhand

furnishings like my house. Gold and turquoise are my favorite colors — no, I have other favorites, too; but I do like gold and turquoise very much."

"Everything in the dream seems special, Sally — the new place with its gold and turquoise, Beth acting older than she really is, and then the celebration commemorating the move . . ."

"Yes, there was a very special feeling about it, you're right."

"Gold is the finest of the precious metals. White means light, as opposed to the black of night. There are now five kittens, and that's a special number. Also, the numbers three and four and nine in the dream are special; the reason isn't important for us now. This dream is a big step, such a positive one; and because only female figures appear, it is concerned with your life as a woman."

I was hoping Sally could absorb the importance of these symbols at some level. Perhaps she did. But because she was so insistent that her interest in religion was an intellectual one, I didn't tell her how strongly I felt that they were connecting her to her own instinctive religious feeling. The kitten in this dream has developed fivefold, supporting my first thought that it is her center-most female symbol. The Mayans and Egyptians since the beginning of time have attributed the characteristic of wisdom to number five. The number nine (nine lives) has always been associated with cats. Nine (three times three) contains the idea of self-procreation. The sign of the virgin is the ninth astrological sign.

Sally didn't seem to be taking in what I said. She seemed to have something else on her mind. When she did speak, her tone was enthusiastic.

"But wait, here's another dream along those same lines.

I was with Marian, my sixty-year-old Catholic friend who also had a mastectomy a year ago. We were keeping vigil in a new house; the room we were in was like a chapel, and it had fresh white plaster walls and a huge fireplace. We sat in silence before three lamps of beautiful, intricate, blue green glass. Outside a storm was raging.

As in the previous dream, this dream stresses the importance of religious feeling. But here the religious setting is more personal—the three exquisite lamps, the chapellike room, the friend who is in the same predicament. The religious approach verges on a Catholic, orthodox one.

Orthodox religions protect the individual from the harshness of reality, and their rituals hold off at a symbolic arm's length issues too hard to comprehend, especially the issues of death. Meditating in a chapellike room with three lamps is a protection against the storm that rages outside. The storm could stand for undifferentiated emotion or for the fear or threat of death.

Nature in a violent mood is a reality that threatens Sally, and she attempts unconsciously to structure the inner chaos through meditation, an age-old form of prayer directed to one's center. Here the meditation is concentration on three lamps, which bring to mind the Trinity in Christianity, which for believing Christians is the self.

Perhaps the dream is asking that she consider death as she would the storm, as a natural phenomenon, and not in her nihilistic "I want out" way. In this sense she still has more to learn, and she has to go ahead in spite of the great difficulty of the task. The dream may also be asking her for a religious approach to death, an approach that would have common roots with the Catholic one but would be her own instinctive, religious way. The chapellike room in a new house, the huge fireplace, and lamps that shed more light than candles, all point to the difference.

Gold and turquoise may be religious colors. Gold is the highest color value and is likened to the sun. White refers to consciousness. The symbols in this dream and the previous one show tremendous progress.

"Does this dream remind you of anything?"

56

"Well, yes. It just occurs to me now that I felt upset when I read the chapter about life after death in Jung's *Memories, Dreams, Reflections*. I don't know why."

"Let's talk about that later, Sally, because your unconscious will take up the issue in a dream, and it will be easier for us then if it does. I like this dream. It feels positive to me, but let's also talk about that later on. Besides, I need to think more about it myself."

In this conversation Sally and I had touched on the delicate subject of her religious feeling, arising both in the dream of the chapel and in her reaction to Jung's mentioning of life after death. I wanted to avoid putting her off with amplifications that might sound strange to her. I didn't want to run into her conscious denial of religious feeling when her unconscious was showing so much interest in it. Her nihilism would only get in the way. I hoped that future dreams might point her more directly to religious issues, making further discussions easier for both of us.

Sally seemed to accept my postponement.

"All right. I don't know why you say that, but I do know that I feel better than I did when you arrived today, whatever the cause. And I feel we're getting somewhere.

That remark, from someone who customarily spoke in understatement and who did not dare to have hope, greatly moved and encouraged me. Perhaps we were moving in the right direction.

CHAPTER FIVE

IT WAS now the end of July and my family plans were finally settled. Today I would tell Sally that late in August I would be going away for six weeks. I had asked a colleague if he would consider seeing her once a week during my absence and he had agreed to do so, but I was concerned about whether or not she would accept this arrangement. I sensed how important my visits had become to her and I was worried. How would she feel about my going away so soon after our work had begun? After our last session she had been optimistic about her progress. Would her optimism depend on my presence? And now there was a danger of interrupting the flow of important dreams. I feared that if this flow of unconscious material ceased, she would feel empty and sterile once more. Besides, I knew of the theory that cancer comes with bereavement. Would my leaving her only destroy what we had accomplished? I would have to be careful today not to place the burden of my own worries onto her.

The door was ajar and I let myself in. Delicate, rational sounds of a Schubert impromptu for piano came softly from a speaker in the corner as Sally, looking particularly worn and strained, sat quietly reading.

"Hello Sally. How do you feel today?"

"Terrible. But here I go again, and you must be fed up hearing about it. Still, that's the way it is, always. Last night was awful again. It was bad; the pain was very bad, and it took so long for morning to come. The cancer's in my head and it makes a pressure that feels like a tight band. Sometimes the pressure's so bad that I vomit. And it gets worse in hot weather. It worries me because last summer I had a spell of vomiting so acute that I had to be hospitalized."

"That must be hard on you, Sally. Are you sure you want to talk to me today? I can come back tomorrow if you'd like."

"No, no, I'm really glad you've come; you take my mind off how awful I feel. I've been wanting to talk to you about Jung's psychology. I finished *Modern Man in Search of a Soul* and *Memories, Dreams, Reflections* in the last couple of days."

"That's quite a bit to read and swallow so fast. I hope it hasn't contributed to your indigestion."

With effort she smiled.

"No, don't worry. I didn't bother with the parts I didn't understand; I just skimmed over them so I wouldn't get bogged down. I always read that way. But, you know, so much of it seems like a foreign language to me."

"Well, you know, each school of psychology has its own language. In fact, individual students of psychology also develop their own language — that is, if they're not too impressed by the established cliches."

"I suppose so, but Jung's language interests me. I was intrigued by his chapter on mandalas,* and I decided to paint some myself to see if anything would happen. Something did. I didn't get the mystical experience I was hoping for, but I did get a feeling of calm that seemed to stabilize me for several hours. I've been painting one or two each day now. They help."

"That's good. I'm sure you know that the mandala is one of the oldest religious symbols. You find it the whole world over — from the sophisticated cultures of the East to the most primitive tribes of the jungle. Painting a mandala doesn't automatically give you a mystical experience, but during turning points in your life — when tension is at its highest or after impressive events — painting a mandala can somehow give you a sense of your total personality. That's especially true when you incorporate figures out of dreams or fantasies, because then the unknown in you is touched."

"Now, that sounds like a bit much to me."

"Well, even a totally conscious design will reveal something of the unconscious. The main thing is to let go and work as freely as you can."

"I've been trying to do just that."

"You certainly hit on an important activity for yourself. You beat me to it. I should have introduced you to mandalas before, but your coming to the idea of doing them on your own makes your discovery all the more real. May I see them?"

I was very concerned about Sally's work because a mandala, if it is a spontaneous vision or part of a dream, may signify completion.

She reached over for a small art book lying on the table in front of her, opened it, and handed it to me. I saw that she had painted bold, well-balanced mandalas.

"These are great. It's certainly obvious that you've worked with paints before."

"Oh, yes, I've experimented with all kinds of media. Jim

60

used to say I had a bit of talent with everything, but not enough to do anything important, and I suppose he's right. But I try a lot of new things; that's always been true. You know, I think I understand what you mean about the mandala giving you a momentary sense of yourself, but Jung talked about it as signifying also the wholeness of the self. What does he mean by that? And what's all this about psychological types? I don't see how I fit them. I have so much trouble seeing into myself. What about them? Can we talk about these things? Will you explain?"

She took a cigarette from its box on the table and lit it, frowning as she moved forward on the couch, closer to me. Then hesitatingly, she asked, "Am I putting you on the spot asking you to explain? It's not done? I've friends in analysis who tell me their analysts only respond to their questions with other questions. But please don't do that to me. I need explanations. I need to know."

"I don't blame you for wanting to know. Illness like yours must create an intellectual desert; and your friends and family haven't helped you with it, maybe because they're too much in their outer world. Remember the book in your first dream? That tipped me off right away to your need for intellectual and spiritual outlets. That's what you're saying now, aren't you, that the dream was right?"

"Yes. And I need something now to counteract the awful boredom of my life."

"All right, Sally, let's see what we can do about that. First, the self. The self is difficult because you have to talk all around it. It is present, but you can only know very little about it. By the way, when you reported your first dream, I thought it was about the self. I would have taken it up then if you hadn't already had so much to get used to. I thought,

61

too, that your hunger to know everything would sooner or later make you ask about it."

"How can you know about the self if you can't know about it?"

Her face now had taken on some color. Remarkably, the strained, worn look had diminished.

"Well, I'll try to explain. Think of it as a sphere that is both its nucleus and the sphere itself, the center of one's whole being, which paradoxically also includes the total psyche, known and unknown. It's also the source of dream images, which function to regulate our psychic system and give a picture of the forces within the process. That's what was so exciting about your first dream, Sally. There was the tower you climbed and the city below it. Together they referred to the self — the tower was the nucleus, the city was the sphere. Or if you think of the four directions of a city — north, south, east, west — the city is also a square. You could also say, as you did once before, that the tower is masculine — you called it phallic. But now think of the city also as feminine, especially because it is a square. The Bible is full of this imagery. The self, you see, as well as being all-inclusive, is made up of opposites."

"Oh, this is all too much. Still, I had a strong reaction to that dream. I was impressed, yes, but I was also afraid."

"You did tell me that. And, in my experience, once there is a need for a connection with the self, a very painful and difficult business begins. And it can be scary. The self wants reevaluation and change, the ego clings to the old ways, and you are torn. It's the dialogue with the self through messages from your dreams that can close the gap and give meaning to your life. Besides, when you trust this center of yours, you don't look out there for someone with all the answers. You know the answers are within you, and that gives you true independence. It may even promote the healing you need for your illness. This is something known by old people who have lived completely. But I feel younger people can know this also, given the necessity."

"I must have been wanting to know something when I began to paint mandalas."

I picked up two from those I had been holding on my lap.

"Look, Sally, these mandalas are essentially circular, and the circle brings everything together. It's all-inclusive, a state of oneness. The circle is certainly a whole, and it stands for the divinity in human beings. Take, for instance, the halo in Christian art. The circle is our highest symbol. And there are squares in your mandalas — squares and circles that can never merge. They're opposites — two opposite ways of expressing the total — just as total woman and total man are opposites. Anyhow, that's the most inclusive symbol that can be given. And you have drawn it. In short, you have expressed your concept of God in these mandalas."

I took a long chance when I told her this; but at least it would introduce, by means of her own creation, the subject of her religious feeling, which she had deliberately repressed.

My words seemed to jolt her, but then she quickly re-established her control by countering disdainfully, "Oh, come on. These are so simple. How can you talk about seeing God in something so ordinary? Anyway, I've no belief in God anymore. How many times do I have to tell you that?"

"All right. Maybe we ought to drop the subject for now. Perhaps your friend, the unconscious, will send up a dream that will make it more believable for you."

I had gone far enough. I had learned from years of practice what Jung had said many times: "Individuals do not come to the fullness of self-understanding until they have accepted their religious feeling." Although I agreed, I did not want to push the subject any further and have her close the door.

With a gesture of her hands she brushed me off.

"Can we move on to the types now? Types seem to be more on my level of understanding than this other subject. I feel at least I have a chance of understanding them."

"All right, Sally, I'll see if I can put types into ordinary language. That, by the way, is good exercise for me because it makes me review what I think I know. It keeps me from being too heady and from bypassing the real stuff. But please remember that no one fits perfectly into one type or another. Everyone's a bit of everything; it's only a matter of emphasis."

"Yes, but why types at all?"

"Well, they help you to know what you may and may not expect from others and from yourself too. For me they helped most in my marriage, next with our children, and then in my professional work. My husband and I wouldn't still be married if we hadn't had an understanding of Jung's types; we wouldn't have had our children and grand-children either. I might not have been here talking with you now. So you can see the whole business of types has been awfully important to me. Using his typology, Jung has made some fundamental distinctions about people, but it wasn't his intention to put people in pigeonholes or to excuse their inadequacies either. In fact, it was more to get people out of pigeonholes."

"What do you mean? How can a system that says some are naturally this way while others are that way get people out of pigeonholes?"

"By making us aware of how much we tend to imprison others in our own prejudices; of how much we tend to judge people by ourselves; and, even worse sometimes, to judge ourselves by others. So instead of saying, 'You're not like me, you idiot,' you might say, 'You're not like me; you're some other way, so I can't expect you to look at things the way I do, although you might try.' But let me try now to give you a very sketchy bit of orientation."

"Go ahead. It intrigues me. And I'll stop you if you launch into too complicated a lecture."

I liked that. She would not allow me to get carried away in my teaching role. She would let me know where I stood.

"Well, first of all, in this type system the population is divided into two groups with two different attitudes* toward life — 'extroversion' and 'introversion.' I'm sure you're already aware of these differences in people. Take you, for instance; you've described yourself to me as having been an adventurous, innovative, gregarious person before your illness. And there's your husband who, you say, keeps a lot inside himself."

"That makes me extroverted and him introverted?"

"It certainly sounds that way, although there is a lot more to it. Then there are four subdivisions of these two groups, and they're much harder to put into ordinary English."

"Give it a try."

"Okay, here we go. Within each of the two attitudes are four functions,* which account for four ways of coping with life. They're labeled sensation, thinking, feeling, and intuition, and they're paired off into two variations of opposing and supporting pairs. Thinking and feeling are one pair of opposites; intuition and sensation are the other. Now that makes how many?"

65

"You tell me. It sounds complicated, and my head just isn't up to complicated stuff."

"But there's a reason for my going at it this way. Let's take it step by step. We have the two attitudes — introversion and extroversion — each of which contains the same four functions; that makes eight possibilities. Then multiply the two variations of the pairs of function to get sixteen. There you are; we have sixteen different kinds of people. And that's a sobering thought. It put me on notice long ago not to be too sure I understood what people were about."

"I can believe you. But you haven't described anything except the two primary groups."

"True, and I have a way of putting it in a nutshell that's worked pretty well so far. It goes like this: Sensation tells me an object exists, thinking gives me a name for it, feeling tells me what it's worth, and intuition tells me what can be done with it."

"That's pretty good, but how do I come out in this?"

"My impression is that you may be primarily thinking and have sensation next and intuition and feeling last. We're similar, except that I have sensation first and thinking second. By the way, this difference between you and me may be because of our backgrounds — mine on the ranch was predominantly physical and yours was intellectual. Those last two, intuition and feeling, for you and me aren't much to write home about. Your husband may be your direct opposite. Mine is to me. In fact, most husbands and wives seem to be opposites, at least in our generations. We're forced to take our husbands on faith until we gradually get to know what they're like by trying to become familiar with those opposite functions in ourselves."

"I wonder if it's worth it."

"Well, since we seem to be stuck with this task for ourselves, we might as well keep the marriage while we're working on it. In such a setup two people can be enormously helpful to each other if they want to be. Of course, they can be pretty ruinous to each other too."

"Tell me more about the four ways of coping and why they're paired."

"That's not so easy. It's as though nature frequently patterns people into these pairs of opposites, who are drawn to each other. Here's a diagram of what I mean."

I came over to sit next to her on the couch and wrote on a corner of a piece of the art paper:

You:	Thinking	Sensation
Jim:	Feeling	Intuition

"This is your constellation and Jim's as far as I can guess, according to your strengths. There would be a similar design for your weaknesses, which, by the way, would be important too because one's weaknesses are what get one married in the first place. And our potential lies in those weaknesses. Two people of opposite types can be enormously helpful to one another; they can bring together two worlds instead of dividing one into two warring halves."

"Mmm. That's interesting. Did I marry Jim because my feeling and intuition and introversion are inadequate? Are we splitting apart our one world? That's a new idea. But enough, now; I'm tired. Maybe later you can spell it out for me."

"Yes, later. We'll talk about the functions as they come up, and that's bound to happen. Then I can hitch these theories to specific examples. By the way, this need to pin things down is characteristic of practical sensation types like ourselves."

I crossed back to my chair and sat watching her as she looked past me, past the redwood trees outside the window, pursuing her own thoughts. After a long pause Sally continued slowly, "I was just thinking. It really is a wonder that two people who are opposites can stand each other for a moment. Yet I know that old chestnut, 'opposites attract,' happens to be true."

"Yes, and there's the rub, at least for our generations. In a love relationship we tend to be attracted to the person who is strong where we are weak; that person rounds us out, completes us. It usually works out all right that way for a while, but at some point contempt for the other person's style may set in, and one may blame the other for being stubborn or unfeeling or rejecting or impractical or whatever. But the truth is that no one can do anyone else's rounding out. If you don't understand that, you can be awfully disappointed in the person you were counting on to do it for you."

Sally sighed, picked up a seashell from the table and rubbed its smooth surface in her hand.

"I'm not sure I know exactly what you're talking about, but what you say made me recall a conversation I had with a friend who came to see me yesterday. She's one of several friends I'm terribly worried about right now. It seems to be such a bad time for so many of my friends — trouble in their marriages, trouble with their children who are on drugs and running away from home. It's just awful. This friend who came yesterday just separated from her husband after eighteen years of marriage. She told me with such sadness

how much they loved and admired each other in the
beginning; they were very young when they married, just
like Jim and me. He's a bright go-getter, a successful lawyer;
she's tentative and shy, different from him in many other
ways too. She was trying to account for the subtle change in
their feelings for each other over the years; she said that one
of the qualities that had attracted her to him in the first
place, his sure sense of direction, she now felt as a fault, a
means of dominating and controlling her and the children.
She couldn't recollect at precisely what point in their marriage this change had occurred, nor why it had, and she just
couldn't understand it. I was puzzled too."

"It is puzzling, Sally. That kind of thing happens between
many husbands and wives over the years, and when it does,
the solution is never easy because it has to do with discovering and then strengthening in oneself whatever it is one had
needed most from the other. And often one person in the
marriage isn't interested in that kind of development and
would rather continue on in the same way, or give the whole
thing up and start again with someone else. Many in the
younger generations might be giving up marriage
altogether for this reason. It's a difficult task, becoming
whole, carrying your own self completely, especially when
you live with someone who is so different. It's the work of a
lifetime. I know that from my own experience. Jung has
termed that wholeness 'individuation,' although it's more of
a dynamic process than a static one; but there are other
names for it also: consciousness, oneness."

"Like satori in Zen?"

"Yes."

"I think I like this typing business. Maybe it will help me
with my family, especially the children. And it gives me

something to hang on to. Jung's psychology does slither around so much."

"Well, he was an intuitive, and he never intended to pin down his ideas. He deliberately kept them fluid, although his brilliant thinking gives a lot of stability to his ideas. It might interest you that Jung's system of types came out of his own necessity to understand why he and Freud simply couldn't resolve their differences. Sensation people like you and me find Jung's types especially interesting and helpful because of our need for concrete explanations. People who do not fit their milieu often want to know why they don't and get reassurance from discovering there are reasons outside of themselves for their difficulties. People who don't want to lose their relationship but are having a hard time of it, or people who've been disappointed in a relationship and need to know what went wrong, will resort to an understanding of types. But more about all this later."

She persisted in talking about the psychology of Jung, however. She told of having been an art teacher at a senior citizen's center, of how reading about individuation had now given her some understanding of what she sensed to be their attitude of detachment and acceptance of fate. She said she found Jung's concept of synchronicity* difficult to understand, and then proceeded to give an outstanding example of it from her own experience. When she first discovered a small lump in her breast, she was worried, told no one about it, and arranged to see a doctor. Several days before the appointment, she and Jim attended a New Year's party where the guests were entertained by a gypsy woman who told their fortunes with cards. When the queen of spades (the death card) came up twice, the woman grew pale, stopped, and refused to continue the session.

70

Sally's thoughts seemed to shift abruptly. "I think I'll stop reading Jung for a while. Anyway, I've a book of my own by Suzuki about Zen Buddhism that appeals to me far more."

It occurred to me then that Sally's attraction to Zen may have been another indication that sensation was one of her superior functions. Zen is a practical religion in which the physical is as important as the spiritual, and it appeals to many people like herself because it is geared to everyday life. Such people are instinctively impressed with the ordinary aspects of life, and they fret less about chores and routine happenings than others do. Their dedication to ordinary living relates to their deepest psychic life. Through the commonplace events of life, they come in contact with the archetypes, although they may not be able to recognize them as such until they are old. If they are in analysis, they mull over dreams for long periods of time, as though the dream clings to them and fascinates them; they do the same thing with life situations. Their concentration (in contrast to the intuitive, who is immediately focused on what comes next) brings about changes, which they recognize and which the analyst sees in their behavior and dreams, even though they themselves cannot explain how or why the changes have come about. I thought that Sally, because she was a sensation type, would have to find out about herself within the context of her immediate family.

I felt the need to stop this discussion about Jung's psychology and Zen Buddhism. My thoughts about having to leave Sally soon kept pushing everything else aside. I had to share them with her, for her sake as well as my own.

"Sally, I have to tell you that at the end of next month I'll be going away for six weeks on one of those trips I told you about in the beginning."

71

She sat up a bit straighter and smiled.

"Yes, you did. I understood it then and I do now. Where are you going?"

I watched her face for signs of the distress I knew she must be feeling, listened for nuances of anger or complaint in her voice. There were none. She seemed simply interested. Her bravery saddened me. Was this concealment of feeling a self-defense?

"To Europe. Zurich mostly, and then to London."

Mine was a matter-of-fact response, matching hers. But I wasn't fooling her either. Just as I knew her distress, she, too, must have known how troubled I felt about the separation.

"I've asked a colleague of mine to come to see you once a week when I'm gone, if you agree to the idea. I think you'll like him, and having someone to talk to will make you feel less alone while I'm away. Anyway, I think it's terribly important for you to continue the work you've begun."

It pained me to see her defenseless body become so tense.

"You must have gathered that I don't see how therapy could possibly prevent the spread of cancer, but I'm glad you've arranged for him to come. It does help to talk to someone."

"I'll write to you when I'm away, Sally. I don't usually do that with people because it's so hard for me, but I want very much to keep in contact with you. I hope you'll write to me, too, and tell me your dreams and how you are."

For a moment she looked directly into my eyes with her steady, hazel gaze. Then she relaxed into the cushions. Her expression became defenseless and sad.

"Yes, I will. Now I want to talk to you about some strange dreams I've had since last time. Listen to this one."

I was in prison, but I received a bouquet of red and white carnations that signified my release.

I felt she was brushing off the subject of my going away but I saw no point in countering her stoicism. It had become her badge of self-respect.

"That was all of it?"

"Yes."

"What do you think about it?"

"Red and white mean something positive to me."

"And prison?"

"I've no association to that."

The red and white carnations, referring to the opposites, could have to do with a positive attitude toward death — a time of the coming together of opposites — but I was not prepared to interpret them as such because at the time I hoped they meant a cure coming out of psychological death and rebirth. Her positive association indicated that if the bouquet did mean death, it was her task to find death's positive aspect, which might be her individuation. In terms of its being a way out of her misery she had already found something affirmative about it; still, she had no sense that death could be the culmination of her life, her crowning experience.

"Let me tell you, Sally from my experience with dreams I think this one's an important milestone."

"But why?"

"You say that the bouquet signified your release, so it must be pointing to a resolution."

"How could it be? In real life I feel as awful as ever. I feel no resolution, no relief."

"Let me tell you why I see it that way. According to Jung, red has symbolized the male and white the female for a thousand years. Can't we say then that this bouquet of the red and white flowers together signifies that the marriage can take place now — at least in terms of deepening your relation to Jim?"

"I don't see the connection. You told me once to let you know when I didn't, remember?"

"Right. Let me try again. Not long ago you had a dream about a deputy arriving with a subpoena to stop your marriage in order to answer charges — to face yourself and go your own innermost way. Now this dream comes up with you in prison, so you must have been convicted. Imprisonment means, I think, being forced, against your natural inclination, to concentrate completely on yourself, and that is another step forward on your road. Now here's another: You're being released. Could we say that now the psychological marriage can go forward? Remember your first dream?"

"I see what you're driving at, but this imprisonment hasn't been my choice. It's been forced on me, and that's different."

"True, but you're the whole dream, so the idea of locking you up comes from your own center. So from somewhere within, part of you has ordered you to know yourself and to accept yourself completely as someone unique and different from everyone else in the world. If only you could make the shift in attitude and begin to see the imprisonment as an inevitable commitment to something in you that's bigger than yourself. The facing of oneself is what human life is all about, Sally, mine as well as yours. Whether we live to be very old or die young, whether we're successful or unsuccessful, whether we achieve much or nothing is all beside the point. It is the consciousness we gain from living that matters. Jung says consciousness is the meaning of existence. The older I get the more I agree with him. This imprisonment of yours, this self-imposed dedication could be your true religious attitude."

"I just don't know."

"Try to look on the imprisonment as having been not only your illness but your fate, your unique psychic constellation that forces you to telescope your life to find yourself, to achieve individuation. This process could result in the sacred marriage within, a kind of completion of yourself that corresponds to what a young bride experiences when she marries the man she loves. Somewhere within you this marriage is now being experienced. Because you are released, it now remains for you to realize it."

"I have to think about this. Give me time. I don't mean to brush you off after going to so much trouble to explain, but I simply have to have time to try to take in what you've said. I can't agree with you just like that. In the meantime I must tell you another dream that's more understandable.

I was at a beach house with my mother. I was going blind. My right eye had been removed; but as I held my right eyelid open, I found that I could see light and that my sight was beginning to return. Then my mother held a diamond-shaped brooch that contained twenty-four one-karat diamonds in front of my eyes to test my vision. A ginger cat was going wild around the house.

"This one is a gift from the gods, Sally! It contains one of Jung's descriptions of the self image—mother, daughter, and symbol; you, your mother, and the diamond. Another dream of the female aspect of the self. In this dream your mother is not authoritative; she instructs by example, not by command as happened in your marriage dream of the father figure. But what are your thoughts about it?"

"I don't see what all the enthusiasm is about. Tell me, why doesn't it mean just what it says—that I'm worried about losing my sight? That's a real, understandable worry. The doctors have told me that cancer might make me blind."

"As far as the immediate, external situation is concerned, you're certainly right. But so much of our conscious life has deep roots leading to the unconscious and sometimes, as in this dream, to the self—to the inner sanctum of one's being."

"Now you're back on that inner thing again. And I need time to think about that. I just don't know."

"Well, let's take it step by step and try to find its logic. Since you're already worried about the possibility of going blind, the dream has to mean something more. Dreams tell us what we don't know or what we're not taking seriously enough. In fact, this dream is saying you've been blind, perhaps since you were born, and are now gaining some sight. You're seeing light, getting more light on the subject. Translated that could mean you are on the road to having a greater understanding of yourself. So perhaps it's pointing out that there are two kinds of sight: the physical kind and the magical, psychological kind. If you were to feel that by going blind you would gain another kind of sight, you might not feel so desperately curtailed if it did happen. I don't mean to seem unsympathetic to what could only be a tragic occurrence; it's just that a change of attitude about the possibility might help you. In any case the dream says you're beginning to see the light. But still more important, it's your mother who tests your sight."

"Mmm. I see, but . . ."

"She holds the diamond brooch to test your sight and you find your sight returning. Let's say then that you can now judge how well you are doing by how you make out with her. The more you understand what she has that you need, the more you will be able to respect her and get along with her."

"Well, I have to admit that things have been better with us in the last few days. Oddly enough, she's pretty well stayed off the drink. But I find it hard to think of my mother as being that important, and even though we're doing better, it's still pretty hard to think of her as anything but a blob. You know, we're so different; she's never in her life known what to do about anything. It's hard to imagine her having any meaning for me."

"Maybe a study of Jung's types might help you to understand her, Sally. My guess is that not only is she different, she's a hundred and eighty degrees different from you, if I'm right about your being an extroverted thinking type. She's probably introverted and primarily feeling, and feeling is your fourth function, your least available one. But it's the one that is paradoxically your lifeline. You cannot afford to lose contact with it. You need your mother for that."

"I can't imagine that being more like her would do me any good though. Most of the time she just sits around looking at me with this woebegone expression on her face. And she's even more bungling than Jim."

"But maybe we need to explore the cause of her bungling. It's hard for me, too, to understand introverted feeling people, but I have a friend who's one, and she tells me what it's like for that type. She says they're able to experience every nuance of feeling, the whole gamut, and I believe her. But she says the trap is that they can't help carrying the burden of the feelings of others close to them, and it makes them feel put-upon. Because they can't detach themselves, they suffer the other's feelings just as if they were their own.

The burden may become so unbearable that they have to withdraw, often with a great final outburst, which the other person can't understand. Or they may feel inadequate about not being able to alleviate the other's suffering; that's probably how it is for your mother. None of this gets articulated because of the introversion, and often the best they can come up with are bungling, inappropriate attempts to help or woebegone looks. Then if the close one, most often a thinking type, becomes hostile and impatient, they feel they are not valued, which of course they aren't at the moment because the thinking type doesn't understand what's going on with them. That compounds everything because, for the feeling person, to be valued is essential. And, incidentally, in my experience introverted feeling people expect you to understand what's going on with them and are terribly disappointed in you if you don't."

"But that describes how it is with Jim too. And I always thought the cause of our difficulty was that we were exactly alike. Something else to think about, and what a speech! But first what is that magical value which my inept mother holds for me in real life?"

"Believe it or not, that's just what I was coming around to. Granted your mother seems inept, but I wonder if it isn't her depth of feeling for you, her total awareness of your tragedy, that immobilizes her so much. Should you let out your feelings, live them, express them, you could be doing for yourself what she tries to do for you, and find a new source of energy in yourself. It would also relieve your mother of her burden. I can't help you here. My own inner feelings are not that available. Your mother is the key to your life. The diamond proves it. You might start by taking on faith the possibility that she has something crucial and important for you, and by keeping open to her you may come to it. But don't expect her to have ideas. You have enough for the two of you. Somehow I think Jim is in all this too. I don't have specific thoughts about him, but maybe they'll come to me later. I thought he was in it when you told me of your marriage dream. You thought he must be the bridegroom and I agreed, but I thought he could be the deputy also on a deeper level. In your dream he was, after all, your link to your governing, regulating center. I get the impression he has a kind of feeling that can take in your desperate situation, and this is why you need him so much. He may touch feelings buried at your center that could provide healing energy. But if he is the same type as your mother, don't expect him to explain himself or be articulate about your relationship. In order to reconcile a situation he would have to express feelings to you by a simple word or gesture, not through a long, verbal clarification."

I suspected that his feelings touched off her emotion, allowing her to be her unreliable, explosive self with him. He provided her with a security that she did not feel with me.

"It's strange. As I said, I'll have to think about that. And about my mother being so important. You say the diamond proves it . . ."

"The diamond is of the highest value in our society. And it is your mother who holds it for your benefit — not just one diamond, but many that are brought together in a brooch that is itself diamond shaped. The emphasis is significant. The diamond has been a central theme in myths and legends, and now here it is in this modern dream, your dream, as a symbol of the self. The diamond is also the symbol we choose for marriage. The engagement is sealed by the diamond ring; and the gold circle, the gold ring, is put on at the wedding ceremony. Both of them stay on for life if the marriage holds, and both are placed on the finger of the left hand — the unaware, 'off side,' so to speak, the side that refers to roots. It is a ritual developed out of deep symbolic experience from the beginning of time.

"We cannot get away from the importance of the marriage theme in your dreams, Sally. This time marriage is being dramatically associated with the symbol of the self through the diamond. Marriage was already implied in your first dream as a sacred event, and it has occurred in some of your other dreams — if not literally, then indirectly. Yes, I think we've been on the right track, and your efforts with Jim and your mother are on that same track."

It is interesting that Jim was present only by implication in the impersonal marriage. This dream is about her personal mother. Both dreams are of the self, but it seemed to me that the female aspect of the self, unlike the male, was finding expression in her family life.

"There's still another item loaded with meaning in your dream. It's a kind of reverse oedipal theme. Oedipus was blinded by his mother's brooch, but in your dream you are helped to gain your sight by means of your mother's brooch. The mother, who drives the son to unconsciousness, helps the daughter with consciousness."

"That's interesting. I suppose that could be so. Yes, but what about the ginger cat going wild?"

"Oh, yes, I forgot that part. Possibly the overwhelmingly positive effect of your dream created a kickback. Your dream is concerned with an enormous spiritual effort that is opening your eyes. In the effort your female, or animal, instinct must be sacrificed. You are, after all, at an age

80

when the biological instincts assert themselves. To gain psychic insight of such dimensions at your age must mean the sacrifice of your warm-blooded, young side. So why shouldn't the ginger cat go wild? Perhaps your pent-up, untamed emotions are wanting out.

"All this takes time to assimilate. I need to understand it in my own terms and that takes so much time. Let's leave it for now."

She had been completely attentive until this time, but now she seemed impatient to put everything we'd been talking about aside. I knew that as a sensation type, she would mull over these points until she understood them.

"But on second thought, there's one more thing. Why should marriage itself be so emphasized symbolically with diamonds and gold rings and the ziggurat and court charges?"

"I can only guess that when marriage was first dreamed up, it must have been looked on as an important step toward maturity, toward development of character that would automatically make conscious much that lies unconscious in us. Marriage, after all, follows a universal pattern of bringing together the opposites — the impossible magically made possible. We all know marriage is difficult and requires a great deal of understanding and effort and faith and struggle, as well as love. That goes for any serious relationship between a man and woman. It is perhaps for a woman, apart from any effort she makes in her professional life, her greatest opportunity for growth. It is important for a man, too, if he wants to become more conscious through a serious relationship, although the man's primary need is for increasing his awareness through his professional life. I believe the frequency of failed marriages only proves how difficult this test in life is and what an enormous achieve-ment it is if marriage works. It may be one good reason why so many young people prefer short-term affairs."

"Well, I know I have a long way to go, with both Jim and my mother. One thing that makes it so hard with my mother is that I can't stand her wanting me to help her face my illness. I have enough trouble facing it myself."

"Of course you can't help her with that. It might help, though, if you could see your relationship with your mother in a different light. I think you may be putting some de-spised part of yourself that you're not aware of onto her. We all do that. It's very common to see in others what we really reject in ourselves, both good and bad, and what we're ashamed of, including our inferiorities that will never im-prove, much like an ugly face we might have inherited. Parts of our outworn personality also get put on other people, outgrown phases that nevertheless still belong to us, like a long tail dragging behind. That's a rather oversimpli-fied version of what Jung called the 'shadow.'* It'll have to do for our purposes. Otherwise you'll accuse me of launch-ing into another speech!"

"But why the word 'shadow'? I've seen it in my reading. Is it because there's something dubious about it?"

It seemed to me that she was now constantly pushing for clarification. It was indeed a miracle that she could be so determined when she hurt so much. I felt increasingly de-pressed about having to leave her at this crucial turning point in her life. I was worried that my absence could feed her old tendency to indulge her self in disillusionment. I was especially eager to go on with the answers to her questions in hopes that they would tide her over until my return.

"Not always. Sometimes our greatest potentials lie in the

shadow because they haven't surfaced from the depths where it is dark—the dark of the shadow. We've all got one. If you regard the shadow as it occurs in nature, you'll get the point; you'll see how impartial it is, even though we project our moral bias onto it. Whatever is in the light casts a shadow; and the bigger the item in the light, the bigger and blacker is the shadow. The more we see, the less we see. Enough to discourage you in your efforts. But it isn't as bad as all that."

"Wouldn't the shadow have to do with one's choice of a partner? Didn't you say nature insists on our being rounded out, so we choose our opposites? Couldn't that be where the shadow goes too?"

"Well, in Jung's terms, the shadow is not represented by someone of the opposite sex. The shadow for you and me has to be a woman. For you it might be your mother, who is your opposite in type. But you're also right about our need to contact the shadow to round us out. It gives us depth as well and keeps us from being too sure that our way is the only way. It gives us humility and sometimes spice. Think how two dimensional a painting is that has no shadow in it."

"But couldn't it also account in some way for disparate people marrying?"

"I suppose you could say that, although marriage technically involves the projection of the woman's potential masculinity onto her husband. And there's the man's projection of his feminity onto his wife also. But certainly the shadow gets involved in the marriage when people are unconscious. It's true, too, that a lot of our inferiorities instead of our potentials come out during the wear and tear of marriage. And when they're unknown to us, we attribute them to our spouses, where they don't apply. So, more often than not, marriage becomes an institution that promotes unconsciousness whereas it is designed to do just the opposite. Certainly the shadow is in all this. It's what I see in your trouble with your mother too."

"Tell me specifically what I'm putting onto my mother."

"Well, those qualities you despise as being 'weak' in your mother. It seems to me you need to find for yourself some of those female qualities, like softness and dependency, that are exaggerated in her. True dependence needn't be a weakness, even though that's the way you see it now. In my experience it often takes strength to admit one's weaknesses. That's a strength too."

She sighed. The liveliness that had been so apparent in her throughout most of this visit had disappeared. She seemed distressed, lost, overwhelmed with grief. Perhaps her feelings were being released a little by all this talk.

"Once I was close to my mother; she was a great comfort to me. She taught me how to sew, to cook, and to do all the domestic things. I loved it all as my children do now. But I couldn't admire her after the way she was when my father had that affair. I had to turn against her."

There must have been more to it than that, I thought. Her having to reject her mother on those grounds hadn't rung true when she mentioned the affair the first time, but I didn't press her. She sighed again, then was silent for a few moments.

"What is it, Sally?"

"I was just thinking. You know, sometimes when I'm just about to wake up and I'm in the half-asleep, half-real state, I hear myself calling out 'Mama, Mama!'"

The color drained from her lips; her fragile face had a pallid, worn look.

Jung wrote in *Shadow, Animus, Anima* that the marriage quaternity for a woman is made up of the woman, the man, the animus, and the chthonic mother:* the transcendent quaternity forms the pattern similar to the self. Without knowing, Sally was seeking what was missing. She had a husband, and she knew about her masculinity. There were, counting herself, three dimensions in her life. But the fourth, the mother, was missing because of her poor relationship to her actual mother and her mother's poor opinion of herself. Society has generally, until now, repressed the chthonic mother. Among the more enlightened of the younger generation of women who like sex and what goes with it, this archetype has recently begun to appear in a more positive way; there is evidence that it is associated with the self in a woman's psyche.

I felt strongly that the mother for Sally, as a modern woman, was of great concern. The mother nowadays not only incorporates patriarchy's chthonic woman but also spiritual woman. If the personal mother is not available, the modern woman needs to involve an older, wiser, more experienced woman than herself. Persephone's relationship to Demeter, illustrated in the statue found at Cyrene, is a significant example of a grown daughter's close relationship with her mother. The fully matured but smaller figure of Persephone reclines on the lap of Demeter, who is portrayed as nearly twice her size. They as an ensemble are the divine goddess, demonstrating the protective, all-accepting attitude of Demeter and the trusting nature of Persephone. The Demeter and Persephone statue of Cyrene, excluding a male figure, can be a guide for modern woman to help her solve the mother problem before she seeks out a man, as well as to connect with an older mother figure throughout her life.

"Sally, are you afraid of dying? Shouldn't we talk about death again?"

"I'm not afraid of dying, I've told you that. It's only the terminal part of the disease I'm afraid of. I've seen patients dying in the hospital; it's horrible. I don't want to be a vegetable. My God, I want no part of that! And another thing, there's a chapter in Jung's memoirs about life after death that really upsets me. He says his dead father came to him in a dream when his mother was dying and asked him for advice about their marriage, as if the father expected their relationship to continue after her death. How awful! I don't want to think of death in those terms. I want death to be the end. I've had enough surprises. I want to be annihilated, to be nothing. I want it to be all over."

"I don't blame you; you must be fed up with the struggle."

"I did not respond to her stated wish for annihilation, feeling at the time that it was a totally negative statement, as it may well have been. But in retrospect I'm not so sure. As a therapist, one learns along the way. The *Tibetan Book of the Dead* refers to annihilation at death as consciousness weaned away from all form, from all attachment to objects, and returned to a timeless, inchoate state. Sally may unknowingly have been reaching for a state, which for the East implies a totally completed life before death. I was asking her to be her unique living self, to work toward individuation — the objective in life. She was seeking the opposite, which was perhaps not to be nothing, but to be eternal and universal. Had I been aware of this idea when she made the statement, I might have pointed out that her attitude was accepted in some cultures, thereby helping her find meaning in her negativism.

"Would you like to stop now for today, Sally?"

"No, not yet. My head hurts, but I feel a little better, I really do. And I must tell you about two more dreams."

Indeed, she looked better; her color had returned. Perhaps her assurances that she did not fear death were false. I think she needed to give vent, at least indirectly, to the fear. She seemed so eager to go into the dreams, as if she now saw them as her own creative production.

"I had these dreams on the same night that I woke up calling out 'Mama.' The people in the first one are Nanny, a close family friend — a funny old, outspoken lady of about eighty who used to babysit for us — and Aaron, who is Mark and Susan's son.

It was Christmas Eve. Jim and Sarah and Beth and I were moving into a new house, a modern bungalow. Nanny and Aaron were with us too. Nanny was silently setting the Christmas table with huge goblets of red fruit juice. She seemed austere and out of character, although she wasn't unpleasant or hostile. Aaron was impatient, so I let him go outside to run and play.

This is another "big dream" of the female aspect of the self. In it Nanny (the English term for nurse, or governess, if one thinks of the regulating function of the self) appears in the role of generalized mother. She is fruitful, protective, silent, austere, and enigmatic; she is probably the mother archetype.* Her advanced age refers to wisdom; she may be the wise old woman.* She is all-inclusive, so much more than Sally's mother. Her importance is stressed by the red — bloodlike — juice, which has a female, earth quality. The image of the vessel is a feminine symbol, a maternal womb in which the figure of the god-man is transformed and reborn in a new form. This motif has historical connections with the gnostic religions as well as with the Osiris myth. Women are associated with blood because of birth and menstruation; Nanny implies the chthonic mother as described by Jung, and in the dream answers the call for 'Mama.'

Sally knew the Bible, so the story of Aaron was familiar to her. He had the power to destroy as well as to create with his rod. The child,

Aaron, is archetypal; male and very young, he is the opposite of Nanny, female and very old. In reality he is the child of Sally's hippie neighbors, and they have already appeared in a death dream of omnipotence. In real life as hippies, they are opposed to the rational and the traditional in which Sally has been contained, and which has made her rigid. This rigidity may have helped promote her disease, for rigidity, requiring an involuntary repression of the instincts, is exhausting. Her potential was too great for so restrained an attitude.

Now she must look beyond into the unknowns of death in order to be prepared for either life or death. Moving into a new house could mean moving to a new attitude. Jung has said and it has been my experience that moving into new places, and journeys also, especially when dreamed by someone so ill, are death dreams.

She and Nanny were celebrating Christmas, which is specifically a ritual of rebirth—the end of the old and the beginning of the new. It could be forecasting a spontaneous cure in life or death as a cure leading to rebirth—a concept that seemed to interest her unconscious. But I was not able to say any of this to Sally; she had just told me of her wish for annihilation and for no surprises in her death.

"What are your associations to this dream?"

"I haven't any, but I do recall that I wasn't aware of being ill in the dream. I could get around."

"I feel this is an important dream, Sally, but I don't think we can do too much with it at this point other than feel its creative implications and be happy with so positive a statement. It certainly is talking about the self again; there's hardly a dream so far that hasn't. Nanny and Aaron couldn't be more opposite, and they come in a pair. The symbol of the fruits of the earth appears with them, so altogether it makes a symbol of the self."

Because I couldn't bring myself to be candid about my fear that she would die, I passed over this dream. But it is significant that she didn't push me to analyze it fully; she must have had the same concern. Possibly I could have talked more frankly about death, and perhaps it would have been better for her if I had. This is one of those difficult questions one ponders in retrospect.

"Tell me the other dream now."

I was in the hospital, terribly ill. My mother and father, sad and depressed, were visiting me. Then you came in. You were matter-of-fact and rational, not comforting in the usual sense. Still, you calmed and cheered my parents. You fed the tiger cat and offered to feed the dog, but my father explained that we didn't have a dog.

This dream suggested that my matter-of-factness, my doing for her and holding things together, my rationality, which made her feel good on awakening, were all part of our relationship. She treated me like a sibling, not a mother. I was more managing than mothering and that she could accept. My relative objectivity was helpful to her. She also needed Jim, with whom her emotions, even though unruly, could live.

"Any associations to this one?"

"No, but when I woke up I felt good about it all."

"You felt good, even though it was a dream of being terribly ill in the hospital?"

"That's true."

"Then try to believe this much from these dreams: a good connection with the older woman is of the highest importance for you now."

I thought again that if this advice were part of the modern women's movement, it would have modified the present drive in women to compete with men, for the sake of competition, rather than find their own true way of functioning.

"But right at the moment the tight pain in my head is just unbearable. And there's a rumble in it like thunder."

She took a sip from the glass of water on the table in front of her, a pill, another few sips of water.

"If only I can keep this down now. We'd better say good-bye for today."

As I was driving home from this visit, I realized that I needed help with the problem of how open I could be with Sally—how far could I go with her in discussing these dreams of death. It occurred to me then that I might contact Marie-Louise von Franz for consultation during my stay in Zurich. Dr. von Franz had been a student and close friend of Jung and was an eminent Jungian analyst in her own right. I needed her ideas, her support. I thought, too, that writing to Sally of Dr. von Franz's impressions of her dreams might help, for to have them taken seriously by so distinguished a person might validate their importance and sustain her interest in them during my absence. I wondered why so many dreams that showed progress had come on the eve of my departure. I found this a depressing stroke of fate, knowing how they might be thrown on the scrap heap with my not being around to remind her of their meaning and importance.

CHAPTER SIX

I ARRIVED unnoticed this morning to find Sally, wearing a short cotton nightgown and wrapper, sitting stiffly on the couch. Her fingers were curled into fists beside her; her slippered feet were tightly crossed. She was looking steadily over the head of the woman who was reading a magazine in the armchair across from her. She seemed to be willing away this presence who was Thelma, her mother-in-law.

A soft ray of filtered sunlight illuminated the dust on the table, accentuating the stillness of the big room. The two women sitting six feet apart could have been strangers. Each of them, enclosed in her own separateness, occupied this space today only because of her tie to Jim.

I felt as though I had walked onto a stage. My entrance would be the cue for another action, freeing them from each other for a while.

"Hello, Mrs. Wheelwright. I didn't hear you come in. This is Jim's mother."

"I'm glad to meet you. I've heard a lot about you."

She put down her magazine. She was smiling and somehow not smiling. She addressed me as I sat down.

"If you're going to be here for a while, I think I'll go down into town and do some shopping."

She turned to Sally, "All right, Sally? Sarah won't be back from riding till noon, and there's enough of that barbequed chicken for the two of you for lunch."

"Go ahead, Thelma. No need for you to stay around."

The slam of the front door signaled Sally's letting go.

"I just can't stand having that distracting, vulgar woman around me! Did you see how eager she was to get out of here? She couldn't wait to be gone. What irony! One of the reasons we got married was to get away from our mothers, and here they are back with us, one right after the other. God, I wish I'd hurry up and die or get better. I just can't stand the waiting. The agony never stops. I feel like a jar with the lid screwed on tight, bursting at the sides."

"You do look so tired this morning, Sally. What happened?"

"I spent most of this morning trying to clean up my house a bit to set an example for Thelma. She's such a slob, it's incredible. No, no, it's not just my projection; she really is a slob and I can prove it. She's completely insensitive about what needs to be done in the garden, and she leaves a mess behind her everywhere she goes. But what I hate the most is that when my friends come to visit, she won't leave us alone. Their visits are one of my few remaining pleasures, and she just sits right here in the room with us, an awful, formless presence. I can't say anything to her so I stew inside. Jim's asked her many times to leave me alone with my friends, but it's no use. She forgets, she says."

"Sally, let me talk to Jim about it, won't you?"

"No, never mind; we'll handle it by ourselves."

For some reason Sally had seemed reluctant to have me meet Jim. She probably had her own reasons for keeping us apart. Our getting together "for her good" would have deprived her of some of her autonomy, and whatever she had left of that was precious to her. Then, too, Jim had been vocal about his disapproval of psychology.

"Everything is terrible right now. You know it has to be because Cyrano has disappeared again, and that's always a sign of trouble. I woke up the other night screaming 'They're killing my cat!'"

For Sally the cat seemed to be connected with her new female psychic life. Perhaps her cry, 'They're killing my cat!' referred to her family's blindness or resistance to her efforts toward becoming a woman in her own right. Cats have what Sally needed, independence and a less suggestible nature.

"Beth's away visiting my mother in San Diego, and she hasn't written. I miss her so much; and on top of everything Jim's going away on one of his business trips. I just hate having him gone. You'll see by my dream how upset I am."

I was all alone on a very pleasant beach that surrounded a body of water. It must have been a bay because there were no breakers. For some reason I had to cross this bay on a surfboard that was like a raft; I had to paddle it with my hands the way surfers do. It was a huge ordeal, a supreme effort, but somehow I managed to get across. When I arrived on the other shore, I felt relieved and triumphant. Jim met me there and told me he appreciated what I had done, but that for some reason beyond his control I had to go back.

It was growing dark and foggy and I was afraid, but I was determined to accomplish the return. I paddled out into the harbor, past a sailboat carrying a handsome couple and their four-year-old son. They waved to me as if they were giving me encouragement, but they didn't offer to help. I awakened before I knew whether or not I made it back.

Her connection with Jim is becoming more conscious. The pattern of this dream suggests that of her earlier marriage dream. Here it is Jim and not a deputy who intervenes, ordering her to go back. Jim is under the command of the self, because the self's demand is beyond his control. On the personal level I feel she is being told she has more work to do before she can be with Jim in the most real sense. I wonder if Jim is sending her back, unwilling himself to attempt to resolve their relationship because he knows she will die. Her death will be beyond his control.

It is also a dream of the male aspect of the self, especially because of Jim's being in the position to command. The coming together of the male with the female aspect of the self is implied in the handsome couple. The sailboat is their symbol of union.

This is the third dream in which the four-year-old boy appears. The other two dreams certainly were concerned with death — the one of ceramic instruments and the one of the celebration of Christmas with Nanny. Sally must be well in this latest dream (another indication of death, if not a miraculous cure, for so ill a person), and she seems to be crossing the bay the second time in a ghostly, archetypal atmosphere. It is foggy and dark; the figures in the sailboat, like Nanny in the previous dream, are noncommittal, are simply there. She is going "out" somewhere. Because she has to return, the going out may mean a brush with death.

The couple and the boy are special because they are above what is happening; they are quite untouched by her excruciating effort and disappointment. There are three of them, like the three lamps that we already associated with the Christian Trinity. The idea of three could also mean death if we include the image of Christ crucified between two thieves. In this dream the three are ordinary people, outside of traditional religion. Jung mentions that the Christian Trinity might have stemmed from the Egyptian threesome: Osiris, Horus, and Isis. Explorations into the neolithic era identify Isis as a descendant of the original female deity, the great mother.

The boy, being four, indicates a totality that projects into the future as another phase, possibly after death. The boy indicates the future because for him most of life lies ahead.

"What are your thoughts about the dream?"

"Jim's reason for having to go away now is impersonal. The trip is beyond his control, just as his reason for sending me back in the dream was beyond his control."

"And in both instances, in reality as well as in the dream, you perhaps feel he's expecting too much of you."

Again, I did not mention to her my thoughts about there being intimations of her death in this dream. I thought then (and as it turned out, I was wrong) that speculation of this nature would have upset her unnecessarily.

"Right. He expects me to tell him that I'll be all right when he's away. It's too much! And I miss him terribly when he goes away because he does so many things for me his mother can't do."

This remark was so typical of a woman who is either too vulnerable or too unconscious of her feelings to express loss. She made it sound as if she needed Jim only for practical reasons; in fact it was the pain of loss, not need, she was experiencing. If only she could have expressed her feeling to him, it would have helped Jim to help her. In her real life he certainly was a possible link to her feelings if she could have honored him with the role. She never confessed to me the intensity of her harangues against Jim. She may have thought the behavior too inferior, and so it was; but it was also behavior that was essential for her well-being. She had to burst out to someone, and she could not do that with me. She seemed to need to brave it out with me and, I gathered as time went on, with her friends as well. That also helped her. She needed all of us.

Sally continued, "Thelma gets frightened when he's not here, and her fears upset me. And if the vomiting gets much worse, I'll have to go to the hospital in San Francisco for intravenous feedings. Most of my friends will be on vacation, and Thelma doesn't drive; so if I have to go, I don't know how I'll get there."

"So many worries for you. But I'll drive you, Sally. I'll be glad to help out in emergencies when Jim's away."

She looked away from me, unable to respond. Perhaps

her conflicting needs for help and independence made her unable to accept or reject my offer; also I'm sure she wanted to be considerate and not make demands. She had to cling to her independence, no matter how isolated, unrelated, and afraid she might have felt. It would never have occurred to her that I would welcome the opportunity to do something concrete to help her.

"Besides expecting so much from me, Jim also puts too much of his worry onto me. I guess he feels that since I'm having therapy I can handle more of it. So he piles it on, and the more I'm able to take the more he dumps onto me. I've got so many worries. You're right about that."

Again she averted her eyes; then abruptly they looked back into mine.

"One of my worries is that we've had no sex now for two and one-half years."

"I'm sure that's been tough on you, Sally; naturally it would be. But there haven't been any dreams specifically referring to sex. Sex doesn't seem to be a problem, at least as far as the unconscious is concerned."

"No, it's no problem for me anymore; I don't have the desire or the energy for sex. But it's Jim I worry about; I wonder how he can manage. He does a lot of running around the track to work off his tension, but that can't take care of all of it. I sometimes wish that he'd take on another woman for sex, but I don't think he'd ever do that. He'd have to be emotionally involved with someone to have sex with her."

"Have you talked this over with him?"

"No, not specifically, and this just isn't the time to do it either. Anyway, the tension isn't all sexual, you know. Our marriage has always been in a state of tension, of working things out. We were only seventeen when we met and fell in love. I guess that's pretty young."

"It certainly is. People change over time and so do their relationships, but the changes you and Jim have had to make because of your illness are far more drastic than they would normally have been. Still, there are some positive aspects, too, if only you wouldn't resist them."

"Ha, what positive aspects!"

"Well, look, the illness gives you a chance first to look at your relationship, and then it sets up things for you to struggle with. You need Jim now in ways you've never needed him before. He's stronger physically than you are; he's not undermined by illness. That's not to say he's stronger than you are in every way. You may be the stronger one as far as will is concerned; the remarkable way you're fighting the sickness suggests that. Few people could do as well, including myself, I'm sure. But yours strikes me as a masculine strength. I feel your feminine strength needs to come along, too, to give you balance. You could, for instance, acknowledge your need for Jim to help you where you are helpless. And through acknowledging the need, you might admit a genuine dependence that Jim could relate to. That's a part of your femininity you've never allowed to unfold."

But she did not understand what I was driving at. She may have been taken aback by my suggesting that she capitalize on her illness and turn her tragedy into an advantage in what could only seem a heartless way. At the time I thought I had to keep her trying, to keep her from giving up. But I had to admit also that I may have been pushing awfully hard, instead of fully realizing the tragedy of my abandoning her. Feelings like these are hard to discover when one lacks the function for them.

She looked at me derisively. "Come on, I despise femininity. The word itself conjures up pictures of sweet, sentimental women I can't stand. What do you mean by masculine strength, anyway?"

"Well, there's a term for it. It's called "animus," and on the impersonal level it's an archetype. Without bogging you down in a very complicated subject, an archetype is a psychic pattern common to everyone. It mainfests itself in dreams as a typical situation like the wedding, but not a specific wedding; or as a figure with universal meaning like the mother, but not someone's mother; and for you just now, as the man, but not a particular man."

"Yes, I've read about archetypes, and I think my dream of standing on top of the tower was an archetypal dream. But still I'm not sure that's really what it was; sometimes I think I dream in archetypes only because of you."

"I doubt it, Sally, but our honoring your dreams the way we do may help to get them going. Anyway, the animus is an inherent male image that lives in the psyche of every woman, just as its counterpart, the anima,* a female image, lives in the psyche of every man. When the animus is driving a woman in a negative way, she's apt to be bossy, inflexible, and opinionated. She may lay down the law, make assumptions, or make judgments she doesn't bother to document. She can be the mother who always knows best. Positively, it gives her courage, the will to see things through, direction and structure in her life, consistency, and so on. Without this positive animus you could never have coped with your illness the way you have. It has given you strength."

I had realized that the negative animus, externalized, was expressed in Sally's resentment toward her children, in preferring a job to domesticity, and in her bickerings with Jim.

At times it manifested itself as a competitive, nonrelating, task-oriented agent that disrupted the home. Had Sally continued to work at a paid job, her animus would have found its rightful place. Internalized, it showed itself in feelings of inferiority and worthlessness, and in a repressive rigidity that she, without knowing, turned inward on herself. I think it put her in a psychic straitjacket that exhausted her and made her vulnerable to disease.

Because thinking was her superior function, she could not fit into the nonthinking feminine stereotype of the patriarchal collective. She had rejected her mother, and being constituted mentally more like her father, identified with him. This masculine identification tied in with her good mind would make her rigid and opinionated, for a woman's animus thinking, unlike a man's thinking, has no heart. It is like that of a computer. On the other hand, with her woman's perceptiveness she could go to the heart of the matter. Because she was not bound to procedure, rules, and regulations as men are, she could, and did, at times creatively debunk people's pet notions. At other times she was only tactless.

"Tell me more about animus strength."

"It's the kind that women look for in the ideal or the traditional man: purposefulness, conscientiousness, the ability to see things through, reliability, courage. I see a lot of it in you, Sally."

"Well, certainly I do admire that much more than femininity."

"But I think it's inferior femininity you're against. Listen, let me propose to you the notion of catlike femininity. It shouldn't be difficult for you to imagine because you're obviously very drawn to cats. Cats are graceful, elegant, resourceful, practical, feminine. Even though they nurture their young, they are not in the least afraid to let them know when they've done their mothering job long enough. That's the instinctual female in them. They're affectionate and responsive, but strictly on their own terms. They're honest about independence and dependence; they can be either when they need to be. They're indirect, unlike dogs; they are discreet and can keep their own counsel. They're able to wait, to bide their time; there is strength in this kind of passivity. There's their dark, wild side too. Think of the emotional, unearthly sounds cats sometimes make at night. And think of Cyrano's arbitrary, independent, and out-rageous habits that he shares with all cats. The cat symbol-izes the female psyche very well because it's never entirely domesticated. Like cats, women keep their roots in the wild; they are somehow closer to nature than men are. Anyhow, I've been describing what I see as true femininity to you, Sally. Do you despise it?"

"No, of course not. I haven't thought about it that way. But look, my Cyrano is a male; and as for the cats that show up in my dreams, I'm not aware of what sex they are; maybe they're all male, then their characteristics would be mascu-line."

"They could be of either sex, and when you can't tell, the self may be involved. Sometimes the animus in a dream scouts and tells us what's coming or could come in terms of experience. It can be presented as an animal, a human, or a symbol; and it often familiarizes us with a problem before we actually confront it. And if the animus were to present the problem of femininity, that problem might be symbol-ized by a male cat because theory and the consideration of problems come out of the masculine side. But femininity

100

itself in the process of solution would show up in a dream as a female cat. The solution itself is feminine business, even though it's sometimes supported by such masculine qualities as will and courage. So you might dream of a cat of either sex or no sex at all, depending on where you are in relation to the problem of femininity."

"Do you really believe all that? I mean, I'd like to, but..."

"But it's not rational and you can't prove it."

"Exactly."

"Well, that's right. You can't. But in my experience with patients and with my own dreams, I've found it to be a workable premise. So why not just consider it a possibility and perhaps let in something new that could help you?"

"I'm sure I could use something new. But speaking of the irrational, I should tell you now about the dream I had the other night, because just by coincidence the cat turned up again. Or would you say synchronistically?"

"Perhaps."

I was in Paris, walking down a boulevard with two women who were my age; perhaps they were friends. We passed a large department store with a sign on it saying Joseph Magnin, Paris. *It was apparently a French branch of the San Francisco store. I persuaded my friends to go in with me.*

The aisles were filled with displays of luxury items, all priced in francs, which I had difficulty translating into dollars. There was one handkerchief that had a black and a white kitten finely embroidered on it. As I tell you this, it occurs to me that I was looking for a gift for my mother. That handkerchief was what I wanted, but to my great surprise, it cost sixty-five dollars.

"And that reminds me, I got a letter from my mother the next day telling me that they'd been adopted by a black and white kitten who showed up on their doorstep."

"That really is a meaningful coincidence, an outer event and an inner theme happening at the same time. And you have to consider how important the cat seems to be for you — Cyrano and the cats in your dreams."

"Yes, I believe it's synchronicity; that's what it is. I really like the idea of that; it makes sense to me because I see it happening to me in so many ways.

"It does give depth to your life, doesn't it. It brings in the irrational and points to the mystery in your life."

"Yes, it helps very much. It's really quite curious."

Synchronicity appealed to Sally as it does to people whose sensation function is strong. Concepts are believable to them if they can be experienced, and synchronistic events need no speculation — they simply happen.

She seemed lost in her thoughts for a moment; she was more moved than I had seen her before. Then she returned to our conversation.

"You'll want associations to the dream now. Well, I've never been to Paris, but I always wanted to go there. I've studied French since I was about twelve, and I majored in French literature in college. In the dream I was happy to be in France, and even though I go on complaining about her, I often think of my mother lately and that dream of the diamond brooch."

"So if going to Paris is something you deliberately prepared for long ago, maybe in some inner way now you might be realizing that old fantasy."

Besides carrying contents of the past and present, the unconscious also holds what is to be in the future. Sally probably would have gone to Paris had she lived; this is why I interpreted the dream as an effort of the unconscious to present to her the future she might not live. If a viable

102

future indeed existed in her unconscious and if she could absorb the messages from that source, she would inevitably experience an expansion of her personality that would occur normally from living a longer life. It may be that this telescoping process is the task of a dying young person — to live psychically into the future.

"Paris is the most sophisticated shopping center of the world, and since you're housebound, it must mean personal expansion for you — something is being added. Can you use this dream to help you feel what it would be like to be there, then let your imagination play around with it? Why not try, and perhaps some concrete feeling of really being there will come to you. Mull it over the way you apparently do the dream of your mother holding the diamond brooch. That can do a lot for you as it has done before."

I was referring to the technique of active imagination,* which can be practiced by sensation people if they concentrate all their energy on a dream situation. The dream figures sometimes behave objectively and convey to the dreamer important messages from the unconscious.

I felt sure that her mulling, typically a sensation habit, would bring her to individuation in the end. It happens in this subliminal way where it cannot be seen. Intuitive types cannot know about this, for it is a sensation phenomenon. The intuitive type, because of an aversion to repetition, instinctively rejects this kind of activity. But paradoxically the intuitive type must experience similar phenomena many times over before the point is made real. The sensation type is repetitive in reflection, but one experience is enough.

Because she was silent, I questioned her, "And what about the sixty-five-dollar handkerchief?"

"Sixty-five is the age of senior citizens when they're eligible for retirement."

In this association she might have unknowingly been referring again to the psyche's ongoing telescoping process.

"So it seems you're concerned with being sixty-five and retired. And how hard that is for someone your age! Once more, as in the dream where the cat kicked up in an instinctive reaction against your having to be conscious, you're being required to sacrifice your young attitude. What a big task! I'm not surprised it costs sixty-five dollars. I also think the dream suggests that you need to get your blacks and whites — your opposite moods — together. That would be the attitude of a sixty-five-year-old woman, who instinctively accepts both the black and white moods and does not get stuck in first one and then the other. And in terms of the effort you'll have to make, the cost will be excessive. That can't be helped."

I looked at this young-old person across from me, saw an almost fleshless, pale woman sitting with her skeletal shoulders held straight in the effort to understand, to connect with her dream, to grow. I was saddened and wished that I could suggest something to help.

"Can't you remember the good dreams and how they've made you feel when you've been so low? Remember your feeling of getting out of prison? Could you try to recapture some of that? It might help now to get the black and white together."

"Ha, you should be in my shoes."

"Look, really I understand. And your dream says the cost is so high. Can't you just try?"

I made this suggestion from my knowledge of Sally and my desire to help rather than out of the content of her dream. Sometimes a dream offers an excuse to present my view of the dreamer. At times these suggestions are helpful; at times they are not. I hated to push her but saw no alternative. I felt I must not let her give up.

"But I don't even know how to begin to try. I actually need some practical solutions. Like just what do I do with the black feelings that rub out everything good?"

"Tell me about them. Describe them to me."

"They tell me what's true about myself—that I'm a fake, a zombie, that I have no real feeling."

It is enormously difficult for a person like Sally, with a strong sensation function, to maintain a connection with the unconscious when her body, her main stronghold, is disabled by disease, pain, and drugs. I sensed that Sally's sterile, negative feeling, amounting to brutal self-criticism, resulted from this loss of contact. It promoted an evil shadowy takeover in her. The shadow invariably hovers over people who are so badly cut off. Also, getting stuck in the present and not being able to see ahead or behind is a pit that sensation types fall into. The past and future tend not to exist for them. Whatever the present contains can be all of life forever.

"Why don't you try drawing or painting those feelings when they take you over, Sally?"

"Oh, no, I wouldn't want to do that. I'd be afraid. I still don't know why, but there's something terribly threatening about that. It's all right for me to paint mandalas; they have a definite structure. But I think it's dangerous for me to probe into my black feelings. I think I'll stop reading Jung too. Maybe detective stories are best after all. They take my mind off myself."

Obviously, reading Jung's work had already stirred some

unknown and threatening depths within her. Painting her dark feelings might take her too close to the unknown. In the past, hard work had enabled her to live through her times of depression and dark intuition. I wondered if she might indeed have been a borderline psychotic who perhaps got cancer instead.

I think one needs some kind of security to tackle the unconscious, and for Sally that security would have been her body. Had she been physically strong, she might not have been so afraid of probing into herself. Faced with death, a person whose sensation function is dominant is extremely insecure psychically. As the disease progressively erodes the body, there is danger that the ego, which is aligned with the body for all types, may also erode, and fear of psychosis is constellated. Her dream of being in a chapellike room with the storm raging outside indicated such fear. One reason I took a directive approach with her at times was that I feared the disintegration of her ego. I felt I simply could not let her stay too long on the side of her despair.

In the next few weeks she would resort to the detective stories she had been reading before I appeared on the scene. They served as a distraction from her depression. Perhaps they shocked into reality a sense of herself and eased the burden of waiting. I believed that through her reading of detective stories Sally was unknowingly assimilating the shadow in terms of murder, brutality, and horror. By accepting her negativism, I may have been helping her to some extent to assimilate the taunting evil within; but I would soon be leaving. The detective stories were probably a necessity. They were a substitute for me by draining away her black thoughts. They reminded her that there was worse evil in the world than hers.

Moaning, she pressed her right hand against her thigh, pushing against the pain; her eyes closed tight in anguish.

"It's your thigh now, Sally?"

It took a few moments for her to respond.

"Oh, yes. It's everywhere, in all my bones, but especially here. It hurts so to move around. Even the pills aren't helping much anymore."

"Is it worse now than it's been before?"

"It's worse in the thigh, maybe, but it's been as bad as this before. I have a hard time reading and concentrating; that's another reason for giving up the heavy reading."

With her elbows on her knees, she leaned forward and held her head in her hands. Then, straightening slowly, she regarded me again.

"It seems so strange to me that sometimes, even in the midst of all this misery, I still have dreams of being strong and well. I had one the other night.

I was dressing a handsome, bright, year-old baby son. He was a blond, laughing, beautiful child with a golden aura about him. It was only eleven in the morning, but he was hungry. I dressed him in his sleepers and planned to go ahead with the feeding.

The beautiful baby encircled by a golden aura symbolizes the self. Once more Sally is well, as she has been in all the dreams of the self so far. The child's hunger for food, like Sally's need for contact with the self, is urgent. It is "the eleventh hour," the last possible moment. The early feeding is another indication of the psyche's effort to telescope the whole life process.

"What are your thoughts about this one?"

"It's Beth's birthday on the thirtieth. I'll be so glad when she returns; she's my one great solace."

Without realizing it, in her associations to this dream Sally was bringing together the concepts of new life and

107

death. New life was associated with Beth, who could be a kind of afterlife for Sally. It is common for parents and even grandparents to expect children to carry on for them. Sally's association of the wonder child was to Beth, her own "wonder child."

I pressed her for more associations to the dream, questioning her about the year-old baby. She told me that one year before, she had become gravely ill from a new drug she had been taking. All her hair had fallen out. It was the second of three times she had felt she was dying.

"From those brushes with death you gained in consciousness. At least, the dream asserts that you did. The baby is hungry, you see."

She smiled. "And I go ahead and feed it, even though it's early."

"You do, so it's a most positive dream, as so many of them have been. I hope you'll remember their messages while I'm away, Sally. I know it's asking a whole lot of you, but I hope you'll continue your efforts in spite of your condition and my absence. Look, I can see you're worn out now, so I'll leave. I'll try to find Sarah on my way out and ask her to come in."

Sally watched me go. Her defenses dropped away and she looked desperately ill. I felt awful.

As I walked out into the front yard, I found Sarah sitting on the dolphin. She seemed to be waiting for me and spoke up at once. She said that her mother treated me like her other friends, never letting me know how sick she really was. With both sadness and anger in her eyes Sarah told me that her mother was different when she was alone with her family. She screamed at Jim and cried in her sleep; she was always in pain and was not getting any better at all.

CHAPTER SEVEN

W HEN I visited Sally for the last time before my trip to Europe, I found her in a deep depression. She complained that each day dragged on interminably. She was engulfed by a boredom impossible to alleviate because she could do little more than vegetate all day. She no longer found pleasure in her friends' visits; she had to pay for them with extra pain. She was unable to take in their confidences; besides, she resented their being in the outside world.

Thelma and the children hovered over her all the time, upset to see her so depressed. She dreaded Jim's going away because the family was so affected by her moods. She wished they could be more independent of her. And the food would be worse with Jim gone. She already had trouble enough keeping food down.

At times the right side of her face and her right arm felt numb; some nerves there had become blocked. No sooner would she accustom herself to one unpleasant sensation than a new one would come along to frighten her. She could not remember how it felt to enjoy life or to be well. She felt dead inside and was utterly and continually miserable.

"Maybe you're suffering so much now because as your feelings come to life you're more acutely aware of your plight. Does our work together make the pain and misery more intense, Sally?"

"No, absolutely not. I swear I've no extra pain after our hours. It's just that I've been feeling so down. I'm not going to promise you that I won't commit suicide while you're gone. If I do though, I want you to know that it won't have anything to do with you." She paused.

I did not ask her whether my going away was getting her down. With more intuition I might have ferreted out what perhaps she herself didn't know about her feelings. Also, I didn't want to stir up in her what could not be dealt with in the little time left. I felt that we both wanted to avoid trouble between us; we both valued her deepening interest in her dreams. They were the liaison between us and could be dealt with by thoughtful and caring letters, which would confirm my warm feelings for her. Few people know how much a legitimate interest or a shared task cements a bond between two thinking types. I tried to reassure myself that her drive to know herself would hold us together for my six weeks' absence. Nevertheless, these thoughts did not lessen my own feeling of sadness.

"But don't worry," she continued. "I feel so low that I doubt I could muster the energy to kill myself. Besides, there's something new now. I've gotten too interested in my dreams and too curious about what's going to happen to me next. Of course, I realize our work together could be only some kind of trick and the dreams could mean absolutely nothing. Still, if they have no meaning, why is it that the children's dreams still seem to be connected with me? The other night Beth woke up crying after she dreamed she was stuck in the top of a tall building at camp and couldn't get home. What do you suppose that nightmare was about?"

"Do you think maybe she's caught by efforts to rise above the situation?"

"Maybe so. Even Thelma's dreams are connected with me. Not long after I found myself crying 'they're killing my cat,' Thelma told me she had had a nightmare about having to drown a batch of kittens."

"Here we go again!"

"Yes, isn't that something? More synchronicity around cats."

I was again reminded of the neolithic matriarchal rule in Egypt under the aegis of the cat goddess and was moved by Sally's synchronistic experiences with Cyrano. I regretted later that I didn't bring the cat symbolism more consciously into our work together.

She took a small, green notebook out of the pocket of her robe.

"Well, trick or not, I've been practicing writing down my dreams. I've been drawing some pictures of them too. Even tried writing out my black feelings. There were three dreams; here's the first.

I was in an enormous partitionless hospital room with hundreds of bedridden patients. The walls were made of brick, and the ceiling was as high as a gymnasium ceiling. I was barefoot and I wore a hospital gown. I wasn't frightened as I really am when I'm in the hospital, and the atmosphere was pleasant.

I noticed a beautiful brown girl. Her name was Narumba, and she must have been in her late twenties. She was ill and very scared. I went to her and comforted her and helped her to settle down. When I walked around the bed, though, I had to thread my way through many broken hypodermic syringes.

Although Sally is ambulatory in this dream, she is dressed like a patient and therefore must be ill; but she is not frightened by the hospital, so the dream compensates for her actual fear. Still, she is concerned with illness, especially in the brown girl Narumba. And she threads her way carefully through the dreadful syringes, which refer to her fear of becoming unconscious or of dying.

The size of the room and the many patients refer to the collective. It is a paradox, but through contact with the collective and through feeling one's closeness to all of humanity, one comes to experience also its opposite—one's own uniqueness. The dream suggests another paradox: Sally assumes the role of both patient and healer, a further indication of the telescoping of her life. The more mature one is the more one is responsible for oneself.

Sally does not totally identify with her illness; she sees it also as being in the brown girl, a definite step ahead in her conscious development. For her to act as comforter in the dream suggests that she is taking on responsibilities of the analyst, perhaps reflecting her brave effort to prepare herself for doing without me.

"Your associations?"

"None, I've none."

"By hospital gown, do you mean the kind patients wear?"

"Yes."

She offered me a drawing from the notebook that contained her mandalas. "I drew a picture of the dream. Look at how it came out; for some reason I had to put the twenty-four diamonds of the brooch into it."

True to her sensation type, she continued to mull over the dream of her mother and the diamonds; in so doing she demonstrated how essential the mother was to her. Something in her knew that her personal mother, inevitably rooted in the archetypal mother, would help her to deal with her fear of death.

"How interesting. You really have been dwelling on that dream. And now you associate the brown girl with the diamonds, so you've given her a quality of the female aspect of the self. That makes her very important."

"Yes, I sense that she is very important to me somehow."

"That beautiful brown girl may be your dark side, your as yet undeveloped side. Somewhere within you're ascribing great importance to that part of yourself now. Do you remember when we talked about introverted feeling, which is exemplified by your mother and perhaps by Jim as well, and how in you this would be the function that would connect you with the self? This dream shows again how the undeveloped part of us is the key to our individuation. Efforts to make it conscious, to live it, take us there. The girl could also stand for the pagan instinctual side — another pipeline to the self — that you've never lived."

The dream reminded me that I have often thought that the women who are most vulnerable to disease are those who are centered in their heads, who are not in contact with their instincts, or in whom the instincts have "become ill" through being cut off.

"I'm so glad you've begun to do some drawings of your dreams."

"Well, it's getting so that mandalas are too difficult for me to draw now. I can't make perfect circles anymore; they all come out lopsided and I've had some tests lately that show my brain has now been affected by cancer."

"Is that so? Are you really sure of that? I certainly get no impression of any mental deterioration. Maybe it's only a muscular problem."

I sensed that she was probably deteriorating physically, but I didn't want to speculate with her about the physical aspects of her disease. Perhaps it was denial or cowardice on my part, but I felt I needed to emphasize the importance of her psychological growth because it was so easy for her to overlook it or dismiss it as not valid. I also felt my own growing urgency to discuss with Marie-Louise von Franz just how much I could talk about deterioration and death with Sally.

She looked at me sadly and was silent for a moment. Then she read again from the green notebook.

My husband and I were sitting at a table in a Japanese restaurant. Our Chinese friend was sitting with us. She is the mother of four children, who are Beth's friends—little girls who are eight, seven, six, and five years old. The food was served on plain oval dishes made of solid black lacquer, and each person had his own dish. It was a course of meat and spinach balls, alternating around the dish. Although the restaurant was dark, there were lights glowing here and there, and it was a warm and pleasant place.

This dream refers to Sally's progress in relation to her husband. The Chinese woman between them represents the Eastern attitude, which accepts both introversion and human irrationality in relationships. It is interesting that Jim is being brought into the process, showing that Sally has accepted some of what he means to her. It may be that she is turning more and more to him now that I am leaving. But the blackness of the dishes and the barely lighted restaurant refer to a partial consciousness, within reach but shadowy. Even though there is good feeling about the restaurant on the personal level, the semidarkness indicates that the actual relationship, an aspect of Sally's inner self, is only beginning to come to light.

"What are your thoughts about the dream?"

"I've always liked the Chinese and Japanese. After the war I had a job helping to relocate Japanese people. I found them most compatible."

"Your Chinese friend who sat with both of you may have been the helpful link between you and Jim."

"That's true, because our relationship is very good now, and I'm sharing more of my real self with him."

"And there are the oval dishes—enclosures, containers.

114

It's as though you and Jim are relating through the self. In my mind in any profound, serious relationship the self is constellated. In the Christian marriage ceremony Christ, through the priest, is the mediator, the one who stands between the man and woman. Here the woman is mediator, and that would be appropriate because yours is the dream of a modern woman."

"I like the way you keep reminding me of the importance of women on those deeper levels. It's hopeful somehow."

"Indeed, the modern women's movement is reflected in the Protestant church as more and more women are being ordained. It's as though we have made a historical spiral toward a more democratic relationship between the sexes."

"Now listen to this last dream."

She handed me a drawing and read from the notebook, smiling.

I'm a little five-year-old boy picking up carrots to fill a large, oval basket. The task annoys me, and I toss an armful of carrots toward the basket; they fall short and land on the ground. Along comes a young man I don't know who's wearing a red shirt. His wife and five-year-old daughter are with him. He picks up my scattered carrots and puts them in the basket. He directs his wife and daughter to add theirs. He says, "See, isn't gathering carrots fun?" I hate him.

"What about associations to this dream?"

"It's really the same feeling I have toward you, the analyst who persuades me to collect my dreams. You're the man in the red shirt because of your Pollyanna, Boy Scout attitude."

The dream takes me by surprise. In her association she shows her dislike of sham and for the first time is openly critical of what seems to her my condescending, "do-good," phony side. She must be angry about my going away, and it is good that she can come out with it if

115

only indirectly. Had there been time, we might have been able at this point to open up the area of her hurt feelings, which she had suppressed for so long.

"You're annoyed by my referring to the good in your dreams, aren't you?"

"Yes, I suppose I am."

"But I have to remind you of the positive things because otherwise you'd overlook them. Besides, I hate leaving you to suffer your pessimism all alone."

Here I was again, pushing for effort on Sally's part to counterbalance her nagging wish to give up, and worrying about whether I was right in doing so.

"Perhaps I feel more secure with the black things of life. Well, I suppose I don't really mean that. Maybe by helping me put the carrots in the basket you're giving meaning to my efforts."

"I can't blame you, though, if you're angry. And to make matters worse, I have to leave early today. There's still a lot to do to get ready. I want to give you this."

It was an envelope in which I had enclosed our itinerary. "Here's a list of all the dates and addresses of places where we'll be. I hope you'll write."

She took the envelope and pressed my hand.

"I will. Goodbye, and have a good trip."

She looked the way people do when they physically brace themselves for separation. I was touched by her effort to throw back her emaciated shoulders. There were no other gestures and no complaints. I felt heavyhearted as I left her. From the time I first told her I was going away she had never once complained. Naturally she was annoyed today by my enthusiasm about her dream. I must have been overdoing the positive for my own sake. I wanted so badly for her to feel better, especially because I was going away. She resented it and was rightfully irritated. Her dreams seemed to indicate that my impending absence may have pushed her further in her progress, and possibly into some independence. But my departure must have intensified the feelings of abandonment that she had been undergoing for some time. Had I sympathized with her instead of trying to bolster her feelings, I might have taken on more of the burden of her abandonment and maintained our connection. One cannot be in contact with another if one tries to pretend things are better than they are. At this point I felt keenly inadequate.

She couldn't express her hurt feelings, at least in my presence, and perhaps I didn't give her enough help. On a feeling level we both missed our chance. Had her feelings been less unruly and more trustworthy and had there been in her life more people with whom she could talk honestly, perhaps she would have risked my displeasure and challenged me. Perhaps because feeling is not my strong function either, I simply did not appreciate any better than she what a terrible wrench my going away would be for both of us. I had not noticed her dependence on me as a person. I construed her attention to the analysis to be more of an expression of interest in understanding her self and her family than one of attachment. This was my error.

CHAPTER EIGHT

A UGUST 7
Dear Sally,
In another day you will be on your own. I wonder
how you are. I hope that you will let your friends know how
you feel. There's nothing like saying *how* things are. The
statement somehow lifts the burden; I don't know why.
Well, it doesn't entirely lift it, but at least it makes the
burden a little lighter.

I was interested in your saying that after friends' visits you
often pay with increased pain. I feel sure the pain isn't only
a result of the effort needed for the visit. Much of it must
come from holding back your own reactions. You've said
your friends are in such awful trouble; they must lean on
you without meaning to. You are nice enough to ask questions and that gets people going, especially when the
questions come from the profound depths you live in. So
many people never see others who are living on such a real
level; and they are hungry for it, even though sometimes
they may not be aware of it. They might possibly fear it.
There is so much superficiality everywhere, not because
there aren't plenty of opportunities to dig deeper, but because there is too little consciousness with which to do it.
I wonder, though, if you might be holding in your own need
to talk about yourself.

118

Hope you won't mind if I write many notes. Please don't feel obligated to answer every one. It would be fine if you could write twice a week. That would give me enough to go on. Good luck and all the best.

Yours, Jane

August 5

Dear Jane,

Cyrano came back to sleep on my bed this afternoon. I feel rotten, so can't tell if this is a good omen. It's surely not of physical strength; perhaps there are some psychical surprises in store. Wonder if I will be able to keep up my faith, for it is an act of faith with Mrs. Wheelwright gone. Carla was here today, and she is a help along this line since she has been through analysis herself and feels strongly about its value. I understand her better, too, since I began mine. I wish the roaring in my head would stop as it keeps me awake and is tiring.

Jim and Sarah are at each other. She is the butt of a lot of irritation but seems to be able to hold her own. Thank God for the horses!

Frank Rice phoned. He and Ruth are coming over. Mixed feelings. Want to see them, but will I have to throw up? Here is one reason I am less eager to see people. The propulsive vomiting gives little or no warning, and I am afraid of being sick in front of them.

August 6. I was sick last night but had enough warning to leave the room. The Rices are good friends. They brought me dried columbine from Yosemite.

Dream last night:

Jim and I are at the Emporium shopping for the children. We buy many items, including games and toys, and I am pleased. I select an olive drab army blanket for Sarah. I take it over to Jim, and he points out that it is a ten-foot size and too large. I say it will be all right, as army blankets always shrink. He says that furthermore it won't do as it isn't an electric blanket. I awake in chagrin.

Associations: None. Has no apparent meaning.

Since the time of her first dream, it is obvious that Sally has cleared away much of the contents of the personal unconscious by herself. Because of her situation, conflicts with the environment, except those with her immediate family, are minimal. We have been working on those mainly for their subjective value to her, although efforts to resolve them have also helped in an outer way. But this is a dream from the personal unconscious, reflecting the constant bickering Sally and Jim must have reverted to after I left. It is a kind of fragmentary dream that lacks theme and content. It suggests that she is at loose ends.

The feeling function is needed for shopping when something of value or something appropriate is being sought. In this Jim is the sure one. He knows best, and that is upsetting to her. This is one of the problems in an atypical marriage like theirs. In a typical one the wife would decide with her sound sense of values, not the husband whose thinking would only rationalize the choice. It also gives us more evidence that he supplies the feeling that she needs to reach her objective.

August 7.

I am a teen-age girl student at an exclusive girls' school. It is mid-morning free time, and I go up to my room to be alone. It is important that I change into a pretty dress by eleven in the morning and play a record on my phonograph. The record is a triangular-shaped LP of French folk songs.

Associations: None.

I am hostile toward Jim this weekend. I am wondering what I ever saw in him; he is just as vulgar and coarse as his mother. Part of it is that he resents all the Saturday

120

chores—shopping, laundry, cleaning—which put him in a low mood. I feel reluctant to ask him to help me bathe and do other things for me, yet I am absolutely helpless. His mother went downtown at nine o'clock, got back at five thirty, and left all the cooking for him to do. We went for a ride through Sausalito (the first in weeks), and I felt nothing but anguished hatred for all the colorfully dressed, healthy pedestrians. Wish I'd stayed in bed. This is *not* a good atmosphere for children.

Sally

The two dreams show how hard she is trying to put into practice what we have been working on and how awkward she feels in these efforts. Typically, she has no associations. Her inability to venture into speculation has presented me with the task of guessing what might reach her.

August 10
Dear Sally,

You are constantly in my mind. I keep wondering how you can get through so many hours of just existing. I don't know how you do it. It must take an enormous amount of willpower, persistence, and courage. Has anyone ever told you this? Maybe people cannot imagine what it is like to be in your situation. Believe me, I constantly wonder how you can stand what you call that terrible boredom. If only you could sense the reality of the unconscious. If only you could tease out your reflections and convey them to your friends. It would make your long, endless hours have meaning. Are you letting out your black thoughts? I hope so; otherwise they will block you and make you feel empty and inferior. I hope you at least get them onto paper for me to see.

Yours, Jane

August 14

Dear Sally,

Your dream of the carrots just before I left: I feel sure the vitamin A of the carrots you showed in your drawing is an antidote for night blindness. Remember the dream of your mother and your sight returning? It becomes more and more apparent that you are well on your way toward individuation. The proof is in the dreams of marriage in the offing, your closeness to Carla, and the bird's-eye view of all the great cultures. Your very brave acceptance of death has to mean individuation. You could not accept death without first having the feeling of completing your life. It seems that in your wish to find peace at last in death you are saying as much in your own words. So many and such positive and constructive dreams in the face of so much pain and distress must be fulfilling your wish.

I have so much I want to tell you, Sally, and I won't always weigh what I say too carefully. I'm just giving you my ideas, sometimes in a very hurried, off-the-top-of-my-head fashion, and I don't speak as an authority with all the answers. I'm sure I once told you this: If any of my ideas don't fit, just throw them out. I know you're independent enough in your thinking to be able to do that, so I don't worry.

But about the carrot dream: It is interesting that you appear as a boy and I, by your association, as a young man. Must we be "objective," which is supposed to be the man's way? Or is the dream indicating that so far you and I have grasped the whole thing intellectually, and we have yet to feel the reality? On the positive side, the red shirt does suggest that feeling is not too far away. Anyhow, for the moment of the dream that might be so.

The symbol of the oval basket, like the oval plates in the dream of the Japanese restaurant, is the mandala. Remember when we talked about the mandala being an all-inclusive symbol? By throwing into the basket a kind of food that helps you see in the dark and with the help of your young man (your mind or will, plus whatever knowledge I have), you are in the process of putting together the insights that are helping you become your true self. Designing a mandala served the same function. The next step is to experience, to feel, that totality. To experience one's true self is the highest objective in life.

Sincerely, Jane

August 9
Dear Jane,

Last night was filled with dreaming. I have the impression that it was *very important,* but memories are extremely hazy. I get only vague snatches of incident, yet I know the whole thing was quite formal and meaningful.

May Hubbert and I are putting on a poetry festival. (She is a strange, lonely, and difficult seventyish artist in Sausalito. I have worked with her in the past and have produced three of her plays. Our relationship has always been stimulating and difficult. I respect her— as the "wise old woman" perhaps—and I admire her work.) I am responsible for silk-screening a program cover. It gives me a lot of trouble but turns out well. It is an abstract expressionistic design made up of red, orange, and pink squiggles.

I can't remember the evening itself, which took place in a large auditorium with a balcony.

In the same dream, there is something about the birth of a new baby girl. I have a photograph of her to show my friends.

Associations: I don't get any.

Cyrano is still sticking close to me. Three days now, and very pleasant. The weekend was not too bad as Jim took the gang to the beach. Much better for all than having them hover around me nervously. The numbness in my face won't go away. This is infuriating. I am finding it hard to enunciate.

Sally

The formal quality of the dream points to its archetypal nature, and the birth of a new baby girl indicates that the analytical processes continue. The juxtaposition of the baby girl theme with the poetry festival and wise old woman suggests two aspects of the female self — the personal progenerative act and a more impersonal, creative, female effort in the exterior world. Male figures are conspicuously absent. The cat, like the self, knows before Sally does that a creative phase is due.

August 9
Dear Jane,

Thank you for your note. What a lift it gave me! I'm afraid to express to you how very much your support means. As a matter of fact, I can't.

Here is a dream.

I decide that I must become a Catholic nun. I get hold of a habit and put it on, but am not sure if it is official. I am walking up Grant Avenue at night and run into Pope Pius. He asks, "Who is your sponsor, my child?" I say, "I have none." He offers to sponsor me. We stroll through Chinatown together. He is cheery and friendly and he stops in a gift shop to bless some Oriental brass crucifixes hanging from the ceiling. Suddenly I am in a convent. There is a horrible war going on, and we are short of bed linen. I awaken in horror.

Associations: My doubts about analysis are similar to

religious doubts. The supreme worldly authority reassures me. Confused.

Sally

In this dream Sally is grasping for a feminine orthodoxy that is not her own. With its help she finds an approximation of a belief to which she can attach herself and which, by her own association, is connected to or comes out of the work we are doing. In this letter Sally honors for the first time our connection with feeling. Our correspondence seems to be taking the place of the analytical hours together.

August 16

Dear Jane,

Guess I'll try writing out some of the black stuff. I'm surely mired in it. Had a visitor Monday, a good friend who brought her baby. Thelma sat in the middle of the floor playing loudly with the baby every minute. "He won't let me go!" she shrilled significantly. With Jim gone she's at loose ends, too, and things are pretty chaotic. She's taking the girls downtown today, which is good, and bad in that I'm nervous being alone for so long.

There's no pleasing me. How can I tell that my unconscious isn't just as rotten and full of holes as my body? Chances are it probably is. I'm not just under the influence of the shadow; I have become the shadow, and everything else is already dead.

Jane Wheelwright's bright, strange world on one side and the vivid, lovely world of reality on the other, and I'm in a strange limbo somewhere in between. Can't go ahead and can't go back. Too curious and cowardly to end everything; also afraid of mucking it up. Funny, but the more pain I have, the more I fear pain. Can't imagine using a knife or,

if I had one, a gun. Certainly not jumping off something.
The doctor told Jim my best bet was pneumonia. Can't
imagine catching that on purpose. Dread the idea of
paralysis.

Thelma is going home this weekend, and my mother will
come for a week. Then the kids go down south for a couple
of weeks and Jim up north. Hell! Hell! Hell! Just get through
one day at a time.

Well, Jane, I promised I wouldn't hold back the trash and
I haven't. But this is even boring trash!

Fondly, Sally

August 18
Dear Jane,

I received your welcome letters. The one from Chicago
came Monday, and today the one from Zurich. It is I who
am burdening you with correspondence, but writing things
out daily is amazingly helpful.

I am actually doing very well this week, despite the sound
of previous complaints. Your suggestion about taking on
friends' troubles may be valid, but I realize that being a
confidante is my usual role, and I respond so gratefully to
people that it is apt to leave me a bit weary and sick. I have
been speaking out this week, and it helps.

Fondly, Sally

Sally realizes her need to have others give of themselves by confiding
their troubles to her. Hers is still a receptive role, which may indicate
that her ego is not firmly established. I, too, find myself having to do
the talking, although unlike her friends, I talk to Sally about herself
through the vehicle of her dreams.

August 19

Dear Sally,

Three of your letters were waiting on my return from Germany this afternoon. It was a relief to know that you felt up to writing.

I'm sure you hate to be sick in front of people, and the will to keep up a good front has advantages; but maybe you try too hard. I hate to see you cut yourself off from your friends. I'd rather you had less will to keep up a good front so that it would be less tiring and less of an effort for you to see them.

Your dream of shopping for the children: The pleasure you receive from shopping for them suggests your need for the children and your ability to give to them. Selecting the army blanket for Sarah may fit in with your wanting her to fight her battles as a soldier would. You may be apprehensive about leaving her when she is still so young and vulnerable.

Your dream of being a teenage girl in an exclusive girls' school: What you are attempting to face psychologically is of an exclusive, female nature. You are learning how to live in the face of a terrible threat to your life, and to make something important out of it. You have to start as an adolescent girl, allowing the true female nature to blossom, rather than trying to live up to what you feel our Christian society expects of you.

Keep on writing me the negative thoughts. There is a lot of vitality in your negativism. I'm sure much of your energy is tied in with it. I like it when you cut loose and am reminded of the rebel in me as well! I'm only sorry you are distressed so much of the time.

Affectionately, Jane

August 20

Dear Sally,

Your dream of May Hubbert seemed to have so much meaning and must be very important. I feel sure the real stuff is only around the corner. You will get it before long. The association with May is in the right direction. And the birth of the new baby girl balances, on the feminine side, what the baby boy represented. It is a new female strength, to balance a new, positive adventurousness. The kitten, your first symbol of the female self, has transformed into human form. The baby girl also provides the opposite of very young to very old (if the two parts of the dream are taken as a whole) and puts the creative, archetypal stamp on that part of the dream in which you are the "wise old woman" (you are also the baby and May, you know).

May strikes me as your version of your potential female self, a figure perhaps verging on what Jung calls the "chthonic mother." She is an articulate contrast to Nanny, whom we already talked about, but is just as strange and dubious. Her age, her difficult complicated character, her concern with poetry, and your being well in this dream seem to refer to you in a distinctly future development. Poetry is an expression of introverted feeling (in your case the fourth function) that in old age wraps up the other three and should do as much for you. Your design in red, orange, and pink squiggles also describes the poetic, impersonal side of your nature that not only might help you to connect with your husband but to connect you with your deepest vital center, where all opposites are reconciled. It is now more orderly; the squiggles are contained in a successful abstract design to make a bridge into the future.

So far we have talked about marriage being your objective. Looking back, we have to see that the marriage theme must also refer to death as well as to your real marriage. The gnostics developed a beautiful mythology linking the theme of marriage to death. Jung also saw the chthonic mother (until recently a more or less underworld figure) as the key figure in the marriage quaternity, which as an archetype resembles the archetype of the self. Because of the women's movement, the chthonic mother has begun to appear in ordinary life. It seems that now all these disparate themes are converging, if only by implication. But this is such a difficult theme that we must postpone it for when I get back.

You and May put on a poetry festival. You are honoring poetry on a large, collective scale; you present it as a festival, which is a happy, lively occasion. Also you round up the works of many poets. This is certainly a statement of your serious acceptance, in principle, of the expression of feeling. If I put on a poetry festival and invest the necessary energy, it is because I certainly think highly of the subject, although I can do little toward writing poetry myself. Since you are your dream, I take this dream as an indication of your accepting the need to honor your own introverted feeling. Had your feeling been readily available, you might have been actually writing poetry in the dream.

Cyrano is a sign of things being better, I'm sure. He, like the self, would pick up the signals well ahead of you. I'm so glad you got at least three good days. And, interestingly enough, they coincide with positive, meaningful dreams.

Don't worry about enunciation. There are many ways to communicate if talking gets too difficult. You must not wear yourself out with worry. But I am sorry that you have to be plagued by so many symptoms. If only there were fewer, you could give over much more energy to the reflection that your unconscious needs.

Thank you for your note in response to mine; don't worry about me. You will have all the support from me that I am capable of. I wish it could be more. You have been going it alone psychically for so long; it's about time you got support.

Your dream of becoming a nun: This is also in the right direction. To find your own religious attitude you have to taste and experience the historical religions, and the Catholic religion is one of the most important. Pope Pius offers to sponsor you, so it doesn't matter whether you have on the correct habit. He evidently does not worry about such discrepancies. He even can bless the Chinese version of the Catholic symbol. The intent is what matters to him. Pope Pius might be a superior religious animus (at least a spokesman for the male aspect of the self) that is trying to help you find your way. And your way has to include the Oriental; Western thought is not enough.

The convent, which implies total commitment, raises conflict on a big scale. To find your religious attitude you must expose yourself to a great deal of conflict. In that conflict your own way gets hammered out. It is never a peaceful or even a pleasant process, but the reward is tremendous.

Of course you have doubts about analysis and you can't force yourself to believe in it. My hope is that when you have more evidence from the unconscious and perhaps even numinous* experiences, you will find a friend and constant companion there who always levels with you and who never forsakes you. That would be far more impressive than anything I could tell you because it would come out of your own experience.

130

Please have faith that your negative periods will last for no more than a few days.

Affectionately, Jane

The war, mentioned at the end of the dream, might be a warning of what is to come. In retrospect, I might have done Sally a favor by mentioning this possibility to her.

August 15
Dear Jane,

It's been a dry spell for dreams. I'm very depressed, feel like I live in the bottom of a garbage can. Thelma left for home this morning, leaving a kitchen full of dirty dishes and Beth with a hundred-and-two-degree temperature. My mother is due some time this afternoon. What an awful life for the kids. Poor Jim seems reluctant to come home. I don't blame him. Received your third note this morning. It's not courage or willpower, just conditioned reflex.

There was one dream.

Thelma, the girls, and I were in an old-fashioned kitchen, similar to mine but older. Thelma was serving supper. She had cooked lima beans in an enamel urinal, and I was indignant. "But I bought it cheap at the Next-to-New Shop," she insisted. "You'll use pans in my kitchen," said I. "I'll cook in whatever I want as long as I'm doing the cooking," she yelled.

Associations: This is a macabre version of the sort of thing that's been going on in reality all week. The meals have been so unbelievably bad. Simple things like hamburgers have been cooked so little that the buns are bloody and the meat is still cold. The kids have justifiably had trouble eating. I wish I could blow up at her, but I fear it would get us nowhere.

Fondly, Sally

This is a typically shadow-projected dream. The deteriorated setting, the urinal, and Thelma's uncharacteristic behavior are classical examples of shadow projections.

August 18
Dear Jane,

Your special delivery note from Munich arrived this morning. Your frequent notes are tremendously helpful in keeping my focus on our objective, which, as you indicated, seems intellectually clear but still emotionally distant.

My mother is here, and this visit is going much better than the last. I feel more free to ask her to do things. She keeps busy and is much more relaxed. Numbness continues to bother me, and the length of the days, but this isn't news.

Fondly, Sally

This letter provides the first indication that the emotional impact of our relationship resides for Sally in our communication rather than in the interpretations.

August 19
Dear Jane,

Your colleague phoned yesterday, and we spent this morning sizing each other up. He seems very empathetic. We discussed my Pope Pius dream, which he considered quite positive.

My mother's stay this time has been much more pleasant. She has been busy teaching Sarah to run the sewing machine. The girls ran up a bunch of bean bags and made $1.50 selling them in the park. Entirely their own idea and very successful. Thelma comes back Monday. Ugh! And Jim will be in Wyoming that week. I feel so stranded with that scatterbrained idiot. Then the following two weeks the kids will spend down south. If only I could work out a decent attitude toward her since we are evidently stuck with each other.

Jim and I are rather hostile these days. He's impatient with my panic and depression. Why can't I simply accept the inevitable and shut up?

Fondly, Sally

Sally's improved relation to her mother indicates that she has been reacting out of the female part of the self. It is not surprising that the male aspect in the form of Pope Pius now demands attention.

August 25
Dear Sally,

I, too, think your Pope Pius dream was a very good dream. The Catholic church has preserved the original symbols from the beginning of time, and that is why the church fits in so well with modern psychology. Being in a convent is a step in the right direction; you are building a strong, protective female wall around you to cope with the storms that threaten you, particularly your understandable ambivalence toward the fear of death. And you are right: The supreme authority is a religious concept that is accepted by millions, although in your dream Pope Pius is more broad-minded. "Worldly," you said, and I feel that is apt because in the dream he seems to represent the universal and what is basic to all of humanity.

This dream reminds me of one you had about you and your Catholic woman friend keeping vigil in a chapellike room while a storm raged outside. Do you remember? You were concentrating on three lamps, and for the Catholic the triad — the Trinity — is symbolic of the self. For someone no longer contained in the orthodoxy it would have to be a quaternity, such as you have shown over and over in your mandalas and now in the four-armed Oriental crucifixes. I think both dreams may be stressing the importance of your making a connection to your own religious feeling by honoring your Christian roots, especially those extending back into ancient Egypt's trinity, which included the female principle.

Zen is undoubtedly a bridge to the unconscious for you. It is a practical religion with intuitive implications. That must be why reading about Zen gives you much satisfaction. It would touch off one of your more unavailable functions, intuition, thereby bringing you a sense of life. Actually, two of our functions are quite conscious; the third can be made more or less so; but the fourth, in the unconscious of young people, will only reveal itself in glimmers. For older people who have matured, it manifests as the sum of all the functions. It is the mediator for the self, and at first is often presented in dreams as an animal. Could it be Cyrano, who knows how you feel before you do? It may be a man also; and this man, in the dream of your putting on a nun's habit and walking down into Chinatown, is Pope Pius. He was, after all, the mediator between the people and God; God is the orthodox version of the self. And, anyhow, your Pope Pius even seems prepared to accept the crosses found in a Chinese gift shop.

Also in your letter you describe how you are at the crossroads between the world of reality and the other world, which I represent. You can't go forward and you can't go back. This brings to my mind the arms of the Oriental brass cross, symbolizing the opposites that immobilize you. It seems you have to "sweat it out" in order to constellate the helpful, illuminating third possibility. We all know that couples like you and Jim suffer because of your type differences. But there is a solution via the third element: first the physical child, later the psychological child, then conscious love. In your dreams there have already been two psychological children — one male, the other female — and I believe because of the way they were presented and because of the seriousness of your situation, they refer to individuation. They are the Christian Logos and Eros, which together include all of life. They are the beginnings of the Divine Syzygy, which represents the androgynous self.

It seems to me your dreams are so alive partly because you feel so empty. The unconscious seems to be trying to compensate for your low opinion of yourself and your negative attitude by putting you in the company of a great religious figure. If in your dreams you feel yourself worthy of the Pope, perhaps awake you won't feel so worthless. I can only hope so. I wonder if your symptoms — the numbness and the stomach upsets — are caused entirely by the physical pressures from the cancer. I can't help thinking that some of the physical symptoms are greatly heightened by your tendency toward self-deprecation. If you say you are no good, empty, and unworthy, then every ache in your body is bound to be exaggerated. I know it's hard to get out of an old habit by willpower, and God knows you have every reason to feel low. But if you can believe the messages from your unconscious through your dreams, willpower might not be necessary. Maybe to begin with you need to believe your analysts. You intimated in your first letter that going along with me is an act of faith. Perhaps you can hang onto that, for the time being anyway.

People who are dying are usually in touch with an instinct that helps them face the threat of death, and that instinct generally appears in dreams as an animal. All life since the beginning of time has had to face death sooner or later, so it is logical to suppose that there are established patterns for doing so. The instincts are coincident with the archetypes, or you might say, come out of the archetypes. So there should be an archetypal attitude toward death that is protective. I would imagine the convent in your dream is a partial expression of that archetype. Being protected by walls is, after all, like being contained within the boundaries of a mandala; and painting mandalas has proved helpful for you.

The process that Jung called individuation involves the development of the four functions and the coming together of the conscious and the unconscious. There is much evidence that individuation brings serenity and peace, two qualities that make death ultimately acceptable. As far as what comes after death, no one knows; but the great religions tell us that, given the right preparation, you can expect the peace and eternal rest that you long for. But those who are not contained by an established religion (especially people like yourself who have been burdened by conflict) seem to find peace through certain efforts toward wholeness in this life. This is why I am so anxious for you to accept the evidence in your dreams of your already being so close to your center. I also hope you can accept the self (in both its female and male aspects) that has been so dramatically emphasized over and over again in the dreams you had before I left. I'm not saying your death is imminent; its time is up to the gods. There seems to be left to you now only one way to make your peace. It is my way also. It is through this work we are doing together. This individuation process seems to be an inevitable one for those who, through early conflicts, have lost touch with their instincts and have dropped out of orthodox religion. If you fear death too much, it is like having an enemy hovering around you continuously, sapping the vitality that you need to find yourself and combat the cancer.

Why don't you choose the mandala you like best of those you have painted and pin it up where you can see it from your bed? If you are now having difficulty painting them the way you see them, it is important for you to have the best one available to contemplate. You could, in a way, meditate on it as they do in the East and as you seem to be doing in the dream of the three turquoise lamps. It could be almost as stabilizing as the actual painting of new ones. There is a good chance that your difficulty in painting comes from whatever is causing the numbness in your face and arms. But that affects only the execution, not the concept, and you should go on with new ones, even though they are cramped and unsatisfactory in your eyes. I feel sure the effort would help you. Effort is what matters. Effort is what makes us equal, even though our achievement is not the same. I believe this absolutely.

As for the conflicts in your immediate circle, I feel sure that they are inevitable because of your husband's trips, my absence, and your being more yourself. Undoubtedly your husband had unconsciously depended on me to release him by carrying the situation. Of course you panic. You are helpless; what else can you do? It's just awful that the practical factors are so miserable.

Thelma probably thinks she has to be self-controlled, positive, and helpful because you are so ill. Being human, she must at times rebel down deep in herself against this role. I can't help but feel she represses her rebellion, then unconsciously reveals it in the unappetizing food, messy, house, and hostility toward the garden. If she could only blow up from time to time without feeling guilty for attacking a defenseless person, all the practical side of things might improve. I asked her once how it was going for her, whether it was difficult. She gave me a totally confused look and muttered something I couldn't get. She must suffer great inner conflicts from a lifetime of repressed hostility. Your dream of her cooking in a urinal and her violent reaction when you complained could be *her* dream, but since you dreamed it, we have to say it's all — the old-fashioned kitchen, the enamel urinal, Thelma yelling, a cheap item gotten in the next-to-new shop — about the shadow. Couldn't Jim get her to blow up openly, or complain to him? At least that might help her take onto herself what doesn't belong to you. Or should you be the one blowing up?

I'm glad you find my colleague empathetic. I felt sure he would be because he was extremely interested when I asked him to take my place. You see, Sally, we all have to face the inevitability of death. If we help you in this, we also help ourselves. And that reminds me to tell you that the more I push you to recognize the evidence and importance of your finding your whole self, the more I am reminding myself that I need to do the same. These efforts with you are so valuable for me. Compared to what you are going through now, the pressure for me is nothing; but we are in this together.

I have much more to say, but I had better give you a rest now. Forgive me if I seem to be making a lot of flat statements in my letters. I feel a pressing need to push you forward because of your situation and because of your tendency to fall back into your old negative world when you're left on your own. And being so short of time, I'm sure, makes me more pedantic than I intend to be. Not being able to register your reactions as I "talk" makes it difficult. Please go on writing about your troubles at home. I need to know about them. Your dreams, too, if you can.

Affectionately, Jane

August 22
Dear Jane,

As I told you, my mother's visit was extremely pleasant. We seemed to be able to come closer together than I can ever recall in the past.

Thelma arrived today, and my reaction of revulsion was immediate and intense. Why should I be so violently intolerant of her stupidity?

Here is a dream.

I check into Presbyterian Hospital to die. I am put in a lovely private room with a glass wall looking out on the city. It is night, and I see the golden lights of the buildings. I am tranquil.

Fondly, Sally

This dream, that comes out of the pleasant ambience during her mother's stay, reveals the deep need of a dying person for the mother or mother substitute.

August 27
Dear Sally,

Your last letter arrived yesterday. I'm glad to get it and to know that your efforts to understand your dreams about your mother paid off so handsomely. Perhaps now you can understand Jim better because he, being similar in type to your mother, would have a hard time with the horrors of your suffering. The drawing you did before I left that included the brooch with twenty-four diamonds must have been part of that effort too. It explains why you have been calling "Mama" in your sleep. The archetypal mother, a personification of the female self, includes the personal mother.

You might try drawing the aspect of Thelma that gets you down so much. Objectification is the thing, whether the issue is positive or negative. Once you get the nagging feeling onto paper or into conscious thoughts, it can lose some of its potency. Thelma must be reacting to some unconsciousness in you, as well as in herself. When we began our work, we talked a lot about the problems concerning both your mother and Thelma, and immediately Thelma seemed much less of an irritation. The talking seemed to help. Remember? So drawing or writing down how it is should help again.

Your positive dream of dying: Have you ever had one, positive or negative, that was stated so clearly before? You told me about a dream you sometimes had before we met about a white ship coming for you and a childhood friend embracing you, but you have never mentioned a literal statement of death before. Anyway, I'm glad you had this dream, for it presents death with peace, beauty, and objectivity — the way you long for it to be. It reminded me of your first dream — the one in which you were climbing by yourself to the top of the Sumerian tower that overlooked the city. But this time you are not afraid.

I've been talking over some of your dreams with Dr. von Franz as you and I agreed I should. She was close to Dr. Jung and has had a great deal of experience in interpreting archetypal material. Together we will go over your first four dreams again. The preliminary dreams are so important; they map out the whole course of an analysis. Dr. von Franz will see them from another angle, and that will give them an added dimension for my own, deeper understanding, as well as for you. I'll pass on whatever is new.

Your first dream of the tower: I remember we talked about your needing to find a more comprehensive view through ancient cultures. That view would include an understanding of death that would not deny the death instinct the way our modern culture has. In some ancient cultures, people believed that they were led into death by a dog. The horse is also associated with death. The point is to face death instinctively the way an animal does. For you the animal must be a cat, and perhaps Cyrano's comings and goings are related to your attitude toward death.

This last dream you have written to me suggests that you have found the right attitude, although the animal is not mentioned. Your hospital room is up high enough to over-look the city of golden lights. Being up high, as you were in your first dream, could mean a broadened outlook for you as a practical, down-to-earth person; the golden lights in the dark suggest that death might be a warm glow in the night.

Your dream of the Volkswagen and the ceramic musical instruments: Your inferior function is at the level of the hippies who are with you. (The dispossessed, the despised, and the underprivileged usually symbolize the inferior function.) In other words, the unconscious does not want you to leave this world until you accept these unacceptable and unknown and even repressed parts. Accepting what is truly inferior in yourself might help you to stand Thelma's "stupidity." And once you accept it, she could become less stupid.

You lift the chassis off its four wheels and set it down on the curb. Dr. von Franz thinks the chassis here is the container of the soul and the four wheels are your body and, therefore, of this world. Four is the totality or individuation achieved in this world. Four wheels are also the means of getting around the space-time continuum.

Music is being played on ceramic instruments, and the idea that ceramics belong to the world of the dead is an ancient one. There are, for instance, the Canopic jars of ancient Egypt. Music is often associated with harmony and rhythm and with the wide world of feeling, from the humorous to the religious. According to Jung, music in dreams, for the intellectual, refers to the other world. Western man traditionally projects onto Christ the symbol of the self, thinking of him as belonging to the world beyond; those of us who find no meaning in conventional religious concepts need symbols that are more basic, general, perhaps abstract. We need something that goes back to our instinctive source—symbols that refer to primitive times as well as to the present. Maybe music, because it came into being before writing, touches on an original expression of the self. Certainly music grew out of religious feeling; in your case it seems to be music with an Eastern quality played on ceramic instruments.

Dr. von Franz told me she had a friend who dreamed her father came to her as a ghost after his death to explain to her that he had gone to a conservatory in Vienna to study music. He had been musical as a young man but had not kept up his musical activities. In old age this interest revived and became a compelling need.

Your dream of the station wagon: The station wagon is a work car. Your efforts to make conscious the messages and material from the unconscious are emphasized here. The kitten appearing in the back seat must be female; it could be the new female instinct now being born, your impulse to be who you really are. This may be the instinct that can show you the simple, right way to death, as we said before. But there is your fear of Thelma. She, in her own nightmare, was killing cats; and once you cried out in a half-waking moment "Someone is killing my cat!" No wonder you are so harassed. The cat obviously refers to your basic female self-realization and must not be killed. Your life depends on it.

In this dream you hope your husband will accept the new kitten; in other words, you hope your feeling animus will let nature's kitten live and be part of your life. Then the kind of love you have for Cyrano will be expanded and become acceptable on a human level. Incidentally, women can do a lot to realize their truest inner sense of who they are through making conscious their feelings for an animal. Feelings of love for the animal, no matter how naively or clumsily expressed, will never be rejected.

You might be interested in my experience of a cat figure in my own analysis. At a crucial turning point I dreamed that a wild bobcat was sitting in my lap. This animal, indigenous to the land where I grew up, is incapable of domestication. My analyst reminded me of the stories of the virgin's taming of the unicorn. In other words, I was experiencing the impossible becoming possible. At this great depth of experience lies the solid base of one's femaleness needed to meet the hazards of life. No wonder you are distressed at the thought of your cat being killed. And remember, a domestic cat never loses its wild nature. Just cross one and see what happens!

I get a feeling that in spite of Thelma you are much more on top of things now. Your continuing grasp and assimilation of your new life must be helping you with the fear of death. Perhaps if you recognize that you are seeing Thelma as the personification of everything within yourself that kills the instinctive solution of your life, she will no longer seem so destructive.

Affectionately, Jane

August 28

Dear Jane,

I can't say these last few days have been too good. I seem to have dried up completely as far as dreams are concerned. I'm sure I have been dreaming but have no memories of them whatsoever.

The pain is so persistent that I'm simply floundering around in discomfort, fear, and confusion. Last night, for example, I was completely out of control with groaning and screaming. It's going to get to the kids. Thank heaven they're going south on Wednesday.

The doctors can only suggest more drugs to put me to sleep.

Love, Sally

August 30

Dear Jane,

Your long August 25 letter opened a window for me again. I've been so bogged down and turned off. I know how fear intensifies discomfort, but I've been prey to all sorts of primitive terrors such as : What if there really is a

144

hell? Life is turning out to be so awful that no obscenity would surprise me.

Your August 27 letter just came. What a whopping injection of energy in these two thoughtful messages! It is most helpful to review the early dreams. I had forgotten some of the most vivid ones and appreciate the new insights.

Jim and the girls left for Los Angeles this morning. I was dreading being alone with Thelma, and suddenly when your second letter arrived, the gloom lifted. I don't know why, or for how long, but I can regard her with a tolerant affection and genuine appreciation. We had a pleasant, companionable meal together.

That death dream is the only specific one that I have had and the last one I remember, although I know they are still going on.

I agree that my intuitive and feeling functions are weakest, but I don't know whether I'm thinking or sensation dominant.

August 31. Awoke this morning and the amicable spell has broken, I hope for the time being only. Thelma couldn't sleep for fear of burglars. My Cream of Wheat, the only food that stays down consistently, was lumpy and needed a steak knife. What nonsense to waste energy on such petty annoyances!

If only I could get some dreams going again. I'm back to trashy mystery stories; can't seem to concentrate on anything else. I have trouble when my stomach rejects the pain killers. Things get pretty rough. The pain is worse in my head and back, so it's hard to think.

This letter doesn't properly acknowledge how much your thoughts and those of Dr. von Franz help.

Love, Sally

September 1

Dear Sally,

I'm anxious that you hear from me by next Monday at least, so here goes. I haven't heard from you about my last two letters, but there hasn't been time, so I'll have to go along hoping they have made some sense.

Dr. von Franz is interested in your liking Zen. She substantiates our feeling that Zen means by "satori" exactly what Jung means by "individuation." Satori or individuation is the whole objective of our work. It does not matter whether it is reached in this life or the next. It is bound to guarantee peace; otherwise what we are taught by the great religions is worthless.

We talked over your feeling that there is a danger of Zen taking you away from your immediate family. We definitely agreed that you should allow yourself to drift into your own world, for their sakes as much as for your own. Your tendencies and impulses (such as the feeling of detachment) are instinctual. Remember how Cyrano detaches himself from time to time? If or when you are gone, your children and your husband must make their adjustments. In the meantime, if you seem to be far away, they begin to get used to doing without you. This argument may seem brutally objective. But fortunately you, too, have a talent for seeing life as it is.

We both feel you are very much on the right track. You have something to solve yet in your relation to your husband by honoring that introverted, feeling bridge to him, for instance. Also perhaps you have to ferret out what irritates you about Thelma, other than what she does that's obviously annoying. You seem on the right road with your mother now, so that's one less problem.

Hoping things are as good as they can be for you.

Affectionately, Jane

September 7

Dear Sally,

It does me good to hear from you, even if your news is so desperate. Arriving back in Kilchberg last night, I found your August 30/31 letter waiting and I read it eagerly. I've worried so much about your feeling isolated again. That was the way I found you on our first meeting. Can you perhaps go over the points in my letters about your dreams whenever you feel terror breaking in on you?

I feel sure that being overpowered by negativism is the hell you fear, and the intuition needed for looking forward registers only negatively. That's the hazard of an inferior function; it must be taken into account and be deliberately counteracted. When I experience the kind of negative intuition that both you and I know well, I try to communicate it to an intuitive person. My husband, for example, can always dispel it by saying "That's nonsense" or "Of course not" or some such sharp remark; and his aplomb is much more persuasive than my nagging black intuition.

You told me so many times you felt like nothing. You wrote once that you felt as though you lived in the bottom of a garbage can. All human life reaches these abysmal depths; one look at a slum is enough. Those who are not twisted and who survive such places are equipped with a deep knowledge of life beyond what most of us know. For you the bottom of the garbage can is your slum, but this is also where the emotion comes from that can be your salvation.

You apparently need someone around to point out your positive qualities, to tell you of your great achievement in facing a terrible fate with such grace. I wish I could be there to remind you, each time you forget, of the wonderful evidence in your dreams, which points to your unusual character and personality. I took to you in the first hour we met because you seemed so real, so entirely lacking in phoniness.

I'm sure your difficulty in reading stems, in part, from not finding material directly relevant to what is going on in your head. The "trashy" stuff, if it helps, must have value. Please don't throw it out as a waste of time. Try to see where it touches on your situation. You have always been such a highbrow that I'm sure your psyche needs to fill in with earthy, ordinary stuff. Also if it's trashy, it is probably collective and belongs to the rich level of humanity that we all need to contact. Our roots, our security, our well-being and health come from the mass layer of humanity. Don't look down on that stuff, please. It may even have roots in the world of nature's lowest depths — where the sources of all life dwell and where all life and all death are indiscriminately accepted. In the dark everything is of equal value. Don't we say all cats in the dark are gray?

Love, Jane

September 9
Dearest Sally,

I was so relieved to get your letter this morning, even though your news is sad. There is so little I can write that helps, but I can at least send you my love and tell you how much you are in my mind. With no word from you this last week I was worried that my letters were making no sense or were too much for you or that you were too ill to write. Incidentally, I'm impressed with the strength of your handwriting. With difficulties like yours it's just wonderful that you are able to come through so clearly.

Don't worry about not remembering dreams; we have more than enough to go on. I hope you realize that you have already accomplished so much in the way of the right attitude. There are only details left, and you can manage those with little effort. So, please, try not to be frightened. You don't have, in the big sense of unfinished living, anything to fear. Naturally, the unknown gets us all down, and you are faced with it in such an immediate, cruel way. You have every right to take it hard. I'm only trying to convey to you that your dreams point to a normal summing up of your life. Even your reference to obscenity has its place.

I have mentioned the chthonic mother before in my letters. She was prominent at the dawn of history when society was matriarchal instead of patriarchal as it is now. She was the dark, female deity who was associated with the moon, fertility, and sex. She was frequently honored by rituals that nowadays would be called obscene. Relegated there by our Christian fathers, she resided in the basement of your psychic house. Perhaps now the chthonic mother has been raised to the ground floor, considering that she also symbolizes the earth. All this is not as farfetched as you might think; otherwise, why would you use the word "obscenity"? It does not really refer to the fear of hell.

Have you put up your mandala so that you can focus on it when you are in so much pain? I hope so. I'm sure it would help ease the pain.

Sally, I'm so impressed with you. I wish more people

could have the privilege as I have to know you and see into your great achievement.

Please remember me to your husband.

Love, Jane

September 9

Dear Jane,

The last week has passed rather unpleasantly, and the girls will be home this afternoon.

I've been wrestling with the idea of suicide, to the exclusion of all others. It seemed such an ideal time and such a logical, merciful solution for us all. Now I've missed the chance. Just couldn't set off a train of events like that. I feel like a coward and a failure.

Had a strange dream two nights ago.

A vicious snake, somehow with the face of Sarah, was fastened to a round tire. I was trying to feed it without being bitten. Awoke in terror.

Your sustaining express letter arrived this morning. Thank you.

Love, Sally

In this dream mother, daughter, and symbol appear again, this time in a dangerous way because the symbol (the snake) is dangerous to the mother and has absorbed the daughter. This frightening dream reflects her regression to the suicidal state in which I first found her. Yet elements of the dream reflect a healing power. To this day the snake is associated with healing through the symbol of the caduceus; hopefully Sally will find this positive aspect. I am glad that we will soon be together again.

September 9

Dear Sally,

Yesterday I spent two hours going over your dreams with

150

Dr. von Franz. We managed to cover them all. I took notes while she talked in order to have her ideas preserved for you.

I will start off with the generalizations first and get down to specifics later. The one recurring theme she finds in nearly every dream is your need to let your emotion live. You must do all in your power to express out loud your feeling. You and I have already talked about this, but I tell you again so that coming from her you can believe it. As we already found out, the ginger cat means emotion. She feels as I do that if you don't worry about how your emotion expresses itself or how it sounds, you can relieve yourself of the tension that accumulates from holding it in. Tension only increases pain. I realize that keeping your dignity is uppermost in your mind, but too severe a control can only let you in for more violent explosions later. The situation is even more serious because your standard of dignity is higher than it would be if you were well.

You need especially to express to your husband whatever good feelings you can muster. It could break your isolation and keep him close to you as well. You've indicated in indirect ways that you need his warmth; you also need to express your warmth toward him, in case of death. The Catholic church, for instance, insists that those who might die forgive their friends and relatives whatever wrongs they may have done. It is a specific, accepted ritual that seems to date back to the most primitive times. In many cultures there are accounts of the dead gaining comfort from the benevolence of the living who were close to them in life.

"Obscenity," the word you use in your letter to me, and which I see as coming out of the repressed chthonic level of the psyche, is another aspect of the hippie theme that occurred in one of your earliest dreams. Marie-Louise von Franz says not to be afraid of it. It is also life. In fact, there is much more earthiness all around us than people usually think. Being so highbrow all your life (undoubtedly a reaction against your mother's disorganized ways and the general ineptness of your parents), you have left a human earthiness out of your life. Your Christian repression of that female earthiness exaggerates it into an obscenity now. Don't you remember how we talked about your being too highbrow?

Try not to worry about the physical deterioration that now so telescopes your life. That's normal, too, although it usually comes with old age. The less you worry about it the less it will hurt you. You could use more of the hippie attitude for this. You know how they scorn physical aesthetics; they don't worry about dirt or messiness. Try to regard the deterioration of the body this way. Of course, you have the added terrible pain, but perhaps the doctor can help with pills. I hope so. Try to think of the physical business of birth, for it is parallel to the physical part of death. And, again, this is what we refer to as the chthonic. It is life in the raw, in its most elemental sense.

Dr. von Franz has spoken over and over of how much you need to do to prepare for possible death. She means you need to fully realize and make completely your own the messages from your dreams. This takes enormous effort. You may have to do it in a hurry. Most of us have much more time.

Your dream of the lovely, big new flat in Sausalito and Beth appearing as a three- or four-year-old with five kittens: The three of the child's age usually means dynamism and therefore an attitude of adventure concerning death; that is what we all need. Three is also associated with the Christian Trinity. Four means individuation, the wholeness you are achieving, the goal of analytical psychology. Beth is an aspect of you, after all, as is the whole dream. You have been ill for four years; desperately so for the last three, I gather. Beth is what you produced in the way of your inner self, through the worry of those years. The five kittens could be touching on the perfection (the quintessence) in nature of your new female instinct, or of its intensification to the fifth power. It comes out of the roots of life, out of the dark, where the cat is so well adapted. The cat's extraordinary eyes, which gleamed like fire in the black of night, were extolled in an ancient Egyptian religious myth in which Bast, the cat goddess, had power over moon, sun, and earth and ruled supreme for three thousand years. Even when the male god overcame the matriarchal goddess, the figure of the cat continued its rule through Ra. Indeed, woman was worshiped at that time, and now our modern feminist movement is concerned about returning woman to her rightful importance, but this time, hopefully, not superior but equal to man. This last bit is my idea; but I'm sure von Franz would go along with it.

Your dream of your mother's bringing back your sight with the twenty-four diamonds: Normally the mother, if she is connected with her own instincts, symbolizes instinct for the daughter and connects her with these deep, powerful roots to her female self and to her divine nature. The positiveness of this dream suggests that this problem is being remedied; you can dream of death positively.

Your dream of moving into a new house on Christmas Eve with Nanny and the four-year-old neighbor boy: In this dream you are not ill, so it suggests what is to come, or at least how it would be. Christmas means rebirth. Your whole family is with you, as they would be of course. They would always remember you in a wonderful way and so be with you always. Aaron is a name that carries a great mystery with it. Being four, he represents a new cycle, and he would be the projection into a new attitude. In the mystery story he carries a staff, which blooms and puts out leaves, which symbolizes a new life. A future life symbol, represented by a boy, also suggests the theme of the adventure in death, of individual enterprise. That theme has come up before. It could mean going out to meet the challenge of individuation that takes care of the fear of death, instead of passively submitting to negative, destructive feelings. Apparently you have been too passive in your illness up to now, but you've had too few tools to help you understand that. Your unconscious seems to want you to take more initiative, hence the masculine symbol.

When I reported this dream to Dr. von Franz, she predicted that Sally would die around Christmastime. I told her that in fact I had been pushing all along for a cure, but von Franz said no. She knew from this dream that Sally would die. In any event we agreed that from now on I should be as open as possible about discussing these dreams of death with Sally.

I cannot predict death for you, but I can point out how much your dreams tend toward adjusting you to that possibility if you accept their messages. Yet the adjustment in the unconscious is absolutely necessary, no matter what happens. Your dreams indicate a big change of attitude.

Your dream of being in the hospital critically ill and your parents visiting: I seem to want to feed the dog so he can lead you. As I wrote you, people in ancient cultures believed the dog to be a guide to death. In Persia when someone was dying, it was customary to take a dog off the street and feed it so it would be prepared to lead the dying person to death. There is also a Mayan belief that a yellow dog always leads one to death. In an Arabic legend there is reference to the philosopher's stone in the shape of a heavenly blue dog who keeps watch on the earth and in afterlife. Dr. von Franz says the cat probably has more to do with your female life, which also needs food.

As I already told you, I'm inclined to think that the cat is also your guide. Your femaleness is crucial in making you a whole person. Once you have that wholeness you are free to die. The cat, your female symbol, would be your guide, as well as the dog who stands for your male side. The dog, representing a less passive, more forward-looking attitude, might now dispel your nightmarish thoughts about hell and so on. In living we need to keep contact with animals as a reminder of our own instinctual life. To be disconnected from them, from the unconscious, is dangerous. In your dream I offer to feed the dog and the cat, who are both on your side.

The dreams in which you appear well must refer to a cure or, in the case of death, to afterlife, if there is one. I'm glad Dr. von Franz made this statement because I have been wondering why, in my own dreams, dead people always appear as younger and healthier than when they died, no matter how severe the terminal illness. I cannot be sure about an afterlife, of course, because no one I know of who has died has come back to explain what happens. If there isn't an afterlife, it must mean that death is the cure. This, after all, is what you've been asking for. In that case individuation, if not preceding, must coincide with death.

As for the dreams in which you are ill, I'm sure they refer to problems of your present illness.

Your dream of paddling a surfboard with your hands to cross the bay: We think this dream refers to your relationship to your husband, as well as to the religious task of finding your true female self. It is, as you have said so often, extremely difficult for you to express your feeling and appreciation for him. But it is absolutely essential that you try. I have spoken about this already. What is important is that Dr. von Franz puts her stamp of approval on my opinion and adds that the having to go back in the dream suggests the possibility of leaving your husband through death. And that makes it still more difficult, because just as you find your love for him in its deepest sense, you may possibly have to leave him. The handsome couple and their four-year-old boy may refer to your future. The couple symbolizes the marriage within that completes the self, and the boy represents the new cycle. I agree, and must close for now.

With much love, Jane

September 12

Dear Jane,

This may not reach you, but I thought I would write in immediate response to your richly detailed report of your session with M. von Franz. How much intense effort you are expending and how I appreciate it!

Her comment about the dog reminds me of a dream I had about a week ago and failed to report. It seems to be a missing piece of the puzzle.

I was fondling and stroking an Irish Setter (that's right, orange again!), and we were simply curled up together peacefully.

156

If that's my guide dog, it was a beauty. I wish it would come back. I've been thinking about your idea of the cat as a guide, but I don't know — this felt awfully good.

Your insights and suggestions about Jim are so true, but it's hard to establish a new relationship under these circumstances. I've come back to the idea that we're both thinking/sensation types, so something is missing. Plus there's the conflict over his mother. Already I see him throwing off my influence, becoming more conservative, less tolerant. It makes me sad.

As for expressing my emotions to break tension — if I do, the family punishes me with neglect. I'll go into this when I see you. Also I discovered that Thelma is using Sarah to unburden herself of numerous (justified) complaints. "I wish I could *like* Grandma," she said to me. "I love her, but I hate to hear her talk."

Sorry my notes are so brief and disjointed. I hope you're having some fun and relaxation too.

Love, Sally

September 10
Dear Sally,

I'll continue from yesterday with our discussion of your dreams.

Your dream of being in Paris, shopping with two friends: Shopping touches particularly on the female instinct. Paris is also a symbol of feeling and good taste. In the effort of choosing something for your mother you were developing your feeling potential to value her. The high price of the handkerchief not only emphasizes the symbol of the cat but also refers to the high cost to you of the energy needed to muster the feeling. Furthermore, making choices and discriminating are feeling activities, especially necessary in shopping. The image of shopping, for a thinking person, brings to the fact of death the aspect not only of adding to one's life (death can be an addition, it need not be a subtraction), but also of increasing one's discrimination.

Your dream of the one-year-old baby son: This boy is a symbol of a new spiritual attitude, the prelude of individuation. A baby girl would mean the beginning of the actual experience of individuation.

Your dream of being in an enormous ward room with hundreds of bedridden patients: Since you are in a big ward, you are with humanity, and this is better for you. Coping with the fear of death is much easier when you are with others. Death is a human event that comes to everyone; it is important not to feel isolated about it. You must look upon it in the broad terms of humanity, as you are doing in the dream.

If only you could translate over to your conscious life these attitudes that you have experienced in the unconscious. As the dream points out, you must liken yourself to everyone faced with death and try to give up your efforts at self-control. You have to let go and allow yourself to experience primitive female (the dark girl Narumba) fate—the way to the self. It means giving way to whatever has to happen, not struggling against it.

Perhaps your emphasis on the importance of self-control lies behind your difficulties with Thelma. She represents, perhaps exaggeratedly, the opposite of your lifelong habit. By concentrating on Thelma as a symbol for what is missing in yourself, you might be able to lighten the difficulty between you.

Your dream of being in a Japanese restaurant with your

husband and a Chinese woman friend: This is a very definite move into introversion (the Oriental would symbolize the introverted side for you). Introversion, like feeling, is terribly important for you now. By the way, have you pinned up your mandala where you can see it? That symbol includes your other side and represents the whole person that you really are, even though you may not have knowingly experienced it.

I wish I could be with you and help you in the effort to hold back the torrent of negativism that seems to engulf you when you are too isolated; your lack of dreams tells me that's the way you are now. Perhaps the isolation has to do with my being away. If so, it can be broken by some feeling gestures toward your husband, or perhaps by the realization that Thelma is acting out for you (again, exaggeratedly) your own potential for being a relaxed, fatalistic person. Sloppiness and carelessness can be expressions of a relaxed state of mind carried to the extreme.

These practical suggestions are mine, but the new interpretations of dreams are Dr. von Franz's. She puts things in a clear, simple way that I like, and I hope you do too. We explain in different ways, but we don't disagree at all. She has an enormous amount of knowledge at her fingertips (her stuff is so much less labored than mine), and she was closer to Jung than any person now living. This is why I was anxious to have her interpret your dreams. I read her your last letter in which you thanked her for her efforts, and she seemed extremely pleased.

Please urge your husband to postpone his trip until after the nineteenth when I will be there. You are too isolated with Thelma.

Love, Jane

September 11

Dear Sally,

One more letter about our reactions to your dreams before taking off for England. I hope they don't arrive all at once. If they do you might get indigestion! They have to be thrown together because my time is so short.

More about your dream of being in a Japanese restaurant with your husband and a Chinese woman friend: We think the oval plate is a female symbol, a yoni, idealized and abstracted. The meat is strong food, and the spinach with its iron is also strong food, suggesting the need to feed your female, subjective side. The restaurant has only dim lighting, which suggests that introversion is still obscured; but it is in the offing and on the way to daylight, or toward being a conscious experience. The separate, individual dishes indicate that introversion, especially for a modern woman, is an individualistic human expression. Extroverts tend to be influenced more by others and are less themselves, less individual.

The meat and spinach balls, being spheres, are symbols of the self. The food means nourishment within, or inner development. Oval dishes suggest egg shapes, too, so the potential for rebirth—immortality—is there. It is significant that rebirth plays such a big part in your dreams that speak so much about death.

We think this dream indicates an openness about death and the acceptance of it. You can talk about it with your husband by adopting an Oriental naturalness. The Chinese friend, whether extroverted or introverted, is at home with problems of the inner life and of life and death, and she mediates between you. This, of course, is excellent. The more you talk about your thoughts and speculations and fears of death with Jim the better for you and him and for your relationship.

The Orientals have a natural acceptance of the inter-relationship of life and death and therefore from our perspective don't value life itself as much as we do. Dr. von Franz told me about a Japanese soldier who was found dead. In his helmet there was a piece of paper on which was written "Night falls, darkness creeps toward me; my life is in the cherry tree; my soul is in the flower."

Your dream of the carrots: In this dream, which has to do with our analysis, you are identifying with your efforts and your enterprise; hence you are a boy. Naturally, being new at this kind of thing, you are impatient; you want results now. You can't wait for things to develop. Also you feel that you are short of time. This is understandable. You cannot afford night blindness (unconsciousness) and need an antidote for it, as we have already pointed out. Consciousness, the effort toward individuation, is the solution to your plight. By the way, if you find these letters full of things I've already told you, it is because I don't have time to check what's been said; besides, repetition emphasizes the important points.

Your dream of being a teen-age girl in an exclusive girls' school: This dream of the young girl in the pretty dress undoubtedly refers to the education of your own, real, female self, which is still at a teen-age level. This would be a necessary development if you are to connect with the feminine aspect of the self. But dream figures can grow up fast psychically, sometimes overnight. The triangular LP record (the number three) stands for dynamic feeling; it could be referring to your emotion that needs to come out in a more structured way. The dream is saying once more that you

161

must activate your feeling for your husband. If he has that from you, his thoughts and feelings will go with you and will always be with you, whatever may happen. That is important for him as well as for the children. The children, for their own growth, need good feeling as well as an image of what it is to be female.

Chances are (if age-old tradition, legend, and religious scriptures have any sense in them — and I certainly feel they do) the good feeling your family and friends have for you is essential to you in your own adventure, should you exit. (I started to write "exist," which suggests, at least for me, how important feeling is in either case.)

I think of you so much of the time. I wonder if you are aware of it. I hope so.

Love, Jane

September 12
Dear Sally,

There's one more dream left to interpret, and then I'll have covered most of them. I skipped over several with Dr. von Franz because I felt they were obvious and I didn't want to waste our precious time.

Your dream of putting on a poetry festival with May Hubbert: Dr. von Franz feels that May, being seventy, difficult, and strange, represents your greatest feeling potential. This would make her the "wise old woman," as you thought. What is deepest in the unconscious is also closest to being archetypal. In this sense she is also chthonian. May represents what you could achieve in feeling. Poetry is feeling, as is silk screening; poetry is also intuition. The baby girl of your dream is your actual expressed feeling and intuition. Logically, then, the old woman is an aspect of your guiding ideal model. She could lead you to your other side, the process being your individuation. The baby girl is your first step into the experience of the female aspect of the self, or so it seems to me.

It is just amazing how much effort you make toward feeling in your dreams. It's quite remarkable. I'm sure it will surface very soon, if it hasn't done so already. Again I want to emphasize the importance of your letting out your emotion, no matter how it sounds. You must not try to hold it in to be considerate to your family. If you express your emotion, the pain might not be so intense.

Good luck and see you soon. I'll be thinking about you.

With much love, Jane

W HEN I returned in mid-September, I made three telephone calls. The first was to Sally, who said she wasn't doing too badly. We would see each other the following day. Next I called Jim and, fortunately, found him in his office just before he was to leave for the Northwest. He told me Sally was now at a low point in both physical health and spirit. She was suffering much more pain, no longer wanted visitors, and seemed to have lost interest in everything outside of her own restricted life. She continued to be gentle with the children, he said; they seemed happy and were progressing well. But he was concerned that the increasing, omnipresent pain would prevent her from remaining patient with them much longer. Her physician had told him that although she was sinking, she could live on for many weeks, or possibly months. He wanted to keep her at home as long as possible, but if her suffering became unbearable for herself and the family, hospitalization would be the only alternative. He felt Sally hadn't really established a relationship with the analyst who had taken my place, although many times she had commented that she was pleased to have him come.

My colleague, when I reached him by telephone, confirmed Jim's statement. He said that the analytical process had stopped when I left and that he had to keep reminding Sally that it would begin again when I returned. The cessation of the process strongly suggested to me the importance of the physical presence of the analyst and therefore the importance of the unspoken relationship between analyst and analysand.

I visited Sally the next day and found that she had indeed become much worse during my absence. She now walked with enormous difficulty; her face was shapeless and pale. She complained of having dim, double vision, vomiting spells, a constant ringing in her ears that sounded like the rattling of a broken electric alarm clock, numbness in her face, and much more pain, especially in her thigh. Psychically I found she was suffering in much the same way as she had been when we first met. She was feeling isolated and was again enclosed in feelings of self-loathing and depression. As she began to vent her despair, I could see how much she was now suffering from the physical pain that attacked her frequently. She said she couldn't stand her appearance; she felt like pushing away everyone, including me, because of it.

Deterioration of appearance is a serious problem for a young woman who would normally count on her outward good looks (the persona*) to help justify her existence and to find acceptance. Although Sally's difficulties surrounding the persona were intensified now, she may always have had them, for women who are atypical and who do not fit society's ideal have trouble adopting an appropriate persona even when they are in the best of health.

She was certain that tumors in her head were causing her mind to deteriorate because she had no memory and was confused much of the time. She was now openly hostile to

Thelma, who continually complained to Sarah about having the care of the family thrust upon her against her will. I didn't doubt that Thelma feared Sally's anger too much to confront her directly with her complaints. Sally no longer wanted visits from her friends; she felt distant from them and burdened by their troubles.

She said the analyst I had sent around to her hadn't worked out well, and she had found little to say to him. This substantiated my growing realization that my taking more initiative with Sally than I would have with any other patient, or even with her had she been physically stronger, seemed to have been valid.

She had appreciated my long letters and was intrigued by many of the ideas they contained, but reading them only helped her for an hour or two. She hadn't pinned up her mandala because she'd given up on all "that mystical stuff." She had put aside all serious reading and could concentrate only on mysteries.

My own thoughts were that by absorbing the experiences and fantasies of others in detective stories, Sally was assimilating evil in more objective terms. She seemed to have been trying to do the same thing subjectively by feeding the restrained, and therefore dangerous, Sarah/snake of her recent dream.

She had lately been ruminating over her early relationship with Jim, thinking of how she had yielded to his and her own desire to have sex before they were married. Afterward she had felt full of rage against him and now was feeling that same anger and resentment, particularly for his absences from home, which made her feel neglected. She needed concrete proof that the people close to her, especially Jim, still cared about her; yet her self-destructive attitude only seemed to invite everyone's hostility. As she expressed all of this, I could see her being assaulted by so much physical pain. Knowing the sensation type, I realized that the pain itself and the drugs she took to subdue it cut her off from herself and probably had much to do with the blackness of her thoughts.

I responded to her complaints, making an effort to dispel her feelings of unworthiness by telling her what I believed to be true: The sooner the rational mind goes and the sooner the body loses its importance the better. Essence matters, not body, facts, knowledge, or reasoning; her remarkable spirit and personality were still very much there. As I praised her, I also reminded her of how often she made it necessary for me to try to lift her out of her self-abasing attitude. I told her I was positive the analyst who had seen her during my absence was genuinely concerned about her, admired her efforts, and felt she remained alive because she had more work to do toward insight and consciousness. I reminded her that her mandala was important and meaningful because it was her concept of God. I tried to convince her that reading mystery stories was not a waste of time but had definite, positive value. In stories of murder and violence the horrors of death were objectified and greatly helped to neutralize her own fears. But she was inconsolable. I knew she wanted to be told none of this. All I could do was to be with her and accept what she was saying.

But something within myself could not allow her to submit to her deteriorated, defeated condition, and I told her I would return the next day. She protested, saying she didn't want to inconvenience me. I knew I might have done the same thing in her position; I, too, more easily expressed my feelings of friendship through being considerate. Still, it was

difficult to say whether she wanted me to come or not. I
would just have to wait and see.

The next day she reported a dream, which she said reminded her of the previous dream about the snake fastened
to a tire.

*Another man and I were walking along a river in a tropical jungle.
We were killing bronze-colored salamanders, which were about a yard
long. They were wriggling along the bank. They weren't threatening
us, but we were killing them anyway.*

"What's your first thought about the dream?"

"The children have pet salamanders; they're smaller, of
course."

She was silent too long, so I gave her some of my impressions about the dream in order to help her expand her
horizon and raise her sights, as well as to reduce her feelings
of isolation.

"You know, to me those salamanders wriggling along the
bank recall the chthonic realm I mentioned to you in some
of my letters. Remember? The saurian, the cat, and the
snake of your dreams belong there somewhere. They live on
the level of our dark, female roots. That makes them essential to our health."

"Yes, I do remember about that and it interests me. I told
you yesterday that reading your letters only helped for an
hour or two. All your glowing interpretations of my dreams
and Dr. von Franz's remarks about how close I seemed to be
to my goal, those things made me feel good when I read
them, but the feeling didn't last. I was impressed by your
comments about the cat and the chthonic realm, though.
I'm not sure why but they stayed with me."

"It could be that they touched you in some deep place.

The chthonic principle would do that for me, too, because it's a basic, first principle for women and needs to be brought back from the dark underworld of repression. It brings to my mind the word 'ground.' We speak of the ground, the earth underneath our feet, and the ground of philosophy and religion . . ."

"Yes, and the ground of salamanders with their soft, moist skin . . ."

"That's right. Salamanders are amphibious, too, and they were supposed to have been able to go through fire without harm. Didn't Christ say 'He who is near to me is near unto the fire'? Salamanders do carry powerful symbolic implications."

"And we shouldn't have been killing them that way. They weren't doing us any harm. They had a right to be there too."

"Who might have been that man you were walking with?"

"I don't know. Maybe he was my masculine side, my animus."

"That could be. But you said 'another man and I' as if you are a man too. No wonder your approach is wrong! You've such an identification* with this masculine force that you've lost your own female point of view that preserves all life. You were being destructive in a senseless way."

Suddenly her hand moved down to her thigh, and she pressed it hard as her face twisted with pain.

"My God, won't it ever let up!"

I made a sympathetic gesture toward her and began to speak, but she protested.

"No, just wait a moment. It will pass. I need to go on about the dreams. The pain is always with me, but you'll have to leave soon."

So I waited, feeling helpless. In a few minutes she continued.

"In my other dream, the one I wrote you about, at least I wasn't trying to kill the snake. Every time I'd reach out to feed it the snake would strike, showing its teeth."

The snake symbol is ambivalent and ambiguous. It has represented the deity and the devil, the hero, spirit, wisdom, fertility and sex, transformation, healing, sensuality, and evil. The snake's evil aspect was represented in that dream, and in trying to feed the snake without getting bitten Sally was paying her respect to it. Since the snake was tied to a tire, a circle, it could also have represented the dangerous potential of the self. In offering food to the snake, Sally hoped to take care of it and to turn an enemy into a friend. I think one can say that, like the self, if the snake is not accepted for its healing qualities, it can be expected to attack in a destructive way. Of all the animals we know, only the snake can form itself into a circle in preparation for attack, and it does so instinctively. Perhaps if Sally had taken a more accepting attitude and had given up trustingly to her fate, the snake need not have been tied down, forced by a relentless willpower — that had become autonomous — into the circle where it would become so dangerous.

I am reminded of a powerful statement attributed to Jesus in a gnostic gospel: "If you bring forth what is within you, what you bring forth will save you. If you do not bring forth what is within you, what you do not bring forth will destroy you."

"Perhaps there's a symbolic message for all women from your snake. Let me tell you about an ancient Egyptian myth that might shed some light for us. It's about the ancient lunar cat goddess, Bast, and the serpent of darkness, Apep.

"Bast was worshiped as a symbol of consciousness, light, and healing. She lighted up the night as well as the day, cast light on things otherwise hidden in darkness, and was believed to have the power to bring the dead to life. The cat archetype has its dark aspect as well; the black cat, the witch cat, and the cat that is an incarnation of the devil point to its destructive power.

"No one quarreled with Apep until the moon goddess, Bast, after centuries of supreme rule, was displaced by the male sun god, Ra. Her eyes were incorporated into his, and that was how she lost both her identity and her connection with the snake, Apep. Then Apep became a terror, the lord of the underworld; and every night Ra, seeing through the eyes of the moon goddess, Bast, would descend to the underworld to engage in a terrible struggle with the snake.

"In a way that myth and your dream may be connected. If the woman loses herself in the man or if the female principle gives over to the male force, then the snake, or woman's chthonic, sensual-spiritual nature, becomes dangerous. Somehow a good contact with the snake has to be restored."

I was reminded that perhaps Sarah's head appeared on the snake because mother and daughter were being unconsciously identified. Sarah, like her mother, has been pried loose from her normal, collective place by the tragedy around her.

Modern women who have been uprooted are destined to lead the way; if they do not they become lost. They cannot find support for their true selves in a predominantly masculine society. They must rediscover their own source, and that would necessitate feeding the snake, our modern Apep. In neolithic times in the Middle East, human biological fertility had been raised to a sacred level; it more than magically promoted the increase of game and agriculture. Contemporary women need to contact this special potential, no longer in biological terms but in psychological, cultural, even religious terms, and not as a regression to the all-or-nothing, ancient matriarchal concept but in a forward movement within the same pattern. To gain their rightful importance women must connect with their chthonic strengths and recover on a conscious, responsible level the religious impact, probably unconscious, which they had at the beginning of history.

Sally sat up. "Oh, I like that myth. It's when I've felt totally trapped in my wife and mother role that I've been most resentful and most venomous! How complicated the snake symbol is!"

"It certainly is. In modern terms I suppose you could say it represents both evil and repressed sexuality, and it has been a god as well. Throughout dynastic Egypt the cobra was featured on the royal headdress. We also know that long ago the snake was associated with the dark side of Christ. But, again, the Romans revered it and believed it protected the home; great danger could have come to the household if its snake was harmed. That reminds me, let me tell you about an encounter I had with my own snake, an encounter that touched in me that same collective place I was just talking about."

Often examples of the experiences of others help people of Sally's type, to whom experience is absolutely necessary, more than myths and legends. The experiences of others are only once removed from their own.

"A long time ago I saw a baby king snake in my garden; he's now grown very large. I see him only about once a year, but I've always had a very special feeling for him. I haven't told anyone about him, and I've kept his whereabouts a secret because I've sensed that if something happened to him, it would be a very bad omen for us. Apparently I was caught by an archetype, because I never read about the role of the snake in Roman times until long after that encounter."

"That's interesting. But I'm caught now in the word 'venomous' I mentioned a moment ago. That's how I am when I'm quarreling with Sarah sometimes, and maybe that's why her head is on the snake. She's not that way; she shows a lot of sweetness when we're arguing. Let me tell you something about our relationship because it troubles me. We're in conflict so much of the time — maybe because we're so much alike in many ways. As a matter of fact, Jim and I feel she reflects the best and the worst of both of us and our marriage."

She was concerned about Sarah's recent demand to be transferred to the first integrated school in her town, a junior high school that was attended by more black students than white. Even though Jim did not approve, she was allowed to make the change.

"I was responsible for her making that choice because I'm the one who's always encouraged her to think and act independently. But I never meant for her to go out courting trouble, and I'm afraid that's what she may be doing."

"Maybe Sarah is reacting to the grave situation at home by seeking this kind of extreme reality in her own life, Sally. And she could be reaching out for the earthy, real world you were forced to overlook because of the times in which you grew up."

Sally had other worries about her daughter. She was afraid Sarah was now praying for her recovery. She didn't want her to lose her strong religious feelings by putting God to a test that would probably fail. She had done the same thing at Sarah's age.

"In what way did you test God when you were eleven?"

"I wanted a brother or sister. My mother had several babies during my childhood. I prayed for each one of them, but they all died in infancy. When the last one was born, I prayed again, but that time I made a pact with God; if He'd let my sister live, I'd always have faith in Him. And then that baby died. Still, I didn't turn away from religion completely until I was in high school and fell in love with Jim. I had a lot of trouble keeping down my sexual feelings in those days; they were very strong. I was often terribly tempted and in great conflict about holding on to my virginity. That was a big thing in those days anyway, religious or not, being a virgin until you were married. I was also very religious. I even considered becoming a missionary one day. But I felt that sex and religion were incompatible, that somehow you had to choose between them. When I fell in love with Jim, I chose sex."

Her sensuality, an important part of her nature, certainly was rooted in the chthonic woman. She could not reconcile this deep female root with the concept of the God she had inherited. In the end she had to give up her strong religious feelings in favor of her sensual side. But because of society's narrow view of both religion and the sensual female and because of Sally's restrictive upbringing, neither worked out for her, and she was suppressed on both sides.

Sally continued, "Now I worry that Sarah might have to suffer the same kind of conflict. You only have to look at her to know she's inherited my sensuality."

So Sarah was implicated because of their similar attributes; her warm physical qualities and her religiosity made her the focus of both Sally's black thoughts and her efforts to come to terms with what the snake represented. It is little wonder that the snake had Sarah's head.

"Of course, I don't think I'd be in that kind of conflict anymore. In the first place the idea of a personal god no longer appeals to me. And I know from my reading that sexual rites, written off by our patriarchal society as temple prostitution, were part of ancient matriarchal religions. Also I know that sex can be a selfless act, much like a religious experience. But these ideas came to me much later. I'm afraid Christian morality didn't help me much with my own conflicts about good and evil when I was young."

We talked about some modern ideas of God and the devil in which evil is included as part of the whole. I referred to the all-inclusiveness of the self through which these images manifest themselves. I told her that I thought it was better to know about evil since the archetype of the self includes evil.

I asked her to speculate with me. If I were to believe that God is good only, then following Him as a model I, too, would be good only. All through life I'd try to behave myself and push down my evil side, which would have to fall back unresolved into the unknown of my shadow. Eventually, however, especially at the time of my death, I would have to come to terms with what I had pushed down — God's evil side; for isn't it His evil side that best explains the horrors of cancer and other terminal diseases? I would have to deal with my own personal darkness and rage, which would break out in times of weakness. And if I hadn't consciously accepted my own evil side, it would remain unconscious and still tied in with society's collective evil. It could only come out explosively in unexpected ways as projections on the world or on people around me. Only when my fury and fear had cut me off from everyone might I become aware of the need to understand evil's superhuman aspect and separate out what rightfully belongs to me. But then it might be too late, especially if cancer had taken over.

"Some believe," I said, "that purgatory is a projection that the 'good' Christian makes. Some go even further, to say that if God's evil side is not acknowledged, He acts it out through Hitlers and outrageous wars. Some even believe that without knowledge of God's evil side, any trigger-happy potentate could set off the bomb."

These ideas didn't seem to engage Sally now. She commented only, as she covered her ears with her hands, that she feared for her children because of the bomb. She said she felt a sense of doom all around her.

The unresolved personal shadow accounts for so much undignified behavior of the dying, such as the last minute disinheritance of innocent heirs, old men pinching the nurses' bottoms, the acting out of all kinds of obscenities.

The chthonic woman is often relegated to the shadow. This is why it is important for us to reinstate her as consciously as possible. If we do not, she joins forces with the inferior and unconscious personality that takes over in compulsive, unpleasant behavior under the stress and strain of dying. She can stay stuck in the "garbage can" instead of emerging as a grounding, humanizing, broadening influence, especially in the realm of morality.

I visited Sally every day during the next two weeks. She protested mildly each time — was I sure it wasn't too much trouble? I knew that being left to herself too much, as she had been while I was gone, made her self-deprecating, lost, and anxious. And I was sure that more pain and new, distressing sensations could only intensify this frame of mind, so each time I would insist that it was not too much trouble. I knew she was really glad to have me come even though she

didn't tell me so. Sometimes at the beginning of our interviews I would notice how ashen and formless her face would
be. Then as we talked, her color would return and her face
would take on its normal appearance. Although her pain
and discomfort remained, our discussions about what had
been bothering her in the previous weeks seemed gradually
to lift her melancholy, as if some aeration of that thick
blackness had occurred.

In one of the sessions of the first week she reported a
dream about Thelma.

*We were having a fight, hurling insults at one another. I com-
plained that dinner was late and there was garbage all over the table
and on the floor. "I do things my own way," Thelma answered. It was
an even battle.*

This is the first time so exaggerated an example of Sally's negativism
has appeared in her dreams, and it demonstrated how the shadow, this
time personified by Thelma, takes over when she is left alone. My
being with her physically is a constant reminder of the good within
her, and my acceptance of her anger prevents the shadow from over-
taking her. I also intercept, in a matter-of-fact way, her unproductive,
nagging fear of the future.

"What are your thoughts about it?"

"Thelma wouldn't ever stand up or fight for herself that
way. And really, things are much better between us now; at
least they are on the surface. But naturally she's happier
and more helpful right now; she's about to go home again."

I knew that frequently, if the relationship is good on the
surface, its negative potential will be expressed in a dream.
As the days went on, she spoke of spending more harmonious time with Thelma. She admitted that Thelma had
grown by being in the presence of illness and by working so
well with the children. She said she could even like her now

because she saw her as someone with an adolescent mentality who was trying hard to be helpful and to understand. Even her cooking had improved. When Thelma left for home, Sally said that for the first time in twenty years they had good feelings toward each other.

Then she became concerned about her mother's having to come so soon again to replace Thelma. Her mother and Jim had little to say to each other. He couldn't stand her helpless attitude and continual drinking. It was an awkward and uncomfortable situation for the three of them.

"Besides, I can hardly bear her sad expression; it makes me so sad. Oh, I know. I do remember what you said once about how she must be expressing the sadness I can't articulate myself; but it's not just now. Ever since I can remember, she's been depressed. Even as a child I couldn't reach her."

"That must have been very hard on you, Sally."

"And the dream I had about her holding up the diamond brooch still haunts me. That was about two months ago; in the dream my right eye had been removed, remember? Now that dream has come true in a way, because the vision in my right eye is almost gone. I can't see to read with it anymore. Look, when I cover my left eye this way, I can see only your outline, and you're sitting just three or four feet away from me. Now Jim tells me I call out 'Mother! Mother!' in my sleep almost every night. It's all so eerie."

She spoke of her father's mother, her ninety-year-old grandmother, who lived alone in a trailer on income from social security. She spent ten dollars a month for food and twenty for the trailer. She saved the rest and managed well.

"You said the spirit prevails after the rational mind goes, and I know it's true from the letters I get from that old lady. Even though her memory and reasoning have gone, *she* is all there. You ought to see those letters; there are jewels in them!"

Many times during this two-week period she spoke of suicide. She had often struggled with the question of whether or not to take an overdose of the pills she had accumulated. She told me she had held them in her hand once when I was away and had almost, but not quite, had the courage to swallow them. At times she said that her suicide would allow the family to get on with their lives and would eliminate the possibility of a dreadful future for her. She feared the gradual deterioration of her body and perhaps a long period of being a nose-fed, paralyzed vegetable. The thought of losing her ability to perceive through her senses was worse to her than the thought of death. At other times she would say, as she had before, that she was too curious about what would happen to her psychically to kill herself and that in spite of everything she had gained something from living.

"Suicide would be so final; there'd be no chance of coming back; it would be the end. At least in life there are alternatives."

She said also that she knew Jim was horrified by the idea that she might take her own life, and it would be hard for the children.

"Your children see you as a heroine, Sally. Your dreams —so many of them—present you heroically. And to me, well, you must know that I see you as a woman of great courage; and no matter what you did, I would always think of you that way."

She asked me softly then how she was ever going to make it. I had to explain that I hoped it would be through our interchanges, our combined efforts to free her natural instincts so they could see her through to a peaceful solution.

"Now that I've begun to know myself I realize how different things would be if I were allowed to live. My new attitude would make my life so much better. I could help others to go through what I am experiencing. I would like that."

She told me that she felt her destructive inner man, the one who had been killing the helpful salamanders, was no longer getting in her way. She again felt that her dreams meant something; she could believe in them. She felt she had accomplished all that was necessary. Her children were all right. Their lives were no longer intertwined with hers; they were close to their father, as he was to them. She was sure Sarah had assimilated the fact of her possible death by now; and, perhaps, because she had begun to understand how bound up with Sarah she was, the tie could now dissolve. She and Jim were in good relation to each other. She was no longer needed.

She was beginning to believe in her mandala as a manifestation of God within herself. She now had it pinned on her wall and looked at it with renewed interest when she awakened, crying out in pain. The contemplation of her mandala helped her deal with her fears of death.

"I can see it now only if I cover my right eye, but even so, I can go into it and then out through its corners in fantasy."

"A gateway, you mean?"

"Exactly. I'm going to put up more of them."

Many times she spoke of her fear of death. She wasn't so sure about her feeling that in death she would fall into oblivion; she thought that life did possibly continue in the unconscious. This idea made her afraid, and for reassurance she said she would return to the belief of the Zen

Buddhists that in death one goes back to the stream of life from which one came. We discussed some ancient ideas that love and death were merely two sides of the same phenomenon; death could be looked upon as the final internal love affair, the mystical marriage so beautifully described by the gnostics.

"Tell me how they described it."

"I heard a famous Dutch scholar speak about it once. If I remember correctly, it went like this. At birth man was split into two halves; one half lived on earth and one half stayed in heaven — or in the pleroma, as they called the spiritual world. So every man had his angel, his guardian angel who was exactly like him but was his counterpart. Anyway, the moment someone died, he would be united with his angel, who would save his spirit; they would be joined together in a sacred marriage. The gnostics believed that Christ, the spiritual man, and Sophia, his female counterpart, came together in a mystical marriage. That was the prototype of salvation; also perhaps the coniunctio* to which Jung gave so much importance in his writings. There was a hierarchy of pairs for the gnostics that consisted of the male and female principle together. At the top of it was male Depth and female Silence, and they were the basis of everything. There was Consciousness and Truth, Reason and Life, and other male and female pairs that continued down the ladder to Christ and Sophia and to man and woman, too, I suppose, although my learned professor didn't specifically say so. At any rate, with the gnostics there was always the polarity of male and female."

"It sounds as though those gnostics were speaking only of the spiritual side of marriage."

"But I think there's an underlying meaning in that myth

181

for everyday marriage as well. They also encouraged marriage right here in this world and not just for procreation. That idea came only with the Catholic church. For them marriage was a setting for sexual love that was beautiful and good because it reflected the love of Christ and Sophia."

"I wish I'd known about that when I was young. It certainly was a well-kept secret in my church!"

"But let's apply this gnostic teaching to ordinary life. Take, for instance, Silence, the female principle. Haven't you known those catlike women who never give the game away? You never know what, if anything, is going on in their heads. On the other side there are the men who might be their counterparts; they seem to have a similar trait that cuts you off when you try to explore the relationship too closely with them. They simply go off the air and leave you feeling guilty for having somehow illegitimately invaded their privacy. And then you, in frustration and with vague hurt feelings, push harder to know what they're thinking; before you know it a tug of war has developed. The man defeats you with his silence and you dig deeper and deeper, invoking male Depth as he invokes female Silence. And we know how formidable the female aspect of a man and the male aspect of a woman can be at times. Does this sound to you like too neat an interpretation?"

"No, because I know so well what you're talking about. You've described perfectly what happens between Jim and me. I know a lot of men who won't or can't talk about relationship difficulties. But there are probably just as many women who probe too much."

"The gnostics were talking about archetypes, just as we are right now. Our understanding of religious concepts has to come out of human thought and imagination, or at least out of revelations from the unconscious. Where else could they come from?"

"Well, I'm not sure. That really puts a lot of responsibility on ordinary human beings. Still, when you think of Job, who behaved better than God, or even when you consider a person in my predicament, who has to muster enough character to kill a saint just to keep going . . ."

She paused for a moment and looked out of the window toward her mountain. Then her eyes contacted mine again.

"I really think we've lost that spiritual connection in marriage. When I think about my own marriage and of all the troubled marriages my friends have, I wonder if the institution of marriage has any value anymore. What about you? Do you think it's here to stay, or even that it's worth the trouble?"

"I don't know, Sally. I think I mentioned to you once before that I have an invaluable friend, a woman who's a feeling type. We enjoy sharing our opinions on this kind of problem because even though we have different ways of arriving there, so often we come to the same conclusion, that is, if we reach conclusions! Her marriage ended in divorce ten years ago, and she's been by herself ever since. But, all the same, she believes in marriage. She feels that the desire for union with that other is so strong in all of us and goes back so far that it must have its roots in some collective, archetypal place and must be connected with the self."

Living out archetypal patterns in ordinary life, striving for completion in a concrete, practical way would appeal to a sensation person whose symbolic thinking and imagination tend to give her trouble. On the other hand the intuitive can vividly imagine a close relationship and believe himself to have "arrived" psychically when in reality he may be destroying a concrete relationship that could round him out. These two kinds of people often marry, causing almost insurmountable trouble. It may have been part of the trouble between Sally and Jim.

"My friend thinks that over time, and with its daily wear and tear, marriage loses for most couples that psychic or spiritual connection that love originally evoked, and often this loss is so devastating that the feeling of love is lost as well.

"Few people enter marriage out of a conscious desire for their own psychic development. Marriage is, after all, a practical solution to the problems of loneliness and of fulfilling the desires for sex and children; it is also supposed to provide a living, caring situation which supports one's work in the world. But if the goal of marriage is not eventually to promote a conscious connection with the self for each person, all the outer rubs suffered during a marriage — financial reverses, illness, job losses, attraction to someone else, necessity for moves to other places — might mean the loss of that original connection.

"The popular culture has never helped people to see marriage as a means of pursuing individual awareness. My friend, for example, grew up in the thirties and forties, when the collective view expressed through popular movies and magazines was that a young woman was incomplete before Mr. Right came along, but once he did and she was married to him, the curtain would come down and, barring accidents of fate, they automatically would become one and live happily ever after. The longed-for union would occur at the outset of the marriage; tangible proof of it would often come shortly afterward with the birth of their first child.

"And just below the surface of this idyll something else

184

may have been happening. Mr. Right, for that woman who married during the forties, may have been her complete opposite in type, which was why she was so energetically interested in him in the first place; but she and he didn't flow together into one stream as the words of their marriage ceremony indicated they might. Instead, the difficulties between them because of their unrecognized differences left each of them isolated. One person, because of some inner stirring for growth, might make a new tributary that the other couldn't follow, and then perhaps the other would withdraw energy from the relationship and place it into work or children or someone else. Worse still, the stream of togetherness may have flowed into one stagnant pool; what a disillusionment for both of them to find their newlywed idyll shattered!

"Not that striving for the ideal needs to be given up! It *is* possible for love to be sustained in a worked-out marriage of long standing. The just-married, symbiotic state is unconscious; a mature marriage requires as complete an autonomy on the part of each person as is practically possible. It requires also a mutual respect that allows for a community of differing tastes, expression of talents, interests, and goals. It requires, as well, the psychological equality that the modern women's movement will hopefully foster, once economic and legal equality are established. The conscious marriage allows, too, for emotional upsets that drain off tensions. This kind of marriage fosters efforts toward individuation in each partner, encouraging the man to be responsible for the woman in him and the woman to be responsible for the man in her. Insofar as each person develops in an all-around way, the two may cultivate a togetherness that is more than they dreamed of when they married.

"Children who are products of these idealized marriages of the forties like her own, my friend feels, will inevitably suffer the break-up of their parents' marriages, or will observe their parents still living in marriages in which there is no vitality or spirit. Obviously they're going to seek their own alternatives. Even so, my friend isn't so sure they'll be aware of the underlying cause of their parents' failures.

"She feels it is that mysterious desire for union with the other that can be the beginning of consciousness for each one. A way can be hammered out between a man and woman in spite of their differences if the two enter the marriage with that same objective."

If she had reprimanded me for the long discourse, I would not have blamed her. But she was looking out toward the mountain again, and when she glanced back at me she said only, "I've never heard of anyone getting married for those reasons. If only there were time for our marriage to develop in that way. Maybe it could be different."

One day, at the end of our visit two weeks after I had returned, she told me her doctors had suggested she be moved to the hospital.

"They want to see if I've broken any bones; they think that's maybe why I'm having so much more pain. The nights are horrible. I can't help screaming out when the pain gets so bad, and Jim says it's awfully hard on the children. But, my God, I don't want to go! I have a hunch that if I go now, this will be it; I'll never come back home again."

"Still, you'll be made more comfortable there, Sally; it's probably the best place for you now. I'll come to see you as often as I can."

"That would help." She reflected a moment, then said, "Now let me talk about one more dream before you leave."

186

I was on a pier at a seaside resort with my father. We discovered a theater where about fifteen young people were rehearsing a play. I think it was a light comedy. The atmosphere was gay. My father and I weren't active in the play; we were simply looking on.

My father went to the box office, leaving his wallet behind. A boy discovered it; he showed it to me and I identified it.

"What do you make of it?"
"I don't know, but the play was *Charley's Aunt*."

For the public the play or festival is a conscious collective effort. It can have deep roots in universal psychic patterns that are unknown to the audience and to the actors who are attracted by it. For Sally, because it was her dream of a play that she consciously associated with her father, it touched on her personal problem with her father. His importance was being depreciated by the unconscious, for he was no longer in the father role. To leave your wallet behind is to leave behind your identity.

Charley's Aunt, a famous play of its time, is the story of a young man who impersonates an old woman. It is a grotesque portrayal of the animus-possessed woman or the anima-possessed man, pitfalls for Sally and possibly for her father. Since it is a light and gay comedy, it is in opposition to Sally's heavy, tragic situation and therefore an essential compensation.

The play is probably archetypal because it was so universally popular. But what makes Sally's association so important is that the character of the aunt contains the archetypal opposites of young man and old woman. This combination, which also occurred in the dream of Nanny and Aaron, was revered in neolithic matriarchal times.

She then told me of having once been active as production manager of many plays performed by the little theater group in her community. Really, she said, she would have preferred acting to production, but she lacked the confidence. The one part she did play was that of Adam in an amateur musical review. She and a friend had written the script, which was based on the Old Testament story. Her father, she said, had also been interested in the theater. Born and brought up in a small town in Michigan, he had earned a university degree in engineering and then had become a singer in rebellion against his engineer father. Married and supporting a young family, he sang in vaudeville with a group called "The Junior Orpheum Quintet." Once, while the group was on tour, their manager had stolen their car and their salaries and had taken off, leaving them stranded in California. Eventually her father had sent for the family in Michigan. That was how Sally got to California and why she could never really believe in her father or find security in him. It was just like him, she said, to lose his wallet in her dream.

In other words, because of his dependence on her, she could not use him as a guide. She would have to find her own way in the theatrical world in order to live out the humorous, Dionysian side of her nature. Participating in drama might have led her, without her knowing, to its deep, religious source. Writing, directing, or acting in plays would have allowed her to express her emotion on a cultural level. Creative women, especially sensation types, tend not to get sick if they transcend their biological function and produce out of their archetypal needs and impulses.

It was time for me to leave, but her sad and thoughtful expression prevented me from going just then. Both of us were silent for a time, and then tears filled her eyes. She said softly, "Oh, Jane, the fourth act of my play takes so long."

"Most people leave after the third act, Sally. Apparently you have further to go."

CHAPTER TEN

WHEN I entered the six-bed ward where Sally would remain for the next two weeks, she called to me from across the room. As I approached, she closed the paperback book she had been reading and placed it with the stack of others on the bedside table. Its cover showed the hands of two brawny arms clutching the throat of a grimacing, thin-faced woman.

"Junk and rubbish. I have a friend who brings them to me by the dozen."

"How do you feel, Sally? You look as though you're doing pretty well."

"I'm not, though. I feel terrible. The pain is much worse than it was at home, and whatever they've been giving me for it, some kind of injection, doesn't work. I was awake most of the night; I just can't sleep. And do you know, you're the first person who's been in to see me today? No, that's not true. The house doctor was in this morning. He had an order to do a lumbar puncture, and I wouldn't oblige because no one had explained to me why it had to be done. That made him angry, but he wasn't nearly as angry as I was. Why don't they tell me anything about what they're going to do to me? I get pushed around for tests I know nothing about; I'm treated like a number, not a human being. Oh, I wish I were back at home; I feel so much worse here. And Jim hasn't come in today either."

It seemed as though she had been abandoned by the hospital staff and in a sense by her husband as well, who later admitted when I called him that it was he and not so much the children who had been upset by her screaming at night.

When she finished pouring out her complaints, she could make her only positive statement of that visit. She recalled a peaceful dream she had the night before. It was "very nice," she said.

I was in the desert with four-year-old Aaron again and his mother, Susan. We had made a round house like a hogan or igloo. It was nighttime and the stars were out. It was a lovely place, peaceful and satisfying.

She had no thoughts about the dream except how pleasant it was. I told her I thought the round house is the universe with its center post or smoke hole, where heaven and hell are connected with the earth. Building an Indian or Eskimo type of house suggested that she was coming to an instinctive attitude toward death such as Indians have, one that has not been trampled down by modern life.

The four-year-old Aaron, who appeared in the surfboard dream, the dream of Nanny, and in her association to the ceramic dream, once more refers to the completion of her life and the beginning of a new cycle. If this were the dream of a young, well person it would mean the rounding out of an old phase and the beginning in life of a new one.

She was pleased and said that these ideas gave her peace, especially the suggestion of the round house as a mandala.

190

Variations of this containing symbol had occurred in two of Sally's previous dreams; in one she was sheltered from a storm in a peaceful room where she sat contemplating three lamps; in another she was safe in a convent as war raged outside. Dr. von Franz told me of a dream Jung had had before he died in which a similar mandalalike symbol appeared. He was surrounded by ceramic pots encircled by trees when a voice said, "Don't be afraid, for you are protected." He saw then that the roots of the trees were gold and surrounded him in a protective net.

She was unable to initiate further conversation about herself so I left early, telling her I would return the next day. As I was leaving, I looked back to her from the ward entrance and saw her reach frantically for her detective story.

When I returned, she was even more unhappy and agitated than she had been the day before. She was exhausted, she said, yet she looked surprisingly well and seemed keyed up and alert. Perhaps her clearheadedness had given the hospital staff an incorrect impression of her condition, for they seemed not to be paying much attention to her. She said she still longed for sleep and hated being kept in ignorance about what was going on.

"And I had such a scary dream last night. I dreamed the radiator next to my bed was on fire and I could see my room being enveloped by a pink firelight. I'd gone to sleep frightened, so no wonder I had that dream. My surgeon came in to see me on his way home last night and told me he wanted to remove my adrenal glands. Also he said I was to appear before the tumor board. I don't know which of those items had me more terrified."

"Did he tell you why he wanted to do the operation?"

"No, of course not. Or anything about the procedure either. He was just like the resident yesterday who wanted to do the lumbar puncture. They weren't about to tell me why."

Without thinking, almost not knowing where my response had come from, I reminded her that we knew now from her other dream that she possessed the legendary salamander instinct in her unconscious and that fire would be no problem for her.

"So it's all right, Sally, remember? You could survive."

She lay back then, relaxed into her pillow, and closed her eyes.

"I'm sorry, but do you mind if we don't talk anymore today? I've been so tired, and I think I can go to sleep now."

I know that bringing a patient back into connection with the unconscious has a calming effect, but I wouldn't have believed that this simple statement could have settled her down so. I walked away quietly.

Outside her room I was approached by the resident, who wanted to talk about her. Somewhat uncomfortably he said that she was an unusual person and a strange and exceptional case. He said most patients with her kind of disease would have died long ago; for this reason no one could predict how long she might live. She could die within a year or live for eight. She had not lost weight since they last checked her and this, too, was unusual. He was afraid that the pressure of her extraordinary pain and distress could easily make her psychotic; only last night she had many times called out "Mother, Mother!" in her sleep. He thought that removing the adrenal glands would diminish her pain, even though no one could say exactly what role they played in the disease. He felt fairly certain the operation would have no adverse psychological effects and would not lessen her sensitivity to life, but he could not swear to it. He urged me to encourage her to do whatever her doctors advised. I told him I could not honestly do this, since I was not a doctor and could not know what was medically appropriate.

For the next week I was unable to visit Sally because I had the flu. Jim and I, with Sally's approval, kept in touch by telephone, and he told me that x-rays had revealed a fracture in her right thigh; the break accounted for the terrible pain she had been suffering in that leg. She would have an operation and the broken bone would be pinned or set and put in a cast. Other x-rays disclosed that her cancer was more extensive than the doctors had realized. She was actually worse than they believed her to be. She could continue to live for weeks, even for months, but not for years. They had now decided against removing her adrenal glands.

The first message she sent me through Jim was the report of a nightmare that had recurred throughout the night.

There was a pogrom. Men, women, and children—masses of orthodox Jews with expressions of horror on their faces—fled in waves, as if on a frieze. Groups of them were chased, and then somehow these same ones chased the others. The men had classic Jewish features; they wore curls, black beards, and black, rounded hats with flat brims. Prayer shawls flying, they belligerently brandished the scrolls they carried.

For a Protestant, so great an emphasis on the Jewish theme, one that incorporates evil, balances the Christian point of view. The Dead Sea scrolls, recently found, trace the Jewish origin of Christianity. Perhaps the men, belligerently brandishing the scrolls, imply that Sally's roots in the Jewish tradition need to be acknowledged. Jew beset by Jew refers to Sally's choice: Either she integrates evil as does the sensitive Jew, or she indulges in it and becomes the insensitive Jew.

There is an interchange of pursuers and pursued in the dream; the chaser becomes the one chased, a subtle implication that one is both the victim of one's fate and the cause of it. This is the psychological dilemma connected with disease.

Jim told me that Sally had likened it to a scene in the film *Potemkin,* in which people were shot down by the Cossacks as they fled down the steps. But there was no bloodshed, torture, or cruelty in the dream; it was only a statement of pure fear and terror, the kind she was trying to dilute by reading gruesome murder mysteries. Jim and I agreed that the dream showed she was being hunted down by cancer, just as the Jews had been hunted down by the Nazis. And, I thought to myself, the theme of being forced to face her responsibility to herself that had occurred in her earlier dream of imprisonment was now, in this dream, turning up again.

A few days later Jim seemed somewhat embarrassed but anxious to tell me another dream she had reported to him. She had told him she would leave it to him to decide whether to tell me about it or not. He said it seemed such a strange dream that he couldn't resist telling me.

An all-encompassing, big voice, which she knew was the voice of God, said, "Let us nourish the arid soil." She awakened, having wet and soiled the bed.

Arid soil and barren lands are symbols of depression common to cancer patients. Out of arid soil and barren lands, however, arise great religions and cultures, such as the religion that came out of the desert surrounding Jerusalem and the magnificent culture constellated by the aridity of Greece.

Symbolically defecation is part of the process of individuation: To attain the highest one must also know the lowest. Saint Simon supposedly spent twenty years in the desert wallowing in his own excre-

194

ment. An attraction to dirt may be associated with a sense of being close to God, while repulsion to dirt may go along with a feeling of being far from God. I have heard some young, counterculture patients talk that way. They have seen the value of the earth principle and consider the adage "cleanliness is next to godliness" appropriate only for a hygenic, sterile society like our own.

In the dream Sally is not encompassed by God, is not one with God, but is associated with him in mutual work. This statement is even more presumptuous than the one made in the gnostic myth we discussed, in which every man saved at death attains the vision of God when he joins his angel in a sacred marriage. For here she is elevated to equality with God as his partner, joining him in the performance of a cosmic task. I felt she had achieved on the religious level the modern woman's ideal to be equal to but different from a man.

In personal terms God's command is that Sally must overcome her depression, or as the Chinese say, turn sadness into strength. Expressions of her emotion in raw, human terms instead of angry, manipulative outbursts might help her overcome the depression. As it is, her only connection to her emotions is made in an involuntary, eruptive way, exemplified by the involuntary eruption of the physical that may have made way for, or possibly have caused, this dream.

It had been a vivid dream, and she had told him she felt good when she awakened from it. "A little closer to the living in God," was the way she had put it. She had also told him that after having the dream she felt she was going to die and it was all right with her.

I believed she was describing the feeling one has after a kind of "ultimate" experience. When Jung had a heart attack in 1944 and was close to death, he had a vision in which he saw the male and female principles, in the form of the all-mother and the all-father, join in sacred union. For him this was a blissful image of the self. I have heard others report this kind of ultimate experience — either on a personal level, as in the coming together of lovers, or on an impersonal one, as in the completion or total satisfaction of a specific achievement. And afterward they have experienced a willingness to die, if not a desire for death. The state of individuation invites death in a positive way. Once the highest is reached, it is as though the secret of life has been glimpsed, if only for a moment.

I thanked Jim for telling me about the dream and mentioned that it seemed to be an extraordinarily female and unusual way to withdraw from this earth or from the personal ego life, and that I felt it even hinted at immortality.

Later Jim called to tell me how interested and pleased Sally had been with my interpretation of the dream. Apparently he had now become interested in her dreams and was trying to make some sense of them. I recalled that when she first entered the hospital, he had complained about her being a difficult person; she was, he had said, a stubborn and uncompromising patient. He had seemed somewhat grudging when I commented on her enormous courage. But since playing his vital role in her psychological development by reporting her dreams and carrying my interpretations back to her, his attitude had changed and his resentment seemed to have dissipated. He seemed much more impressed with Sally now and spoke readily of his great admiration for her. He was spending more time with her, and he thanked me for now being as helpful to him as I was to her. My absence during this week turned out to be fortuitous, for it had obviously served to bring them closer together. Closeness in their marriage was the essential outer expression of the deep-level theme that was our objective, and this theme was enigmatically implied by the joint venture in the dream of God.

During that week Sally's thigh was pinned successfully.

When I talked to Jim after the operation, he said her pain now overshadowed everything. She was being given morphine for it and cortisone to shrink the tumor in her head, but morphine was not as effective as they hoped it would be, and the pressure in her head had not improved. He said he thought the end might be near.

She was not in her bed in the ward the next time I came to see her. On my way to the nurses' station to find out where she was I was surprised to meet her sitting in a wheelchair in the hall. I hadn't expected to find her out of bed. We were glad to see each other, and I wheeled her around the floor while we talked. She was communicative and seemed exceptionally lively, even though she said she was in terrible pain. Her head, she said, felt like it was being squeezed tighter and tighter in a vise, and morphine took away only the edge of the pain. But she told me with obvious pleasure how much better she and Jim had been with each other during the past week; they had often discussed her dreams. Even her mother had gotten interested in dreams; just yesterday she had told Jim about a marvelously funny dream she had one night.

"Imagine! It's unheard of for my mother to talk about anything personal, or even to talk to Jim at all. Listen. She dreamed she was on a grassy slope, and there lying in the grass was something that resembled a large, stuffed cat. She went up to it and found it was a man, a famous song-and-dance movie actor. Except for a patch on his left loin, over his genitals probably, he was stark naked. He got up and chased her, then jumped off a cliff."

"Isn't that something, Sally! You've so often described your mother as a sad, withdrawn person. It's not surprising she'd been that way with her cat —her female symbol —

turning out to be a man. Apparently in spite of her warm nature, she has no female instinct. No wonder you couldn't model yourself after her! In this dream she was taken over by the man's idea (the stuffed cat) of what she should be."

"But I feel sorry for her now. It's too much for her, all of this. Maybe she should go home now. Wheel me back into the ward, would you? I want to lie down."

I did and helped ease her back into bed. With sorrow I observed the useless, wasted remnant of her body. Her eye protruded grotesquely from its socket. In spite of her pain and the deterioration she had so often anticipated with abhorrence, I had the impression that she was happier than she had been before; possibly morphine, which also may have connected her to the unconscious side of her psyche, made her feel that way.

She seemed eager to talk again and returned to the subject of dreams.

"Your way of interpreting them is so different from what I expected. I always believed dreams were nothing more than disguised wish fulfillments with only the most personal kind of meaning. But I keep thinking about some of my dreams; they've moved me so much and have been so far removed from my personal life that I can't help feeling they're valuable and must have come out of something else. Then I come to my senses and tell myself they're really nothing more that very peculiar dreams."

What a discouraging remark! After all the work and all the evidence, why was it still so difficult for her to take hold of the reality of her dreams? What made her resist so stubbornly? She was so bright; why couldn't she understand?

Oh, I was tired of this battle; and then it came to me. She might have been suffering from a thinking function that worked *too* well. Jung has named thinking and its opposite, feeling, the rational functions because they arrange data in orderly, acceptable, understandable ways. I like to add to his definition and call them "organizing functions" to emphasize that aspect of their role. I find it helpful also to label the irrational functions, intuition and sensation, "gathering functions." Jung called them perceptive functions.

When the organizing functions are too dominant, they can prevent the flow of intuitive data or sensation from entering awareness; this means that hunches or even actual experience and observation are not accessible when needed in order to come to more comprehensive conclusions. A strong thinking person, especially if she is already biased, might discredit her evidence by pulling it all together too quickly. The thinking is not checked; it is too imminent and forces itself onto the situation, demanding expression. Bright people like Sally sometimes come to superficial conclusions or seem to be obtuse when considering issues that should not be at all difficult to comprehend for a person with such good thinking. Those who have excellent feeling and are also considered bright might behave in a similar way. If, for example, a feeling writer evaluates his material too soon in terms of style and form, the result might be a story lacking in depth, subtlety, and content.

For those whose irrational functions are too dominant, material comes through in an arbitrary way, and these people get lost in their material, unable to organize or evaluate it. The ideal is a balance between the rational/organizing and irrational/gathering functions.

To explain my idea to her would have meant launching into another discourse on psychological types, so I restrained myself and responded to her doubts as best I could.

"Oh, Sally, if only I could dispel your doubts! Of course your dreams are products of your own life, and in that sense they may be peculiar. But can't you see that they also connect you, through all the ages, to people everywhere who've had to face the same problems you're facing now? If you could know this idea and really accept it, you might be less afraid."

"The only thing that would make me less afraid now is if they'd give me more information about what's happening to me medically. One thing I really do know is that being uninformed this way exaggerates my every symptom."

So be it. Clearly she wanted now only to talk in an extroverted way about what was going on in real life. I wouldn't push.

"Tell me then, besides giving you more medical information, what do you think the hospital staff could do to make you and other patients with cancer more relaxed and comfortable?"

The issues concerning this subject were obviously clear to her, and she seemed eager to discuss them.

"Well, first of all, people around you have no idea how much guilt you carry around for having cancer. You feel as though you're being punished for some horrendous crime you committed, yet you don't know what the crime was. When strange technicians and doctors and nurses come in and without a word stick needles in you or insist that you take pills without telling you what they're for or wheel you somewhere on a slab to wait in a hallway for God knows how long and for what kind of test, it all gets to you as being part of the punishment. Have you ever seen patients lying on tables in hospital halls waiting their turn for some ghastly procedure while people walk by and ignore them? Can you imagine how lonely and scary and undignified it is to be on that table and watch healthy people whiz by without so much as a glance; and, you, wondering why you're there and they aren't? It *must* have been something you did; you must somehow deserve it. Honestly, patients need to be reminded all the time that just as earthquakes and floods and famines are random acts of God, so is cancer."

I felt that Sally had made an important point, suggesting that people who are ill might on some level know that illness has to do with unconsciousness (again, one is the victim of one's fate but also the cause of it). In a letter Jung wrote in response to a question about the psychological causes of cancer, he said that he had seen cancer arise in a person who could not overcome a certain psychological obstacle, but that each one of us was stuck somewhere, after all. At another time Jung said that guilt is often the result of un-consciousness rather than of wrong doing. (Of course one could speculate that wrong doing is always itself the result of unconsciousness.)

"Of course, Sally. If only people could remember that . . ."

"And then there's guilt about letting the family down, about causing them so much trouble. If only people would help us deal with those feelings."

I had an impulse to make notes on what she was saying so I took out pencil and notebook from my purse.

"I want to write down what you're saying, Sally. Who knows, someday I may have the opportunity to let people know how you feel."

"I hope you will because then maybe this hideous suffer-ing won't have been a complete waste. Yes, it's letting people know how you feel that's so important. I wonder why people who work around patients with cancer don't seem to understand how angry we are and how scared. It would help so much if they wouldn't leave us stuck with those feelings. What a relief it would be to let them loose! I need to be reassured that if I blew up at one of the nurses or screamed out because of some huge, nameless fear, she'd still come around next time I pressed the button."

"Perhaps the only reason she might not would be because she was so scared herself."

"And then there's the asking for help. It would be so much easier if only my family and the doctors and nurses would tune in to my needs more so I wouldn't have to ask so often for help. I feel like a beggar — so unworthy when I ask for something."

"It's probably far worse for you, Sally, because of that exaggerated spirit of independence of yours. You've never been comfortable asking for help."

"Well, that's true, I suppose. But, you know, the whole business of the way drugs for pain are dispensed fits with my feelings of being a beggar. What's the sense, tell me, of withholding narcotics from people with cancer? Does addiction matter? Sure, drugs should be given on time, according to an impersonal schedule; but if we ask for them more often, then of course we should have them. As it is, we not only feel like beggars, but there's some implication that we're cowards if we ask for our medication too soon. Very often because they're short of staff, the medication comes late; we're always so anxious about its being delayed that we can't forget about narcotics, even when we're not in pain. Fighting for drugs becomes an all-engrossing issue that distracts the patient from her personal thoughts. I'll give you an example of how it goes. Last night the nurse came in to give me sleeping pills for the night, but she wouldn't give me any medication for pain because it wasn't time yet. Her attitude made me think she was trying either to improve my character or punish me. If I'd been given both morphine and sleeping pills at the same time, I might have slept through most of the night. As it was, I woke up at midnight with excruciating pain."

A few days later when I visited Sally at about noon, I found her moaning in agony. She cried out as soon as she saw me.

"Oh, I can't stand this! Can't they put me out? I swear I'll kill myself if it goes on much longer!"

I left her room, found the resident, and told him she was suicidal from being in so much pain. A nurse, one whom I recognized as a favorite of Sally's, came and gave her an extra dose of narcotics. In a short time she looked like a different person. She wanted to talk to me about the recurring dream she'd had throughout the previous night. An oxygen tent had been placed in the ward for another patient, and she had been forbidden to smoke.

"I needed a cigarette so bad I was just frantic. I kept having snatches of this dream all night long.

I was in Chicago with Jim. There were flashes of us in different parts of the city—on street corners, in the theater. Suddenly Jim forbade me to smoke, and I yelled at him for it. I cried, "You are stupid, Jim!"

This personal, quarreling dream points up a negative aspect of their marriage of which she seemed to be unaware. It also brings into focus a fine distinction: A kind of undermining goes on here that occurs in many marriages in which one partner seemingly has, by all outward appearances the upper hand, but in reality it is the other—often a feeling type—who possesses much more power and uses it in such an unconscious or covert, subtle way that he or she cannot be confronted openly about it.

Sally has always presented herself to me as the shrew who heaps her anger on Jim. She may complain to me about his bungling and may in her dream yell at him that he is stupid, but really she is flailing at phantoms because no matter what she says, how she acts, he calmly holds his ground. His saying no to suicide, no to her selection of an army blanket for Sarah, no to smoking somehow gets to her where she is vulnerable. He prevails. The dream also points out her projection onto Jim; the hospital forbade her to smoke, not Jim.

"That was just because I had been forbidden to smoke, I'm sure. It was a terrible night, and when morning came I could barely see it."

"I've noticed how little you see now, Sally. Shall I try to get some taped books for you from the library for the blind?"

"Yes, I'd like that."

"What kind of books do you want?"

"Fiction. Detective stories — well-written ones, I mean — not trash. But nothing technical and nothing inspirational."

Saying she did not want trash seemed to be for my benefit. Detective stories were obviously helping Sally to assimilate the shadow, to feed and tame the poisonous snake. I feel a sadness now that I did not fully understand until after her death the meaning of her snake dream or the deeper implications of her obsession with reading detective stories. If I had, I might have helped her to indulge more wholeheartedly in her "trash" and encouraged her in her craving, or at least have given her a more satisfying interpretation of its meaning. It seems we must do as the primitives did for their evil spirits: Put out food for our unconscious evil impulses, honor them, bring them into our awareness in any way we can, and never mind how lowbrow, trashy, wasteful, or demeaning the activity might seem to be. I suppose I may have been trying to discourage what appeared to me at the time too debilitating an attitude.

Outside the ward after this visit the resident approached me and thanked me for telling him about Sally's suicidal feelings. He told me they had now done all they could do for her, especially because she had rejected some of their suggestions for further treatment. Since it was the policy of the hospital not to treat patients with chronic or terminal disease, a bed for Sally could no longer be provided. They were now investigating nursing homes for her where she would be given therapy to make her more ambulatory and where she could bathe in showers especially equipped to accommodate patients in wheelchairs. She could maintain more of her independence in such a place. A convalescent home, he assured me, would now offer the best solution for her care.

When he left, the nurse who had given Sally the injection at the beginning of our visit stopped to talk to me. I recalled that she was the one who had once given Sally a patch to cover her blind eye, making it possible for her to read with her good eye. She spoke sympathetically about Sally and asked if there were any way she could make things easier for her until she left the hospital.

"I think it would be very helpful if you were to give her medication for pain more often, whenever she needs it, in fact."

"Oh, now I couldn't do that. There's a lot of life left in her yet, you know. She could still surprise us."

CHAPTER ELEVEN

I N THE middle of October Sally was moved by ambulance to a convalescent hospital near her home. It was a new nursing home built on a flat, arid site that had not yet been landscaped; its stucco exterior was painted some un-namable shade between the color of hot dog mustard and pea soup. The interior walls were a sparse institutional green. The place had, in fact, the feeling of an inexpensive-ly constructed motel, where, lacking an alternative, one might spend a night on the way to somewhere else. Inside, the atmosphere was unsettled and noisy even though the floors were carpeted and the ceilings were soundproofed. Because most of the occupants were old and needed extra heat, the temperature was excessively high. Patients, many of them senile, called out to each other and to the nurses from their rooms; some of them wandered about aimlessly. Since the place was understaffed, it was not unusual for a patient to be abandoned in a wheelchair, left uncovered after a bath, or ignored when calling for help with some eruptive bodily function. The thought of dying in such a place would be abhorrent to anyone.

The first day I came to see her I found her alone in a double room. She told me she would be by herself until a suitable roommate, one who was about her age, could be found for her. She was in misery again. She loathed the cold, modern decor of the place and longed for the comfortable and spacious atmosphere of her own home. She even preferred the hospital to this environment. She was now constantly in a state of anxiety about not getting a sufficient amount of morphine. She had received increased doses during the last two days of her stay at the hospital, but here they had been reduced. When she eagerly described a dream that had followed an extra dose of morphine during her last night there, I realized that her preference for the hospital was based on her increasing need for narcotics.

I was riding on a cart like one of those in the Persian miniatures. Two corpses rode with me, and they were dressed in white tunics, which were beautifully embroidered around the neck. The cart jogged along through a Persian landscape of vividly colored pools, hills, and flowers. It was a long and pleasant ride.

The quality of this dream verges on the psychedelic. If morphine has contributed to this pleasant atmosphere surrounding death in the dream, the psychological effect has been positive, for the dream compensates for her suffering and anxiety in reality. In experiments with dying patients who have been given LSD, similar effects have been noted, except that the visions seen after the ingestion of LSD may seem more real because they occur when the patient is awake.

"What do you make of this dream?"

"I really don't know what to make of it. Riding on a cart certainly is a journey, isn't it, and this one seems to be referring to death."

"In a serene and beautiful way."

But apparently these positive feelings about death were not lasting; she told me that during her last few days in the hospital the thought of coming to the convalescent home would send a rush of fear over her, and she was still terrified to be in the new place. A second dream, which she had on the night before she was to leave the hospital, showed the kind of apprehension she felt about being here; she somehow sensed it would be her last stop in life.

The new place was like a huge gymnasium. The floor was spread with straw mats, each one covered with only one rough army blanket. I was pushed around and poked by malicious nurses. One of them lifted my blanket and exclaimed, "You have two legs. Good. Two arms. Good. You won't be much of a problem!"

This dream is permeated with the fear of the process of death; since the unconscious moves from one opposite to the other, it is not surprising that a dream in which dying is depicted as a peaceful journey should be followed by one in which it is experienced as a terrifying new place dominated by evil women.

Sally's dislike of women in uniform, women in power, is shown in the dream. These domineering, malicious women, imitations of inferior men and negative aspects of herself, are also aspects of the negative mother,* the mother who destroys. These are the negative figures that lurk behind her mother's benign, helpless personality as her shadow, reinforced by a self-demeaning animus, to whom Sally must have related throughout her childhood. These women, lacking the healthy instinct for which she was groping, have remained a lifelong problem for her. The authoritarian woman, the pseudomale, the witch, the evil side of earth woman, have been constellated during her short lifetime because Sally has suppressed the chthonic element. The solution to this is an essential part of her individuation. It has to be faced before her fears will abate.

This is a collective dream because gymnasiums are collective places. The hugeness of the building refers to dying, for one envisions the going "out there" as going into limitless space. The army blanket, prominent also in her dream of shopping for Sarah, seems to be some kind of bedrock symbol for Sally. The army, the soldier in the field, stoicism, self-control, combat, all are collective representations of the animus.

208

Sally continued excitedly, "It's those vindictive nurses again. And the dream has turned out to be more or less true too. It's so hard to get used to the new faces and the new routine. That feeling of being helpless and at everyone's mercy is always with me here, and I know it will only get worse. I'll break more bones; I'll be blind and maybe deaf. And with all that, always the pain. I'll come to depend more and more on these people to help me; they pay no attention to me now when I call for help. How will it be later on when I'll need them even more? Why did he do it, Jane? Why did Jim send me here?"

Then quietly, miserably, "I know the answer; he couldn't stand to have me at home. He doesn't care for me anymore."

"That's not true. You know Jim cares for you; he's with you in your suffering. But you need too much care to be at home."

If I had known at the time what I later realized—that this convalescent home was not actually as bad a place as it seemed to both of us at first — I might have been able to help Sally relate to what it was really like and to help her see that she was projecting onto the convalescent home her fear of a miserable death.

She was crying now. Why had she been singled out for this terrible agony? Why now, before her children were grown? She feared for her children, for Sarah especially, who would need her even more as she grew up. Who would be there to give her that special understanding she needed? She had begun to dread the children's visits; their enthusiasm about their own lives made her feel excluded. She could find nothing to say to them.

Her bed was near a window. She turned her head toward the light, away from me, and spoke softly.

209

"I'm desperate. Suicide seems to be the only way out for me now. Yesterday I almost slashed my wrists with a piece of broken bottle glass, but finally I didn't have the courage. I have no courage left."

For a moment my own courage seemed to ebb away; then the thought occurred to me that in many of her dreams her unconscious had pictured quite clearly the other side of that despair.

"But, Sally, there have been so many positive dreams that have said you have more work to do before you bow out. You've been distracted from your tasks lately because of all your practical problems and this is why the woman in your unconscious has turned sour. But now we'll be able to concentrate on the psyche again so your body can release you."

She looked back at me, slowly nodding her head.

"I know. You're right. And then when my psychological tasks are over, perhaps I may die. I hope so. I've been living on a superficial level for a long time now, off the track and far away from what matters. I wish I could be relaxed again about being on my way to death the way I was at home before I went to the hospital. Remember?"

"I do remember, yes."

She sighed.

"Maybe talking about my dreams might help me get back again. I've had some since I've come here; let me tell you about them."

I'm sure she really felt her dreams would get her back on the track again. But also I think her eagerness to tell her dreams was connected to her feeling. She knew what an important language dreams were for me; in sharing them with me she was beginning to rebuild our relationship.

"One was about my father."

I was with him in Northwood Park, a park where my mother used to take me during my preschool days. Only I was my present age and I was well. We were having a pleasant walk along the paths around the edge of the lake, and we were exploring the grottos. I felt reconciled with him; I had forgiven him for causing me to be born.

"My father created me in a moment of passion, when he was thinking only of his own gratification. But in this dream I'd forgiven him for his selfishness. Everything was all right."

This dream in which she is well may be her fantasy of how it will be after she dies or a fantasy of what is to come, should she live. It may also be that she is unconsciously taking her father with her. A daughter who does not finally value the personal father may be seriously involved with him on an unconscious level. Sally must settle her father problem somehow because he is a component of her male side and therefore part of the ongoing marriage theme which has appeared in her dreams.

"I know how that must have been because I had a kind of half-waking dream myself about my own father the second night after his death that was a bit like that. In it I felt his presence in the room, and we were reconciled too. Somehow he knew then that I'd played fairly in my dealings with the family and hadn't gone against him."

Although she said nothing, the expression of hopelessness around her eyes was gone and she regarded me with interest, so I went further.

"Sally, doesn't it seem a bit curious to you that in this dream you were well? There have been other dreams, too, in which you've been well."

Still she seemed attentive but did not respond.

"Did it ever occur to you that death may bring a solution to the most nagging problems of your life? In this dream you were well, and your disappointment with your father was

211

resolved. If you consider that neither of those things is true in reality, death may be the healer."

"Oh, I wish you'd stop hinting around about life after death! I've told you I don't believe in any of that. I hope there's no such thing as life after death or reincarnation or any of that nonsense. I only want complete annihilation in death. I want to be a rock and nothing more."

A rock, I thought, is certainly a symbol of the self. There are many examples, including the philosopher's stone of the alchemists, the rock of the sacred temple in Jerusalem, the black stone of Islam in Mecca, the stones of Australian aborigines that were supposed to have contained the spirits of the dead. But this was hardly the moment to tell her these thoughts.

"Well, you certainly make your fantasy about death perfectly clear, and I can't quarrel with it; but at least let me have my own."

"What is your fantasy about death? I remember when you first came to see me, you told me you needed to know what I was going through for your own sake. I know you've had thoughts about what happens when you die. What are they?"

"I've had thoughts, yes. I don't pretend to know any more than you do, but I'll tell you what I think. So many of my thoughts about death have come to me when I've been by myself on long walks by the sea or in the hills where the terrain is unfamiliar. Sometimes when I've started on one of those trails, I've thought that maybe death is the ultimate unfamiliar trail—frightening, arduous, possibly dangerous, but perhaps also beautiful, and certainly interesting. In any event, I'm sure it takes an adventurous spirit—one that doesn't hold back—to get the most out of it.

"Psychological death is an experience in life that I'm familiar with; I've observed my patients go through it, too, and there's something about it that makes me think it must approximate real death. In psychological death an old attitude, an old way of being in the world, has to be given up because it's worn out. It doesn't work anymore and it makes you stuck in your life. But your ego is invested in that old way, and it doesn't give up without a struggle — a struggle between it and the self, which is making its own demand that you change. Take for example the kind of woman who has lived her life being cooperative, helpful, and obliging and who's been easily divested of her natural negative impulses. Old, suppressed hatreds and resentments emerge against people whom she feels have put her into her present stuck situation. She's angry and she needs to put blame somewhere, so she puts it onto people in her life who personify her own unrealized potential or who exhibit the same kind of unconsciousness that she has had throughout her life. Once that anger is activated and lived through it goes away, but it might be replaced by feelings of sadness and emptiness that may last for a long time. And then one day — she may not even know why her ego finally gives up and releases her from the anger, the need to blame, and the depression — there's a feeling of peace, of reconciliation, of freedom. She feels different, for a while at least.

"Another kind of woman with a strong ego and a sense of her own superiority could one day collide head-on with someone who personifies all that she has considered inferior. Suddenly she may become aware of her own weaknesses and doubt her own judgment. She sees that she does not know enough to evaluate others; she hardly knows who she is. And then one day, also perhaps not knowing why, she is released from both the struggle and her old attitude of arrogance. She becomes a new person.

"Well, I fantasize that my real death will go something like that, only on a much grander scale. Once through the portal of death — and that may be the worst part of the experience — I like to think I'll go to the place of the collective unconscious, which has become familiar to me over the years because I've been there so often in my dreams. When physical death confronts me, perhaps my giving up of life will be much like the giving up of an outworn attitude in psychological death. Not bothered with the ego, I could be part of all life: the trees, the winds, the water, and all wild things. And on the other side of that struggle called dying, who knows? Maybe there will be that same sense of reconciliation and peace that comes when the ego gives up in the psychological struggle.

"Naturally, I have serious qualms about what will happen. I can imagine having the same kind of qualms — nothing as serious, of course — about taking LSD for the first time. There's the possibility of having a bad trip on the one hand, but on the other there's the possibility of a marvelous expansion of consciousness. I'd just have to take the attitude of trust and belief in the constructiveness of nature and of my fate. This would be true of any adventure into the unknown, so why not take that attitude toward death?"

"But for that one has to have faith."

Again she turned her head toward the window. When she looked back at me, she asked only if we could go on now and explore another dream, one that had come to her in flashes.

I was a high school student in a classroom with one other girl. Some great calamity—probably an explosion—was about to occur. Each

214

time the disaster threatened I held my hands out in front of me and
willed the calamity back. As I did so, my terror would diminish, but
disaster kept pressing in on me again and again. I didn't know the
other girl. I couldn't see her, but she was my age.

An explosion sometimes stands for a collision or a coming together
of opposites, in this case the conscious and the unconscious—a dramatic, important experience. On the other hand the result of this
collision could be insanity. The thought she had expressed some time
ago—that the unconscious was too dangerous to probe—may have
come from an underlying fear of insanity. She may have used "willing"
in the past to hold back the threatening unconscious.

Explosions also signify proliferation in the sense of too much
happening too rapidly to be controlled, such as population explosions,
nuclear fission, malignant cell production in cancer.

The only association she had to the dream was that for
some reason she had felt as though she were in school the
night she had it.

"Were you afraid for yourself?"

"No, I was trying to protect the other girl. Somehow I
had endangered her life, and I was willing disaster—probably death—away. As I think of it at this moment, that girl
must have been Sarah, even though the dream said we were
the same age. Yes, I'm sure it was Sarah. She was here last
night. I'm so afraid she may be the one who will inherit the
tendency toward cancer because we're so close. Yes, that
was the disaster I was trying to protect her from—death
from cancer."

I wondered if their being the same age in the dream
suggested Sally's identification with Sarah's independent
decision to attend one of the first integrated schools in their
district. I also wondered if perhaps, more than the possibility of cancer, Sally may have feared that her blond
daughter would marry a black man. Such a union would

215

provide one of the most dramatic, problematic, unpredictable settings for the bringing together of opposites that one could imagine and would carry in it the elements of both creativity and destruction. So radical a step might be symbolic for Sally of what she was facing herself.

I said I thought her strong connection with Sarah might be keeping her alive.

"But I do worry so much about what will happen to her when I'm gone."

"I'll try to keep in touch with her, Sally. Perhaps she'll come to me if she's in trouble."

"That's good of you. She did mention last night how fortunate I was to have you."

"Then maybe she'll remember to come to me if she needs me."

I commented that I thought acts of will came out of the ego; therefore, it was the ego that was keeping her alive. I suggested that the ego and body are usually symbolically identified and that both have to give way to the self, but never completely until we die. Then, noticing how tired she seemed, I stopped. She was rubbing her arm.

"Oh, it hurts, and so does my head. I can hardly concentrate on what you're saying. I wish it were time for my pain medication. But no, please don't go yet; there's one other dream I need your thoughts about."

I was in an enormous hall where hundreds of people were voting. The voting place was like a ticket window, and there were so many people milling around the window that I couldn't get to it to cast my vote. I completely missed the opportunity.

"It was Pat Brown again who was running for governor in the election. Which reminds me, Jim was late when he came to see me yesterday, and by the time he got here the pain medicine had worn off, so it was a bad time for me."

"In other words, he bungled again."

"That's right. You remember that old dream too."

"Yes, but this one's different, isn't it. There's the suggestion here that you'd like to vote for this person and show you've confidence in him, but somehow you're blocked by an attitude, represented by the multitude. You need to be more discriminating."

"But how can I have confidence in Jim when he does such stupid, thoughtless things! Listen to this. Later he brought the children back to see me. He arrived with them during my dinner, just in time to watch me spill food all over myself because I couldn't see to prevent it."

"Come on now, Sally, Jim's not perfect, but who is? Sometimes he's bound to make mistakes; how could he know your feelings if you don't tell him? At times we're all inadvertent bunglers. You might not be aware of how much he helps you just by allowing you to get rid of so much of your tension when you direct all that anger his way. And I know you'd be the first to allow how thoughtful and giving he's been through all this."

Tears came to her eyes then.

"I know he has. Why do I have to dwell on those negative things? Why did I tell him not to come back tonight when I miss him so much already? Why is it so hard for me to express my feelings of love and warmth for him?"

"I don't know, Sally. It's strange how some people can love others in the face of the most glaring faults, while others just cannot. In your dream your human attitude, which the crowd also represents, wants to vote for the human, bungling Brown or Jim; but somehow you, as an individual, just can't get there to do it. It seems as though your unconscious puts you in connection with humanity, but there's something wrong with your connection to the crowd that prevents you from contacting Jim. I suspect the dream is telling you that in your terrible isolation you're expecting Jim to be everyone for you. And, naturally, he can't be; so he bungles, or worse, he cuts himself off from you and that leaves you feeling even more isolated."

"But what can I do? I miss being with people so much; I envy them, I envy Jim."

"It must be just hell for you, being so alone. But if you could try to see him as just one individual and not burden him with having to be the whole crowd for you, perhaps you might be able to make it to that window."

"And give him my vote."

"Yes. I think we agree that the struggle of relating to him in the marriage is terribly important; it's your individuation at stake here. But that ticket window has a second meaning as well. You could, once you expressed your real feelings for Jim, buy a ticket for a trip at that window—a trip to the most unfamiliar places. I always take my own dreams of going on trips as death dreams because of my age. I think travel for old people is actually a way of making real the symbol of death that pushes at them. Did you ever notice how much they travel? You see them compulsively trotting around the globe, vying with each other about who's been to the most and the best places. Sometimes they seem just about worn out from the strain of it but they keep on going."

She smiled and interrupted, "You seem to have done quite a bit of traveling yourself."

"Yes, and I know it's that same symbol that pushes at me, but I would like to think not so unconsciously. There's only one major trip left that intrigues me; it's to Egypt where I'm beginning to feel that my deepest roots lie. I'm sure one thing that keeps me going is that when it comes time for me to leave this globe, I'll want to have seen and experienced as much as possible of what I'm leaving behind. When I'm traveling and I'm having trouble getting used to the feeling of a new place, I sometimes think that having to make an adjustment is a kind of individuating preparation for death. At least, that certainly gives travel another dimension for me."

"The dream did say I missed my chance."

"Not necessarily for long, Sally. I remember the dream you had of being in Paris — your lovely, long-cherished, star-shaped city. You certainly managed a successful inner journey then. You may be waylaid this time, but maybe that's how it is only for now."

She seemed exhausted, so I said goodbye to her, telling her we would see each other soon again. As I was leaving, I could not help commenting on a picture I noticed on her wall. It was one of those paintings of a bowl of gaudy flowers that one finds in motel rooms.

"I wish you'd replace this with one of your mandalas."

"I wouldn't want to do that. If I were to put one up, I could hardly see it; and if I could, I'd be embarrassed. On your way out would you please ask someone if I can have my pain medication now?"

CHAPTER TWELVE

T HROUGHOUT the next three weeks her mood of
depression and despair remained essentially un-
changed, although for brief moments I would find
her calm, almost serene. I visited her about three times a
week; when I entered her room she would ask me to roll up
her bed to a sitting position before we started talking. But
before going in I would first learn what I could about her
from the head nurse. During the first week she told me that
Sally often cried, especially after visits from her children.
Since this nurse seemed eager to have my suggestions, I
mentioned that she could feel free to talk openly to Sally
because she was now quite able to speak about her fears of
death. The nurse responded regretfully that she and the
staff were not.

Sally was walking a little, with great difficulty, and spent
some time each day out of bed in a wheelchair. I noticed she
was often in pain in spite of the heavier doses of drugs, but
even so, as time went on, she became more relaxed and
would report having slept fairly well at night and easily
during parts of the day. Her failing sight was increasingly
worse. She could hardly see her children when they came,
and she could only tolerate visits from them about twice a
week. I saw her having trouble lighting cigarettes and was
concerned that she could easily set herself on fire. I began as

unobtrusively as I could to light her cigarettes for her. I also noticed that she had lost her sense of time. Once when I asked her for the date, she brushed my question aside with "I don't know," as if I should have known better than to ask.

I found her acutely apprehensive during this time about physical deterioration, and I always tried to encourage her to talk about her fears. She was having pain in her right arm; she was afraid it would become paralyzed, and then she would have to learn to use her feeble left arm. She was worried, too, about breaking another bone as she walked the few steps she took each morning—steps she resented being strong enough to take. The thought of being unable to communicate terrified her. If she were in a coma and unable to talk, could she be certain she would be given morphine to keep her out of pain? Perhaps some of her fears were unfounded, she admitted; but five years before, when she had expressed worry about her bones breaking and about going blind, the doctors had belittled those fears. She could not trust them now.

I knew Sally's addiction to morphine must have been pressing on her mind, but her guilt about dependence on drugs, reinforced by institutional policy, prevented her from conveying her thoughts to anyone. I believe doctors would do well to encourage their patients with terminal cancer to discuss openly not only their fears about death and pain but also their preoccupation with obtaining sufficient doses of drugs and their fear of addiction.

"Sally, I assure you that if you were in a coma, I would do all I could to see that you would be put on a strict routine of drugs. And I suggest that you make a good connection with your physician, so he'll take care to give you morphine if you are in a coma."

"I don't think I need to worry about that; we do have a better connection now. Only yesterday he told me he no longer had any desire to try out new drugs on me. He's content to leave me in peace."

Again and again she would ask why she had been singled out for so much torture. I thought perhaps I could lessen her despair by suggesting that she see herself in an archetypal role, perhaps the female version of Job, whose story we had often discussed. I offered her Jung's idea that Job marked a turning point in the religious drama which led to the incarnation of God in man. God had been divinely unconscious before his encounter with Job. Because of God's unconsciousness, Job had been forced through torture into a higher state of awareness — into individuation — and then God had to catch up and in Christ become human. Jung suggested that those who are forced, through pain or conflict or psychosis, to a higher state of consciousness are those who carry the burden of the future. But Sally could not see herself in this heroic role.

"No, that just doesn't seem right for me. It doesn't fit."

"Because after all, you're not a man? I think that's why it doesn't fit. How can we as women experience ourselves as heroines in masculine terms! It's like being given a theory to follow instead of a warm, all-around, human model. That is the curse of the Christian myth for us. We lack God's female counterpart. Perhaps one model you can follow is the one that came in the dream where you and God were partners."

"Well . . . I don't know about that."

Sally trailed off, obviously taken aback. I was reminded of her reaction when I had explained that her mandala was her concept of God.

Sally finally spoke again. "Another thing, though, Job was all right when he accepted his fate. That was his solution. But I can't accept mine."

In these weeks she had three dreams to report; two were of her father, who would arrive during the third week and whose visit she anticipated with such dread that she was puzzled by the joyous dream.

I was on stage during the filming of a musical comedy at a Hollywood studio. I was in my early twenties, in the middle of it all, dressed in black leotards and a turtleneck sweater. Evidently there was another number needed to complete the production. I suddenly burst into song and with great showmanship sang a Rodgers and Hart tune, "My Funny Valentine," all the way through. I made a great hit, was offered a part in the film, and accepted.

Everyone rushed into rehearsal. My father was W. C. Fields. Ed Wynn was my coach. Together they taught me all the subtle details of comedy. In one scene I was to jump over a tray of sandwiches, and Ed Wynn showed me how to pretend it was a pool of water by dipping my toe into the sandwiches.

The father's importance is emphasized again in a "well" dream. He first appeared to her as he watched a rehearsal of *Charley's Aunt*, then later at Northwood Park. Here he is as W. C. Fields in the role of teacher to Sally. In all of the dreams of her father, or father surrogate, except for one that came long before this series, Sally is well; she may be finally recognizing inwardly her paternal heritage.

Dreams of being well refer to the future. She may now have to live out these potentials in her imagination as she did in the Paris dream, or even in her afterlife if such exists. Whatever the implications, I could not speculate about them with Sally.

The clown, respecting no boundaries, brings opposites together. He is at once wise and foolish, clumsy and exquisitely agile, tragic and funny, outrageous and appealing, cowardly and courageous. He whacks away indiscriminately, laying low whatever is in his way. He tends minutest life with infinite tenderness. He is archetypal — a personification of the trickster.* Since the beginning of time the clown, like nature's elements, has promoted new life by sweeping aside the established, outworn conventions. He is able to take risks, to stick his neck out without knowing the consequences. He is the embodiment of the life force, but he also has a connection with death. He risks his neck and miraculously escapes. He plays with death.

In a sense this figure is a male part of the chthonic world, reaching us from below, coming in through the back door, touching us without our knowing. He is spirit itself—spirit with its own laws that comes and goes according to its own will. He is Coyote for many Indian tribes. Greek fertility rites, undoubtedly originating in matriarchal times, out of which it seems drama and comedy arose, honored the phallic fertility god, Dionysus, with revelry, hilarity, comic antics, and clownish obscenity. These rites had to do with life and regeneration, as opposed to death.

Had Sally's true nature been allowed to flourish as a girl, her basic reductive, "misanthropic" nature could have led her to be a comedian. She could have creatively turned her jaundiced views into humor as W. C. Fields had done so successfully.

Her undeveloped feeling would be appropriately expressed through the sentimental song "My Funny Valentine." An undeveloped function that turns up in a dream breaks through in a fresh, childlike way, and with youthful energy.

The figures, W. C. Fields and Ed Wynn, must refer to the clowns who bring together the opposites and in this role represent the transcendent function. Certainly they could be helpful dream figures to contemplate, to incorporate into consciousness. The more relaxed, less constrained attitude of the comedian could be helpful to her.

In this dream she is part of a collective, popular gaiety. In life she bears alone the heavy burden of impending death. These two states are opposite parts of her whole being. Can we not speculate, then, that in death there may be something beyond or above the sum of these parts?

"What did you make of it, Sally?"

"It was a wonderful dream. W. C. Fields actually is my favorite comedian. I think he was very clever. He was truly a great artist. And I loved Ed Wynn too. My father was on his radio program once during the thirties. He was zany and ridiculous."

"Yes, in my youth those two were the clowns that made us laugh no matter how bad things were."

She said she had been very happy when she awakened from this dream, but the contrast between it and her real life had left her feeling let down and depressed for days afterward. It was in vivid color; it was a thrilling, intense dream, full of humor.

"I'm sure it was an attempt to balance the sadness of my life with hilarious, comic fun."

It was indeed an illuminating statement of joy from her depths. Apart from ego influence, apart from the horror of her physical condition, the psyche was sending her this joyful message through the dream. It so clearly illustrated Jung's idea about the objectivity of the psyche, because this dream was so foreign to the soberness of her situation. Unfortunately, at the time I didn't have time to explore the dream, so she could only partially feel its impact.

She told me she was sure she had inherited her father's sense of showmanship but had never allowed herself to follow her inclination to be a performer. The joy and gaiety that was part of her had been buried by inhibition and burden. She knew the comic side of her nature would have come out had she been given the opportunity to express it.

"Perhaps in this dream you're going back to fill in what you didn't live, just as you were in your dream of going to Paris."

For someone not faced with imminent death, dreams that take the dreamer back in age may only signify regression, since psychic energy is normally both regressive and progressive. Or a dream of being much younger may presage a consolidation, a filling in of gaps. It can also signify that the dreamer is taking one step back in order to take two steps forward, especially in regard to an important central problem. But because Sally was dying, I speculated that her dreams of going back in age meant that, in the process of dying, she was experiencing an agelessness that is common to old people who have lived deeply. She was close to the collective unconscious, as are old people, wherein the past, present, and future become one.

"Life is normally both bad and good. And something else too: W. C. Fields and Ed Wynn personify the chaos that has to come before change. Their foolish antics break down what's fixed, so something new—maybe a new attitude—can enter."

The unlived artist in her seemed to come alive for a moment. "Maybe so, but to me they were only pure fun and laughter."

"Do you think your overseriousness compensated for your father's irresponsibility? Did you associate his singing career with his unreliability?"

"I might have; I don't know," Sally said impatiently. "But I do know I always loved to sing. Not for others, just for myself. Secretly I used to see myself as Lotte Lehmann, the great German songstress. I memorized all the popular songs and many of the French folk songs. I loved the songs of Schubert, Schumann, and Hugo Wolf. Remember my dream of the triangular LP record of French songs? I've always loved music. But I know now that I couldn't live out the lightness in my nature because I had no security from my parents."

The second dream she reported during this period had been a recurrent dream during three or four nights. She

226

had failed to report it because she considered it unimportant. It was, she said, half-fantasy and not quite a dream anyway.

I was moving into various large, old houses, making one move or several moves each night. My mother was with me, helping me to place the piano and to choose the rooms for Sarah and Beth. In each house the children's furniture was already in place; there were dressing tables and other feminine, frilly objects that were unlike their actual furnishings. Old, floral paintings—unlike anything I own or would choose for myself—hung on the walls of the living room. A soft, blue green carpet covered the floor from wall to wall. The furnishings were early American in style, typical of my mother's taste. The colors were blue— like a blue mist in the wind—gray, green, and stone. In all the rooms femininity and feeling were accentuated, and the atmosphere was pleasant and comfortable.

"What a positive dream of your feminine inheritance, Sally! You're certainly not wasting time. A change of home in a dream usually means a big inner change. Moving, like traveling—an individuating effort—also can foreshadow death. After all, we go somewhere new when we die."

"If we go anywhere at all . . . but let's not get into that again. I want to talk about my mother; I felt so good about her. The dream made me appreciate her good taste; she is really in tune with what's warm and human. My taste has always tended toward the functional and sophisticated, but I think if I could have been myself, it would have been more like hers."

She told me her mother had been orphaned at the age of three. We agreed that she probably lived out her mother's initiative and potential for accomplishment because her mother couldn't. This could have explained Sally's striving so hard for intellectual achievement, to the detriment of her own personal feelings. Sally's mother once more had entered her dreams significantly, this time to set up for her a warm, human, psychic home.

Sally would often talk about her children, grieving for their futures, which she would miss, and for everything she missed even now. And while the awareness that they had become totally absorbed in their own lives pleased her at one level, at another it continued to hurt her. I sensed she may have feared that the children were indifferent now about coming to see her. I tried to emphasize that they were busy, happy, and free only because of her good relationship with them. If she hadn't allowed them to be themselves and get on with their own lives, they would be bound to her now and caught up much more negatively in her illness. I tried to show how she and Jim courageously avoided placing on Sarah and Beth the kind of burden she had carried for her parents.

She seemed comforted and commented that Jim had a more broad-minded attitude toward Sarah now and was doing a marvelous job with both children.

"They're so much more open with Jim and me than I was with my parents. It makes me feel good that they've had a better background than we had; it gives me some assurance that they'll be all right. Certainly I felt deprived when I was a child. I don't remember ever getting what I asked for. I felt especially deprived because I had no brothers or sisters. I was completely alone with parents who could do so little for me."

"But your children aren't deprived, Sally, and probably won't be susceptible to cancer. It's true they'll lose their mother, and that's a deprivation; but your brave cutting of your bond to them should free them. By giving up your expectations of them, you'll release each of them to stay close to her own true nature. They won't be constricted by having to live out your needs instead of their own. I think that will be very important for their good health."

She seemed pleased with the way things had been going between herself and Jim. She had openly expressed her wish to see him in the evenings and no longer left it to him to guess her feelings. She said his visits had become more relaxed and that sometimes they would talk intimately late into the night. Still, she wondered if they could ever really know each other. I suggested they might try telling each other as truthfully as they could and at times when they were in rapport how each one saw the other. That would mean describing one another's negative as well as positive traits. I said I thought that might be a way to clear up their perceptions of each other.

"The better your relationship to Jim, the better the girls' image of a woman's relation to a man will be. Their chances of making good marriages will be better, and they won't be forced to live out too many unlived parts of your marriage. I think marriage has ramifications that go far beyond the couple involved."

I knew Sally's father had arrived for his stay with the family that third week only because Sally would say I had just missed seeing him or that she expected him to come right after my visit. He appeared in the third dream she related to me during this period. It came five days after the second and was about moving into another old house.

This one was a big, old white house—probably a frame house. It had huge rooms with paneled walls, painted white. The largest room, which could have been the music room, had a square piano—a Bechstein—in the middle of it. This room opened out into another one, probably the living room. No other furniture was evident, and there were no pictures on the walls. The floors of each room were covered with Persian rugs called "isfahan"; they were older and more abstract in design than the ones I have. I was looking through some sheet music in the piano bench, trying to find some unfamiliar popular music. My father, his father, and I were members of the household. My mother and Jim and the children were not there; at least, I wasn't aware of them.

In these two dreams of moving, which came only five days apart, one finds similarities and differences; but the most important element I find in the combined dreams is the drawing close of the opposites, particularly a positive coming together of Sally's female and male heritage. Her parents, now equal in value, have become the democratic psychic background for Sally. The presence of the Persian rugs recalls her recent dream of riding with death through a Persian landscape and may imply that the peaceful death scene has now become part of her psychic house.

In this dream the square piano, unlike the conventional triangular one in the dream of her mother, coming to her through her masculine inheritance gives her an intellectual and artistic grasp of the meaning of totality. Playing popular music on this instrument connects her talent with her human, feeling, feminine inheritance. The piano, then, is her instrument of individuation.

Meaning has been attributed to numbers since the beginning of time; the number one is implied in dream symbols such as Sally's tower. The numbers three and four have frequently occurred in Sally's dreams. In the first of these consecutive dreams of moving, four people and a triangular (three-sided) piano appeared; three people and a square (four-sided) piano appeared in the second. The numbers three and four have also appeared in dreams of the four-year-old Aaron; Beth, three or four, behaving as if she were nine (three times three); sitting in silence before three lamps; a sailboat carrying a handsome couple and their four-year-old son (three people in all); and a Chinese mother of four children.

According to Jungian theory, three stands for activity, process, movement, struggle, effort, and understanding. It is associated with the masculine and the spirit because of its dynamic nature. Christianity, a religion dominated by the patriarch, is symbolized by the Trinity which, unlike the religion of ancient Egypt, excludes the female aspect of divinity. For someone not threatened by death, three also refers to the temporal, dynamic, developmental, growing, vital, and creative. In its structural form three is a triangle. It moves because it is incomplete; it forecasts the square. Three also signifies the solution to the conflict or stalemate posed by dualism by positing the third element between or in addition to the two. Three emphasizes the theological as opposed to the emotional experience of religion.

Four signifies completion. It is also feminine and symbolic of earth; the points of the compass are four. It is the square, which does not move; it has the quality of coming to rest. The female figure in Navajo sand paintings is identified by a square head; the male figures have round heads. The four structured as a square is used for meditation; it is basic to the mandala, as is the circle, which is also the whole. Four is a number that is common to the East, as opposed to the active three of the West. It represents a state of being rather than a state of doing.

"Tell me your thoughts about the dream, Sally."

"The house might have been dated 1905, sometime around the year my father was born. His mother was musical in an old-fashioned, ladylike way; and my father probably took after her. She saw that he had voice lessons when he was very young, and it was pretty unusual for a boy in those days who lived in Big Bend, Michigan, population two thousand, to take singing lessons."

"Indeed it was. That kind of nonconformism must have been really something then. But what strikes me about the dream is that it's again about moving. We've already talked about the connections in dreams between moving and traveling and death. And this time the new house is white everywhere. Did you know that white is the color for death in China?"

"In China, yes. Why do you suppose China comes into

231

some of my dreams? I walked with my pope in Chinatown, had dinner with my Chinese friends in a restaurant."

"Not so surprising. In California the influence of the Chinese has been around ever since pioneer days. In our culture white is associated with marriage rather than death; the wedding dress and bridal veil are white, for example. And sometimes it refers to consciousness, so one could say death, marriage, and consciousness are connected. Consciousness could include sex, too; to know someone in the biblical sense is to know that person sexually."

"Death, consciousness, marriage, and sex. These odd connections you make. I wonder."

"Also the dream is almost a reverse image of the one you had a few days ago."

"Reverse image?"

"Well, the last one was about the distaff side of the family. As I recall, you and your mother were choosing rooms for the girls in a house whose ambience was feeling and feminine. But this one has a masculine tone. There's nothing of the female around except yourself. It's a no-nonsense place. The link connecting both dreams seems to be the piano."

"The piano in the other dream was just an ordinary one, though. This Bechstein grand was very rare and special. It was the kind of piano you had to care for meticulously, day by day."

"The way you say that makes me think of a meditation or a prayer, something one would do devotedly each day, such as the mandalas you used to paint that seemed to get you squared away for the day."

"Yes, that's right. Caring for that kind of piano takes the same concentration you need for painting a mandala. I can still clearly see that exceptional piano there in the middle of the huge white room. And that's the second time I've associated music with my father in dreams. Remember my W. C. Fields dream? Only that one was full of fun. There was nothing amusing about this dream."

"Nothing at all; I can see that. And you said the house was stark and white. There weren't any pictures on the walls and nothing to give it warmth. And yet in that serious atmosphere you looked for unfamiliar popular music to play. What a contrast! The care of the piano is serious business, too, as you just said. This has to be a very serious dream."

And now her expression was also serious.

"Yes, I think I understand."

After this discussion of the dream she wanted to talk about her father. She had been especially disturbed by his comments about suffering from a heart condition that would probably prevent him from living much longer. He had said he would leave his estate to Jim and the children if he were to die. In the first place, she said, she knew there was no physical justification for his fears. The family had gone through this bad heart business with him before. Also, if he were to die, her mother would be entitled to whatever was left. If Jim were to inherit anything at all, she said, it would probably be a business mess, debts, and the problem of caring for her mother and grandmother.

"You see, I've seen him cry for himself before. I remember his crying over not having work. The family would have to sit around for days sometimes, waiting for that call to come that would offer him a singing job. It rarely came."

Sometimes people like Sally's father are unconscious of the strong tie they have to a dying person who is close to them; they become vulnerable to feelings of being taken away into death by that person. Sally's dream of being well and taking a pleasant walk with her father may have been a preview of this situation. Moreover, people in close contact with those who are dying can feel it to be contagious; this may help explain why nurses and doctors so often avoid the dying person. Anthropologists acknowledge this reaction in primitive peoples, but the issue has not been taken up in modern society. Perhaps funeral rituals and mourning involve the attempt to cope with the contagious effect of the dying person. They offer a kind of protection to keep the living person psychologically separate from the one who has died.

I was not surprised one day when Sally's father came in, bringing a slice of cake for each of them. He was an attractive, charming fellow, but he did seem somehow lost. He spoke nervously, darting from one superficial subject to the next. He ate his cake and left the room. Sally sighed.

"The big baby. Doesn't he plead for you to take care of him?"

"And yet he turns up as a positive figure in your dreams?"

"Yes, I know," she sighed.

On my way out that day Sally's father rushed up to me in the hall. He looked searchingly into my eyes as he grasped my hand and held it hard.

"If only you could have seen her before all of this."

"But I see her now and I think she's marvelous. I admire her so much."

"She's always been my strength . . ."

He seemed to want to say something else, but his eyes filled with tears and he turned away.

CHAPTER THIRTEEN

D URING the next month I went to see Sally as often as I could. Not that she asked me to come more frequently. When I offered, she told me that she didn't want me to waste my time. I had to convince her that I wanted to be with her, that I was reducing my practice and felt many of my analysands could do just as well, if not better, with my colleagues. Not only was I personally interested in her but also in what she was teaching me that might help anyone, myself included, faced with the same reality. I let her know that I especially wanted to be with her now as much as possible because I would be leaving her for a two-week period in the middle of December, when I would be traveling to Bora Bora with my husband for his much-needed rest.

So I was with her frequently in these weeks, sadly observing her tangible gifts of life drain away. Even at the beginning of this time she could hardly see; she said it seemed to get darker sooner each afternoon. At first she could enjoy the box lunches which Jim frequently brought in as I was visiting her. But at the end of this period she was totally blind and could not manage her food by herself; yet she would reject my offers to feed her, and she would not eat in front of me. At the beginning of the month she was taking a

few steps; she would sit for short periods in a chair or wheelchair, and often I would find her sitting up in bed when I
visited. Later she became completely bedridden and at
times was so exhausted that she wanted only her head raised
a little when I visited. Her pain was increasing, especially in
her head; and now it was in both thighs. She had been given
pills for pain along with injections of morphine, but taking
medicine by mouth became problematic because of
frequent periods of vomiting which weakened her even
further.

Sally had been in the double room by herself for many
weeks, but when the nursing home became crowded, a new
patient, a forty-year-old woman with Parkinson's disease,
was moved in with her. This patient was incontinent,
unable to feed herself, and unable to communicate her
needs to anyone. At first Sally was acutely distressed and
complained that she couldn't even die in privacy. Sleep was
difficult for both of them because the two women kept each
other awake throughout the night with their various needs.
Her fears of helplessness were intensified in the company of
this dependent, deteriorating woman whose incontinence
was especially difficult for Sally to bear. Apparently this
patient was treated like a child by the nurses, who would tie
ribbons in her hair, talk baby talk to her, and cajole her
into eating. Sally found their behavior repulsive. However,
these nurses were considerate about giving us our privacy.
When I came, they would roll the woman in her bed out of
the room, and I would open the windows wide to freshen the
fetid, warm air.

At first Sally complained bitterly about conditions in the
convalescent hospital. In the evenings, she said, the place
was filled with the noisiness of an insane asylum. She was

resentful and irritable about the slipshod attention paid to her physical needs. But over time her attitude changed and her complaints became less frequent, less intense. She got used to her roommate; I believe they even developed some means of communication. She came to understand that she was not the only one suffering neglect; she could hear others calling out repeatedly to the nurses for help.

For at least half this time, however, she seemed to be in an extroverted phase. She was interested, lively, and articulate about her friends, whose visits she seemed to need and enjoy perhaps more than ever. She still maintained her role of confidante; I was sometimes amazed at how many of their own troubles her friends brought to Sally, but she seemed grateful for their confidences. She would talk to them about their activities, their mutual friends, art, and things going on around town. Clearly, now that her powers of observation were gone and most of her avenues of extroversion were blocked, her friends provided an important outlet for her.

She took pleasure in talking about her children in this outgoing way. She spoke animatedly about Sarah's pioneer spirit, so different from her own at that age. Sarah dared to follow her own interests and feelings, had a crush (imagine, her first one) on her black teacher. She spoke of Beth's pride in her good grades, her adaptability, of Sarah's horseback riding, sewing, making things with beads, new play at school, sophistication.

The quality of her contact with Jim varied. At times it was comfortable, at others it definitely was not. She would explain the difficulty between them also in an extroverted way: He was frustrated by not being able to correct the situations that so distressed her, and his frustration blocked their contact; they were both doers and were hostile toward each other because both were impatient that things were going so slowly.

I thought that she was again projecting her own psychology onto him as she did when she wrote to me saying that they were the same type.

The one element that escaped her extroverted attitude and remained almost constant during this time was her all-engrossing concern with evil. It permeated her total existence. Her life, she felt, was entirely evil; good had absolutely no reality for her. She said she could now remember nothing good in her past, and although she knew there actually were good times, she could no longer trust her memory. Even in the existence of her children she could find no good, for they were subject to evil and could not be protected from it. I reminded her that she herself had once told me about the many nonselective, random, destructive acts of God that occur. An "act of God" in legal language connotes a highly destructive act. This phrase is a slip of the Western tongue, an unconscious recognition that the concept of God may include both good and evil. I spoke of the evil that hundreds of thousands of Vietnamese people had suffered, saying in this context that she had not been singled out for evil. But these remarks did not help at the time.

Her negativity strengthened my idea that it is important for the families and friends of very sick and dying people to know that they often seem perverse. I wondered then and still do now whether at the end of one's life evil can break in and take over with an all-encompassing power over which one has no control, or whether, instead, this problem is one that comes out of the shadow and can be analyzed, allowing the person to be responsible and do something about it.

Sometimes when I was at a loss to know what to do about this problem of evil, I would talk it over with my colleague who had seen her during my absence. He would often ask me about her; his interest in her was unfailing. He said I should try to convey to her that somehow she had to accept evil as a normal part of life, as in the *I Ching* where light and dark alternate. She must rise above good and evil, for her place was beyond that. The animus, now that its usual outlets were blocked, must take up the spiritual problem. Were she to accept her fate, stop struggling against it, give up to God, "think with her heart," as the Chinese put it, she would be above the conflict of opposites. She would then be thinking spiritually, not intellectually, not as a thinking type. I thought that it might help if I were to suggest that she meet evil head on, struggle openly with it, and give over to it with her fantasy and imagination instead of trying to nail it down, like a man, through understanding. This would be the woman's way.

She reported several vivid dreams during the first of this month, then later complained about not being able to recall them because of the dulling effects of the many drugs. The first dream she told me was a nightmare that puzzled her.

I was walking on air about two feet above the ground, down a narrow alley between two houses. I was carrying a lot of big packages filled with household things, and I was having great difficulty squeezing between the two buildings because of the packages. One of them contained a huge jar actually like the one in which I used to make pickles.

"Your walking above the ground reminds me in some way of the dream you had about riding on a Persian cart. The drugs might have had something to do with both of them."

"That could be. About all the packages, though, when the children visited this weekend, they had so much to say about Thelma and all the household problems. I guess the dream was all about that."

Because I wanted her not to be stuck in her literal interpretation, I mentioned that having to get through the narrow passageway probably also referred to her letting go of the life of the household, or the earthly life, in order to get on with her own objectives. If that were the case, it would mean a radical change of attitude. Her next response startled me.

"Yes, squeezing through a space that's too small is much like physical birth. Don't you think it's strange that all the dreams seem to be saying the same thing? It's always rebirth."

This was her first admission of such an idea.

A few nights later she had a more frightening nightmare.

I was crippled as I am now, sitting in a wheelchair out in the hall waiting to stand trial. I was afraid. I thought, "Why should I stand trial when I can't even stand up on my feet?"

Two women wheeled me into a large room and then joined the others who confronted me. There were fifteen people, about half men and half women, dressed in police uniforms, except that they were yellow. They were seated on wooden folding chairs, and I sat on one also in the midst of all of them. The people were completely noncommittal in attitude, and the atmosphere was not threatening, but somehow I felt I had to get out of the place, so I made myself awaken.

This dream of a trial suggests the religious theme of ultimate judgment, a theme which occurs in all religions around the subject of death. The Egyptians had a myth that the powers of the next world put the soul on one side of the scales to be measured against a feather on the other to judge its purity. In this dream she is ill, so the ordeal belongs to her worldly consciousness and no longer to that of the future.

"Your thoughts about it?"

"I just wonder why I had to get out of that place — why I had to run away. Maybe I didn't have to, but . . ."

"That wanting to run could come out of your old authority problem, Sally. To be judged means having to acknowledge authority and to submit to it; that's hard for you, especially when some of the people in authority are women who have been too often, in your experience, inferior, pseudomen."

"That's true; besides, I remember in the dream thinking, good God, I'm so weak. Why should I even have to stand trial?"

I couldn't help thinking, why, indeed? She was so thin now and so brittle, like a leaf about to be blown away. And that terrible eye, bulging and sightless.

"You must feel that same way about being so incapacitated and still having to confront yourself in an individuation that never seems to end. I think the dream is saying that too. But also I believe beneath those messages is another, deeper-level one. The judgment scene gives the dream an archetypal setting, especially with the non-threatening, impartial atmosphere you describe. This isn't the only dream of a judgment you've had either. I think the first one was about the postponement of your marriage, remember?"

"That's right. The deputy with a summons. And then imprisonment."

She perked up, drawing, it seemed, from a special source of vitality. I felt I could continue in the same vein.

"To my mind the authority referred to in this dream is your fate. It is nature, so you have to accept it just as mother earth moves in tune with the unwavering course of the sun, moon, and stars. Have you forgotten your dream of God? The off-gold uniforms must refer to the sun, and the sun has been worshiped as the supreme authority, male and female, from the time of earliest man. And when death is your fate, you need not fear it; death is to each life as the setting sun is to each day."

"Yes, but the yellow of the uniforms was an unpleasant, off-gold color."

"Well, yellow is also supposed to be connected with imagination; if it is, maybe it would appear in your dream in a negative way. You're faced with something in your life now that requires a broad understanding. If only you could find a way to deal with the unpleasant aspect of the gold so that it could become the true color of the sun."

"I know. It still casts an unpleasant light and makes me fear the future. No, really I don't get any clues I can cling to from this dream."

Her remark cut off that momentary affirmation. The fear that had awakened her from her dream was with her still. I thought it best to give her time before taking it up again in some other way.

Color symbolism has been used universally since ancient times. In Jungian psychology colors are often associated with the four functions. Usually blue, the color of the clear sky, stands for thinking; red, the color of passion and pulsing blood, symbolizes feeling; yellow, the color of the sun and its rays, is likened to intuition; and green, the color of vegetation of the physical world, stands for sensation. Variations in color also have meaning. Pale colors can refer to lack of vitality. Combinations of color, such as purple (blue and red), suggest the opposites are together, as in royal or hieratic themes. Orange (yellow and red), for those who are not at home with emotion, seems to refer to instability and unpredictability. Negative variations, like the off-gold of this dream and an unpleasant mauve or raspberry, point to trouble.

Later when I discussed the dream of the trial with my colleague, he said he thought my association of yellow with the sun was appropriate. He broadened the idea with what he knew about the ancient Incan and Egyptian cultures in which the sun god reigned at the top of the hierarchy and represented the epitome of order and obedience to the laws of the universe. Sally, he said, was definitely at odds with the natural laws of life, not being able to accept life as it is. In spite of my efforts to convey to her the chthonic ingredients of her previous dreams, she was still against the rich, dark aspect of life. Her darkness was still evil, and since one has to accept the dark to accept the light, the yellow in the dream — the light — had to be unpleasant. She could not rise above both the dark and the light as long as they remained negative. In her dream of God, acceptance of her fate had been forced on her. But now, in her longing for death, she had lost sight of the meaning of that dream; she had returned to her nihilistic, defeated state. The off-gold had taken over.

Away from her, as I was going about my own life, I kept thinking that we needed another way to approach the dream. For some reason my thoughts kept focusing on the number fifteen — the fifteen judges in the dream. I had a memory of her having dreamed about this number before; and when I checked through my notes, I found her dream of fifteen young people happily rehearsing *Charley's Aunt* in another archetypal atmosphere. I found something else in my notes that seemed appropriate, and I probably men-

tioned it to Sally only because of her question at the beginning of our next visit.

"I've been thinking about the fifteen people. In the first
place, why fifteen of them?"

"I've wondered that too. Dr. von Franz once told me a
story about the number fifteen that I found so fascinating I
took it down in my notes. It seems that in ancient China
fifteen represented the matrix of symmetry, which was the
same as harmony, order, and peace."

"Harmony, order, and peace in a number? How can that
be?"

"It seems there was once something called Lo Chou's river
plan, which was ancient China's numerical conception of
the universe. It was a square divided evenly into nine small,
inner squares, each one containing a number. Any three of
those numbers in a line in any direction added up to fifteen.
It was the only set of numbers that could be arranged in
that way, so it was unique. The Chinese claimed the plan
was presented to Lo Chou by some great tortoise or dragon-
like creature who emerged out of the depths, so it may have
been a spontaneous product from the deepest unconscious
level, perhaps from Lo Chou's unconscious."

"Do you suppose that's why numbers have always had
meaning for me? Because they come from out of those
depths?"

"It could be. Certainly they've always had meaning for
me too. It seems that nothing's more immovable, more
uncontaminated, more whole than a primary number. Jung
has said that numbers appear in dreams spontaneously but
they only disclose themselves symbolically when we discover
their primary factors. Your fifteen, for example, is three
times five. Jung was intensely interested in numbers, espe-

cially at the end of his life when he thought they may be the connecting link between the psyche and the body, between spirit and matter."

"Oh, that does interest me; it seems to go so solidly to the very bottom of things. And just think of it: In my dream I was part of the principle of order. I was right in the middle of it!"

"You were, indeed. Also, your dream was saying the same thing twice, because that same principle also applies to the symbol of the sun. The sun never fails, no matter how off-color it is. It is predictable. Its course is as steady as time and space."

"The noncommittal atmosphere is still puzzling to me, though."

"Well, we've talked about other dreams of yours that have had the same atmosphere; I'm thinking about the couple in the surfing dream and of Nanny and the goblets of red juice. But in those I believe you were well, so they must not have had to do with the present. Here you're ill; this dream might be suggesting a brush with death. If it does, then no wonder you had to wake yourself up and get out of there."

"But those fifteen policemen and women were noncommittal. They weren't threatening me. And it's strange that police people in uniform should be noncommittal."

"Well, when you think about it, shouldn't the police stand for law and order just as the sun and the stars and the seasons do?"

She nodded and seemed satisfied.

"I suppose I should try to find something positive in the staff aides here in spite of their neglecting me at times. They're in uniform, too, but that doesn't necessarily make them bad. Still I go on resenting them, and no amount of explanation helps. Also I have to admit that there's a part of me that resents my family, too, for doing so well without me. It's as if I'm already gone; I'm no use to them at all anymore."

This statement made me realize how real the brush with death in the dream had been for her.

"No, Sally, that simply isn't true. You're still very much a functioning member of that foursome even though you can't see it that way. Granted the others are better off than you, but you're not an outcast. Your role is to carry the burden of facing death for the family; how you accomplish it is very important for them. They may not know it now, but perhaps when your story is told, they will."

She made no comment but seemed to want me to go on.

"Let me tell you one of the ways I see the family. I think families are archetypal as in your two recent dreams. They represent a whole that not only includes the opposites, of men and women, but also the elements of success and failure. The member who carries the burden of failure, sometimes in illness, is like the fourth function or the inferior function of the family; and he or she can either drag the family down or be the solution to its problem. Most often the sick one or the one who "fails" is disparaged unconsciously by the others as the family's shadow and is never recognized as the carrier of its solution nor appreciated for carrying the burden of its failure. The clown or the comedian, in carrying this burden, fulfills the role for society. Looking back on your W. C. Fields dream, I think that's why it was such an important one. It was a validation of this profound truth because the figure of failure was represented positively, as it always is with the clown. It makes me think

246

that had things been otherwise, you might have turned your life around by using your comic talents as you did in that dream."

A great deal of energy must have been stored where her real talent was blocked; being blocked it may have turned against her in the form of cancer. The proliferation of cancerous cells is after all a kind of negative show of energy.

One afternoon, about five days after her dream of being on trial, she told me of a dream she had had during the middle of a nap.

You were visiting me in the nursing home. I was dying and you were holding me in your arms. You were telling me an old Indian story about the Diggers. I felt at ease about dying.

She seemed somewhat embarrassed as she told me the dream, and I recalled her telling me, when we first met, about a dream of her friend Carla holding her in her arms. She had been embarrassed, but much more so, when she had reported that one, which had come at a time when she had rallied from what seemed a certain death. I felt that this dream, coming as it did so close to the one of being on trial, suggested she had learned from that dream. I reminded her of still another dream she had of dying when it was night and she was looking out over the glowing city. It had been positive, too; everything was all right. Then I asked her for more details about this dream.

"You were telling me a story about 'Coyote,' or 'White Wolf,' or 'Frog Woman.' Anyway, it was one of the Indian legends I had been listening to on the radio before I fell asleep."

I was somehow in tune with her dream then and found myself talking about the Chumash Indians, erroneously called the Diggers in the early days, who were familiar to me in my childhood. I told her about the white coyotes on our ranch and about my childhood quest for white deer. They were rare, those albinos, but there was always the possibility of coming upon one. Her dream revived many of my own memories of wilderness, which I then shared with her. I explained that the white wolf, or white coyote, was a symbol of the highest importance to the Indians as gods or aspects of the self. Coyote symbolized creativity; he was an earth symbol who incorporated both good and evil; he would know about the chthonic world. He was to the Indians what W. C. Fields and Ed Wynn were to our society during the twenties and thirties. He was beyond beginning and end and was outside of the law, stirring up things with his pranks, making people think in a new way by putting them in awkward—sometimes terrible—spots. He was a central figure in many Indian legends.

"I haven't had a dream about an animal in such a long time. You know, I'm glad my children live where they are so close to nature. I think it's so important."

Always having been a city person, Sally perhaps needed this more natural side of life to round her out. It explained an aspect of our contact; my wilderness background made me familiar with the animal world. The animal could be her connection with the self. In this instance it would be like the fourth function.

I told her about an old Indian woman we had seen in the southwestern desert. She was sitting before a brush hut, alone and miles away from her people. Our Navajo Indian driver had told us she was waiting for her death.

Sally's face brightened.

"That reminds me of a book I read once called *Eskimo*.

In it an old woman went away alone to meet death. It's better to go out and meet it, I think, than to let it catch up with you."

"Maybe that's what you were doing in your dream of building a hoganlike place on the desert."

As I approached Sally's room for our next visit, I heard her cry out, "My God! When is this ever going to stop!"

She was thrashing around in her bed. A nurse came in with me and gave her an injection to relieve her pain. When her suffering had subsided, I asked her if this was now some new pain she was experiencing.

"In my sleep last night I must have twisted the thigh that's been pinned. It was hurting me so much the other day I had to ask them to get the doctor to help me. He said that even if the bone was broken again there wasn't anything to be done about it; I'd just have to do my best to bear the pain. So that's it; it's turning out to be just as I expected it would. Right after I talked to the doctor I had a dream that confirmed how deteriorated I've become. But also there's this strange twist. Listen to this."

I was participating in a medical conference in a large room. The walls, ceiling, and floor of the room were darkened with black felt; and I was in the middle of it all, dressed in a uniform or gown of luminous, iridescent white. Equipment and all kinds of gadgets were visible in the center of the room. About twenty-five doctors, all around the age of forty and dressed in white cotton tunics and pants, were milling about. They were on the brink of discovery; the air was charged with excitement.

This dream and the previous dream of judgment have similar qualities, but this one is hopeful. The mood of this dream resembles that of the other, and the atmosphere is equally strange. Again Sally is the central figure, and, as in the court dream, there are uniforms. Here she wears a special one, and the others wear their usual whites.

249

The black felt walls, which absorb every vestige of light, suggest a blackout. Her luminous gown of iridescent white is the extreme opposite of that black; thus the opposites appear more dramatically here than they ever have before. She wears the strange white light of consciousness against the black of night. Could this be a prediction of death? Could death be the discovery, the final liberation? If so, then indeed it would have magical and miraculous implications; it would be something to look forward to with excitement. In this dream she accepts death because she is within the drama of opposites. She has moved on from the off-gold attitude.

Most important, she seems to be an equal participant in the conference. There is an implication that instead of being the helpless, dependent patient, she is now on the road to becoming her own authority. This is a condition of individuation. Another hint of individuation is that the age of the doctors is forty. Forty is not only a middle age, the mean in life, but is made up of four, the number of totality, times ten. I have heard many dreams in which forty has been the age of those who have died.

"Sally, can you see that the dream might imply that it doesn't matter if the body is deteriorated because the solution is almost at hand?"

"That's what seems so strange."

Around this time she reported another dream.

I was at an outdoor auction on the beach and I bid on three ornate, Victorian-style chairs for my dining room. Jim and I argued angrily over my intended purchase. I admitted I neither wanted nor needed the chairs, but they could be had at a bargain price. Jim told me it was a great mistake to buy anything for that reason. "Buy what is appropriate and right and never mind the price, or don't buy it at all," he said. "There it is; now do what you have to do." I decided not to buy the chairs.

"You know, it's only in the last few years that I've been able to wait until I had enough money to buy the right thing rather than compromise and buy the cheap thing I could afford."

"Well, shopping can be a thinking-feeling problem, it seems to me. It's easy for thinking people—sensation people too—to get hooked on bargains. They're not as impressed with the intrinsic value of objects as feeling people are. So often bargains are compromises, and the feeling function is not really on the side on compromise. It's either for or against a thing; it considers something appropriate or inappropriate, of value, or not."

"And I've come around to thinking that Jim's not the same type as I am. Perhaps he is a feeling type after all, and that's why I gave over to his authority in the dream when I decided not to buy the chairs."

"Yes, but remember Jim in the dream was you also— your feeling effort. You finally let yourself be influenced by your inner feeling guide."

"That might be true; yet we were fighting, so there's still some kind of rub between us. Actually we're not very close right now. I know my letting my anger out on him doesn't help. Still, if only he'd express himself about what's going on between us that prevents our being close."

"I agree with you that he's a feeling type, Sally. I think he's also introverted, and people like that are often inarticulate. Also, because he is that type, he can't stand the criticism and anger you have to throw off from time to time. When you're negative, he's bound to withdraw from the contact, but that can't be helped."

I thought if she could understand the trouble in terms of their being different types, perhaps she could avoid having hurt feelings; then she wouldn't complicate the relationship from her own side. They didn't have time to do much about the rub between them, and I was anxious to have her understand that much of their trouble occurred because, like other married opposite types, they had very little objective insight about each other. I didn't want to burden her with a sense of failure, thereby feeding her nihilism.

She returned to the subject of her old worry about having no sex in the marriage. I reminded her about one of her first dreams of marriage, which by her association was her marriage to Jim. I told her that apparently her unconscious had made marriage the most important item on her agenda, and it didn't matter to the unconscious whether it was spiritual or sexual.

She was unusually tired during our last visit of this period, and that day while she rested, I read excerpts from Jung to her about the archetypes. I took up the theme of the trickster figure in mythology and filled it in with my own thoughts about Coyote and a similar figure from Roman mythology called Mercurius. She smiled when I said the word "trickster" and said, "I knew you would mention Coyote next." She had heard on the radio more Indian stories, written by Jaime de Angulo, about Coyote as the trickster. I told her that the trickster—Coyote and Mercurius or Hermes—is a figure who can bring things together. He reconciles opposites; therefore, if death is seen as the opposite of life, he functions to reconcile death to the living. I reminded her that in her dream where she was dying in my arms, I was telling her a story about Coyote; she responded to this comment with a sound of pleasure.

Suddenly, in a quiet voice, she began to lament that her life was entirely evil. She said she knew she should believe in the existence of good because of the goodness of Jim, of her friends, of me, of some of the aides who were warm, help-

252

ful, and caring even though she was a stranger to them. But in spite of this evidence, good was never quite real.

Good was never quite real for her because she could not accept its coming out of evil. She had just made a connection between Coyote — a figure that attracted her — and the evil in her life. Had I possessed the wit at the time, I might have helped her to move further along in her acceptance of evil by emphasizing that Coyote's creativity usually has little to do with conformity, with "being good."

Sally continued, "I had all the good early in my life. Now I'm getting all the bad. It's like being in a black, narrow corridor with no end to it."

The words came from far away. At that instant she seemed barely present in her wasted body.

"You're in a tunnel, aren't you?"

"Yes, that's just where I am."

I told her what came to my mind about tunnels. They seem to appear in the dreams of people who don't know where they are going, who feel stuck and don't know where to turn — people whose lives are in transition. All is black, unknown, and senseless, and remains that way until one comes out into the light again at the other end; that is when the depression lifts. Tunnels refer to the theme of psychological death and rebirth. I spoke of the birth canal, which is like a tunnel, and I reminded her of her dream of squeezing between two buildings in a narrow alley, which was also dark and difficult. Her silence and inaccessibility compelled me to become more positive.

"Sally, don't you see, if there is darkness, light will come; if there is evil, there has to be good. Everything has its opposite. Your dreams have been so superbly creative. I know they must be compensating for the evil that you face daily; in that respect you're right in saying that only evil is real. But I have to keep reminding you of what is missing. Remember your dream of the medical conference? There was a breakthrough at hand!"

She snapped back from her faraway place and looked at me angrily.

"Breakthrough? It could only be bad. Surprise? It could only be evil. Can't you see? I'm totally centered in evil. It's where I am; I'll never be anywhere else!"

The color returned to her face and her voice was strong, almost gleeful. I could not understand her orientation to evil. But the energy in it had brought her back to life.

CHAPTER FOURTEEN

As Sally's preoccupation with evil grew, I came more and more to realize that the archetype of the trickster was our avenue into this darkest area. She seemed to know instinctively that this figure could now help her to transcend the rigid boundaries of her mind. Evil, at once outrageous, unpredictable, subtle, and clever — personified in Coyote — could perhaps be assimilated. As I read to her about him, I would look up and see her face brighten with interest, so I knew we were on the right track. Not only had this figure turned up significantly in her dreams, especially in the one about W. C. Fields, but also in the mystery stories, which she now enjoyed on phonograph records.

I then began to read to her about other archetypes, trying whenever possible to fit my reading to the subjects she talked about. When she told me about Sarah's horseback riding, for example, I read to her about the symbolism of the horse. She seemed to have a great need to get close to the symbols of nature — the stars, moon, sun, ocean, animals, trees, and earth. Indeed, she seemed now to be living deep within herself much of the time.

I read to her about the mother archetype. From Jung's *Symbols of Transformation* I read Hiawatha's "Song of Death" and a paragraph about the sun's sinking into the night to its death. I read about Nokomic, Hiawatha's grandmother, who represented a kind of earth wisdom. Sally said it all felt good, so I knew that in spite of the pain she suffered, she obviously needed psychic food and was receiving it this way. Even if she could not concentrate enough to reflect on the readings between visits, the momentary experience of just listening to them seemed to be enough.

During the next fourteen days I visited her for a short time every day, knowing that it was a constantly wearisome, often painful, often fearful time for her and being conscious of the fact that I would soon be leaving for a two-week period. She often expressed the wish to die, to die gracefully, to fade into peaceful oblivion. Although there were times later during these two weeks when all I could do was read to her briefly as she, with her eyes closed, would listen and comment only when something touched her deeply. She told me many times that my reading to her about the archetypes helped very much. I became more and more convinced that this material drew her into the other, archetypal, world that she needed to enter; it may have been a way of introducing her to individuation and to death.

She said she still called out "Mother!" in her sleep and that a dying man down the hall did the same. For this reason she particularly enjoyed hearing about the ocean as a symbol of the mother from which life comes and to which it returns.

The calling out to mother by so many dying patients suggested to me that there may be a connection between death and the mother archetype. It strengthened my growing belief that women might be especially good as therapists for dying people.

She commented that she had dreamed of the ocean many times. We talked about the phonetic connection between the German, Latin, and French words for "sea" and the various words for "mother." We agreed that possibly because she had an inadequate mother, she may have been searching for the mother archetype through "mother church" when she thought of becoming a missionary.

"All life originates in the ocean. Science agrees to that. I wish you could try to visualize the ocean as the mother you call for in your sleep. Then perhaps the unconscious could do the rest and bring about the peaceful oblivion you long for."

"No, it could never be that easy for me. Nothing good will ever happen to me. Dying will be a ghastly struggle. Death will be the end."

"Oh, Sally, how I wish you could broaden your outlook! I remember you once admitted that the theme of many of your dreams was rebirth. The ocean implies rebirth as well."

"All I want is eternal sleep, nothing more. I only want to fade back into the ocean. Nothing good could ever happen to me, even in death. I'm certain of that."

Again she had to dish up the negative, and again I had to be positive for her. If she had been the usual patient and not someone for whom death was imminent, I would have left her alone to get to the depths of her negativism. But she had never been the usual patient, and I never dared. I always felt she might not have the strength for that; so I continued to carry the positive for her, never knowing whether my decision was the right one.

One afternoon as she was silently resting, I read a passage to her about the regressive longing to return to the mother. For people who needed to take up the challenge of life rather than retreat, I read, this kind of longing constellated the archetype of the terrible mother — the devouring aspect of the mother — and symbolized the most frightful danger. She opened her eyes and exclaimed breathlessly, "Yes, that's the way it is!"

Once again I was impressed by how much more attracted she was by evil than by anything else and how it seemed to rekindle her vitality. It was almost as if she were addicted to it. Perhaps the idea of the terrible mother activated Sally because it filled in her psychic gaps. Her own mother lacked any of the human manifestations of the terrible, devouring archetypal mother. If she had displayed more of them, she might have been more real and a better mother for Sally; something positive for Sally might have emerged out of her mother's unknown side.

I found myself beset by many questions. How could this evil that held Sally transfixed be comprehended? Had her repressed chthonic sensuality hidden in the shadow become contaminated by this evil power? Was her resistance so badly broken down by the cruel, long illness that to deflect its power through consciousness was out of the question? Could whatever it was that once pushed her to become a missionary have had as its underside this attraction to evil? Was her alliance with evil, for some unknown lifelong reason, basic to her nature? Was it an alliance with laws of its own, far more inclusive, impersonal, superordinate to anything we know in human life? In her dream of God she was his equal. Was she now aligned with God's other side — evil?

I recalled her dream of the snake tied around the wheel. She had been mesmerized by that snake as she was now by evil. Remembering how she had to feed it at the risk of getting bitten, I told her that perhaps her compulsive "everything as evil" attitude had something positive in it. In accepting everything as evil she would be in for no surprises, no disappointments; she would be prevented from hoping and striving. If things were so bad that they could only get better, then death, in a subtle way, might be positive. Perhaps, I said, it was her way of giving in, of melting into the landscape, of becoming nothing at death, so that finally she would find peace and rest. In paying her respects to evil this way she may have been unconsciously hoping to insure some good — a rebirth — after death.

"Maybe you concentrate on evil in order to make certain of finding the peace you seek."

"In a way, yes. But it's also to guard against being taken by surprise during the time I have left."

I could only sympathize with her feelings. I finally understood that she had to keep evil before her. Her negative attitude, she said, had begun when she went to the hospital and was operated on for the broken thigh. She had begun to lose her sight then, and the high hopes that were there when we first met had crumbled, because she had been cut off from reading and from painting mandalas. I could not help thinking that my having left her during the late summer might have contributed to her feelings of hopelessness. Now the time dragged on so slowly; the monotony of her life was very hard to bear.

Once during this period she said, "There are only two things that help, the books for the blind and you."

Then she smiled.

"I don't mean in that order. But the books last longer than you do."

Her well-founded fears of deterioration continued to

haunt her. She told me she had been unable to change the phonograph record of a mystery story because her arm had been too weak. She repeated her fears of being kept alive as a vegetable if she were to go into a coma. Once more I assured her that Jim would never allow this; her doctor, I was certain, would take care of her if that were to happen. She told me the doctor had come in recently, bringing her a special lunch with a glass of chilled white wine. She had been touched by his gesture. Still, she could not be certain he would do what she wanted.

Because she was often dehydrated, she found breathing and swallowing difficult at times, and she would become especially frightened when she could not breathe easily at night. We agreed that her fear of not being able to breathe was a fear of death. I felt it was absolutely necessary for us to keep talking all along about her fear of death. In fact I now believe Sally's efforts to confront death and to talk out her fears in our visits helped her to maintain contact with her immediate family and her friends. If she had not had the opportunity to make these efforts, her fears, stated or not, would have created a barrier between herself and the people who came to see her. They could not have coped with her repressed fears because of their own fears of death.

Early in this period she reported a vivid dream. The locale, she said, was unfamiliar to her.

I was in a nursing home, fancier and more luxurious than this one, but otherwise the same—modern and totally lacking in charm. I was ill but could move around. I decided to go outside to the pool and found that it was almost like an indoor pool—it was covered with a canvas pergola. About fifty or sixty crippled, deformed men of all ages and shapes were lying around the edge of the pool. They were scarred

*and had limbs missing, but they were not in pain; evidently what
happened to them had taken place in the past. The men were sunburned.*

*An old, frail, thin nurse came out of the building. She grabbed me
and pulled me away, saying, "This is just for men!"*

In the Near East during the first centuries after Christ, enclosed
swimming pools were often a part of church buildings. The basilicas of
Rome also had pools for baptism. The crippled men symbolize the
animus going through a kind of regeneration or baptism. As repre-
sentative of activity in the outer world, the animus has been whittled
away; the arms and legs have been cut off to allow for spiritual
development.

Sunburning is an imprinting, a marking. These sunburned men
represent her animus, as yet unrealized because they are in a group,
but at the same time emphasized because they are in a group. It is as
though these men, who had been as tortured as she was, had "seen
God," had faced the sun and were healed by its rays, were healed also
by submersion in the pool. It is my fantasy that had Sally "seen God" in
a waking experience, she might have had a spontaneous cure.

Much later when I discussed the symbolic meaning of sunburning
with Dr. von Franz, she said it may refer to a kind of driving within of
values. Darkening of the exterior implies that what was once outside
has gone inward or has been transformed into a value within. In death
it is as though the outside has been darkened while a secret of life has
been driven inward. Death is the dark outside.

She is under the domination of the old nurse once again, the controlling, threatening woman who, like an inferior man, stands by the
rules regardless of circumstances and keeps her from the potential for
cure that exists in the pool. Her unconscious identification with the
negative side of her mother, internalized as this witchlike woman, the
woman without instinct, may be the true evil that keeps her from the
depths that the men around the pool would want for her; it causes her
to belittle herself and to fear physical deterioration above all else
because of feeling that without her body she is nothing. Sally's own
mother, I am sure, would have echoed the nurse's orders; she would
not have approved of Sally's joining the company of men who had been
in the depths and had "seen God."

"Early the next morning I woke up with this horrible throbbing pain, that same pain in my head I've never been able to stand. I rang for the nurse but no one came. I went into a panic. I called out 'Mother!' I wanted out. I longed to die."

"You called out for the mother who would be like Nanny for you; the nurturing mother who would help you to die instinctively."

"Oh, yes. And who would take me away from that awful woman. The nurse was letting me know that I had no business in those healing waters — it was exclusively for men. Something good was there that was only for them, but I could have no part in it, just as I can have no part in much of Jim's life now. Why do women have such superficial, boring roles? Jim's always had a better life than I have. Even when I was well it was that way; he always had more freedom. And now there's no question about who has a better life. He gets to go away on business trips — he's leaving in a couple of days for another. He can be with friends and go to parties; he can't come to see me tonight because he's going to one. I hate him for it. I envy him, that's what it is. I just wish I were able to get around."

"Well, no wonder you're jealous; who wouldn't be! But look closely at your dream; the men don't hold you back."

"True enough. It's the woman in me who does society's bidding. If it weren't for her vindictiveness, I might have lived my own life long ago. Maybe I wouldn't be sick now."

Her dream in the beginning of December was the last one she would report to me.

Jim and I were at some kind of Jewish charity bazaar. I was ill and in a wheelchair. There were people there who were selling their handicrafts and also many others who were milling about. We ran into old

*friends of ours—the Beckers—who found a place for me to lie down
and then disappeared. While I was lying down, Jim wheeled my chair
over to a table where refreshments were being served, found a chair for
himself, which he placed next to my wheelchair, and came back to get
me. But by the time we got to the table, we found two old ladies sitting
in our chairs. I recognized the one sitting in my wheelchair. She's an
active clubwoman in our town and I like her. But she refused to get out
of my chair because she said she was there first.*

*Two policemen arrived and offered to remove the clubwoman if I
would press charges, but I refused. Jim and I decided to go home.*

"Your associations?"

"Hanukkah comes next week. Our friends, the Beckers,
who visited last week are Jewish; and they told me about
celebrating Hanukkah for their daughters, who are the
same ages as Sarah and Beth. I think the holiday com-
memorates the flight of the Jews out of Egypt. Anyway, it's a
festival of light and dancing. A candle is lighted each of the
eight nights of the holiday."

The clubwoman is also Sally, the part of her who won't give in and
seems to be saying, "You can't put anything over on me!" Sally cannot
seem to get out of this old bad habit. It is probably now too late. She
suffers too much pain, exhaustion, and hopelessness to have the
strength to change the habit.

Once again the police are not threatening; she can accept authority
on this level.

The flight out of Egypt, Sally's erroneous association, may have
represented something new in her unconscious which was moving away
from the pseudomale, authoritarian woman (the clubwoman), a
female counterpart to King Herod. (Hanukkah actually celebrates the
rescue of Israel by the Maccabees, who were looked upon as messiahs.)
She, like the witch-nurse, would represent the negative, patriarchal
effect on women that threatens the new female beginning. Sally had in
the past negated the inward life with denial and sarcasm. Now in the
unconscious the old order (King Herod) was on the way out.

In our discussion of the dream the idea of monotheism arose, and we talked about the story in which the Christ child (symbolically the self) was taken into Egypt by Joseph and Mary to escape King Herod's edict, or evil. Herod, the temporal power, feared the competition of the spiritual power in Christ; thus it was a war between the temporal and spiritual worlds.

I told her I thought the clubwoman in the dream was a kind of "animus hound" who was blocking her progress.

"She is a very nice woman, though."

She made this reply sadly.

After this regressive dream of giving up, both Jim and I noticed a change in Sally. She seemed to have lost her will, and from then on she seemed far more quiet and remote. Jim told me he would hold her hand at her bedside, and she would have to struggle to talk, but she seemed to want him to stay close by and would take longer and longer to tell him to go. Their physical contact now seemed to be the most important aspect of her life. Jim knew this and began to question whether he should take the business trip he'd planned. But I told him to go ahead; we had his itinerary, and I would call him back if necessary. I desperately hoped that he would comprehend that one of Sally's last tasks in this life centered around her relationship to him.

Soon it would be Christmas. Sally told me it meant nothing to her, and she wanted no part of it. Jim's asking her to share in decisions about family presents only irritated her.

"I can certainly understand how you feel, Sally. It must seem superficial to you. Your feelings are on a much deeper level now and collectivity isn't important."

"That makes me feel better, especially because I've been

feeling a little guilty about what I did the other night. Some schoolchildren came to the nursing home to sing carols and bring us presents, and I threw them out."

"I don't blame you."

She did tell me with some pleasure that she and Jim had in the past given each other tropical fish for Christmas and for birthdays. That was many years ago, and they no longer had those fish, but this Christmas they would begin to give the children tropical fish as presents. She listened attentively as I described the beautiful fish at Bora Bora, where I would soon be going.

The next day she told me she had awakened during the night in a panic. It was not unusual for her to awaken in fear, but the fear had always been unfocused, and this time it was precisely because "her tropical fish needed attention." She found it difficult to explain her fear to the nurses because it was only an illusion. We pondered over what this fear could have been. I made a guess and interpreted it this way: She and Jim had given each other tropical fish over the years and this year would give them to the children; I had mentioned I would soon be seeing the beautiful fish of Bora Bora. The fish symbolized her contact with all of us; and now she had, to a great extent, lost contact with the children. This explanation made sense to her.

I read to her everything I could find then about fish symbolism in Jung's *Symbols of Transformation*. Much of it was concerned with the death and rebirth theme, and this time she did not oppose the idea; she only remained silent and attentive.

She spoke very quietly; her eyes were closed.

"Strange how much children like the story of Jonah and the whale. I suppose this theme must be there at the bottom of the psyche the world over. I am looking at the aquarium glass; it casts a pattern all over the wall."

She was glimpsing the world of the archetypes.

On our last visit Sally said, "It's all right for you to go away. All we've been able to do lately is to spend time together. I'm glad that your analyst friend will be coming by again."

I told her I had asked Jim to come home a day early as she had requested; he could manage it, his most important meeting was over, and he would return the next day.

"Was he mad? Am I being the devouring mother by asking him to return?"

Although her words implied guilt about making this demand, I heard overtones of her pleasure in being on the side of destruction.

"No, Sally. Jim has to know you want him and that you need him and care for him. You are showing him your true feelings when you express your desire to have him close to you now."

When I offered to bring something back from Bora Bora for the children, she consented with pleasure. I was touched because she never before would accept things from me.

Her consent seemed to be her way of telling me to go. I sensed that she knew, as did I, that we had finished with each other in terms of the analysis but that we would always be friends no matter what happened. During the last three or four visits she had asked me to read to her, saying that she was too heavily sedated to talk. She was uncomplaining and warm in her contact with me. She no longer spoke of the evil that had been plaguing her. She let me know that holding hands with Jim had now become the most important aspect of her life. I knew that I would write to remind her that I was thinking about her; I so hoped I was right in thinking that she would want no more from me at this point. Although I had given to Sally all that I could professionally and all that she could accept, I was desperately saddened by having to leave this friend who was so very ill.

When it came time for goodbye, I took her bony hand. Her essence was still faintly there; there was almost nothing left of her bodily presence.

"I will be thinking of you all the time."

"I will be thinking of you too."

CHAPTER FIFTEEN

I N A LETTER to a friend in late December I wrote from Tahiti, "I had a dream of Sally last night. She was getting well, recovering. The color of her skin was like that of the Polynesians — dark and coppery, as though she had been sunburned. I've had similar dreams of others just before they've died. I feel she has either died since I left or will be dead any day now."

Death came to Sally in the early afternoon of the day in January when I returned from Tahiti. On the telephone Jim told me that her weakened condition had finally resulted in pneumonia three days before her death. He said she was in a coma, so he didn't know whether she recognized him or not, but he was with her when she died. He had taken time off from work when I was away, he said, and had gone to see her twice a day, but they had talked only about superficial things. I told him I thought they had covered all the important ground. He seemed anxious to know that he had made a good connection with her at the end and that he had done all right. I praised him sincerely. To have seen Sally through to the end as he had done was a real achievement, and I wanted him to know how strongly I felt about that.

When I called my colleague, he read me Sally's last dream, which he had recorded.

I was a palm tree, the middle one of three trees. An earthquake was about to occur that would destroy all life, and I didn't want to be killed by the quake.

When he had asked for her association to the dream, she had said she was somehow reminded of her first dream, the one about the Sumerian tower. The palm trees, she told him, brought to mind the hanging gardens of Babylon. I was immediately reminded of my own dream of the brown-skinned Sally, who might well be living in a climate where palm trees flourished.

The earthquake might have been cancer, and her wish in the dream not to be violently destroyed by it had come true; she died quietly of pneumonia before the earthquake could kill her. An earthquake would actually mean the demolition of the earth and the house, which for her was her body. Her physical being had been the only truly stable element in her life; it was also her bastion against insanity. Her dying before being destroyed suggests her preparation or readiness.

The most impressive fact of this last dream, whose message seemed to lift her magically to the level of myth, was her association of the palm tree to the Sumerian tower of her first dream. The hanging gardens also referred to her first dream. Many centuries before, these gardens were considered to be the gardens of the gods and were part of the ziggurat that originated in matriarchal, prehistoric times.

The powerful impact of tree symbolism has been apparent from the time of earliest civilizations. The cosmological, or world, tree reached above to heaven and below to hell, unifying both with earth. The tree is a product of nature and as such is basic to human life; the palm tree contains both food and liquid and in that sense can be looked upon as the original tree of life. In ancient times the palm tree was the symbol of Ishtar, the goddess of love. In one legend Mary was born under a palm tree. In the dream Sally has become the tree, an enduring symbol for all time. And she is the middle tree, standing between the opposites in a pattern similar to that of Christ on the cross between the two thieves. There is no book or other mediator here as there was in her first dream. This dream brings her through the place of human suffering into the realm of the archetypes, where as in nature all is in balance.

The tree symbolically contains many pairs of opposites: male and female, life and death, growth upward and downward, vertical and horizontal growth. It is an androgynous symbol that signifies a harmonious coming together of the male and female. The drama of the opposites and their reconciliation is both the theme and the ideal of a true marriage; certainly marriage was Sally's constant concern throughout our association.

Appropriate to Sally's dream is an account of neolithic Middle Eastern matriarchal societies in which the tree, called the Asherah, was the symbol of the supreme goddess. The tree trunk was also used as a tomb by some of the earliest known tribes. I once saw in a museum such a tree trunk which had contained a dead body. These associations support my idea that Sally, at one with the tree as she was dying, had become the mother to whom she had called in her sleep, the mother who both gives life and lays it to rest. She had come perhaps to the eternal rest for which she longed.

In a seminar Jung once paraphrased a Germanic tale: "The last people disappear into the tree out of which originally they had come forth. The world of consciousness gives place to the vegetative. The tree is the regenerative, unconscious life which stands eternally when human consciousness is snuffed out."

Her last dream, along with evidence in earlier dreams, suggested that she had achieved a kind of full circle, a summing up. It is my hope that having finally accomplished the task laid out for her in her first dream and again in her dream of God, she returned peacefully, as the mother goddess, to unconscious ongoing life.

I sat quietly in the midst of these thoughts, overcome by strong emotions that stayed with me until the next day. My acute realization of how heroic she had been, my excitement over the possibility that she may have resolved her life and that everything was all right now, and my relief that she was finally beyond physical suffering would partially explain the compelling emotions that held me in such a strange way. I even had the curious feeling that she was close by and was trying to contact me.

There are questions posed by Sally's life and death that are ultimately unanswerable. Obviously her unconscious had taken up the process of preparing for death and brought her life to completion in the last dream. I feel that during her final weeks, when she was living so quietly, she could have been living close to the unconscious in the realm of the archetypes, where all was prepared for her death.

Many circumstances of her life mitigated against her. She was young, and grasping the archetypes can be difficult for a young person, yet she had been forced into the attitude of old age in such a short time. Her psychological naivete, lack of parental security, loss of touch with her instincts, her intense pain, and even her brilliant mind were against her. Being a practical person with a strong sensation function in some ways also mitigated against her; intuitive people grasp possibilities through messages from the unconscious (what she called "all that mystical stuff") much more readily. But in her hard, sensation way of living in the here and now she seemed to be experiencing everything in the world in preparation for her death. She was living more intensely than the intuitive because of her experiential relation to every inch of her own destruction and may have covered more ground and thus gone further toward achieving consciousness than she could express. She was more thoroughly experienced in the life she was preparing to leave. She may not have accomplished consciously all of the work that her dreams set for her; but if one accepts the impartiality of nature, then it is effort that matters in life, and her effort toward accomplishing her tasks was indeed great.

Both Sally and I found numbers compelling; we were both fascinated by them. After her death I was haunted by the frequency of the numbers three and four in her dreams and was particularly puzzled by their meaning in her first and last dreams. These opposites (even and odd, passive and active, female and male) appeared with equal importance and seemed to be interwoven kaleidoscopically throughout her dreams. In her dream of moving into her mother's house there were four women of three generations, all under the aegis of a masculine symbol, the triangular (three-sided) piano. Five days later in another dream of moving there were three people of three generations. She was active, looking for unfamiliar popular music to play under the aegis of a feminine symbol, the square (four-sided) piano. In Sally's life before her illness, the three had taken precedence over the four. She was, until her marriage, a devout, believing member of the Christian faith in which the Trinity is a primary symbol. During the last six months of her life, Jungian psychology introduced to her the idea of individuation, symbolized by the number four, multiples of four, and the square and the circle. She reached out for these new concepts by drawing mandalas during times of stress, and these drawings brought her peace and a sense of order. She became interested in Zen Buddhism, which brought her to Eastern thought with its stress more on inner experience than on outer activity in the world. The interplay of the three and the four had finally become apparent in her daily life.

In her dream of the tower, Sally experienced the number four. She climbed to the top of the tower and could survey the city-world below her. It was an achievement; from on high, her view included everything within the four points of the compass. Except for the appearance of the book, which indicated there was more to be studied — a beginning — it could have been her final dream. Paradoxically, her last dream is of the three. Yet in her last days she was serene and peaceful, as though she had at last come to a full acceptance of herself and was ready to die. Was she at the time of her first dream in the state of three consciously and four unconsciously, at the time of the last dream in a state of three unconsciously and four consciously? Perhaps for Sally the numbers three and four were opposite but equal, were two different symbols of completion. The three had to be with the four and the four with the three to tell her whole story.

The question of rebirth is a haunting one. Her unconscious seemed not at all concerned about death being final; there were too many indications of rebirth in her dreams. One makes infinite conjectures; the mystery remains unsolved. But this much is absolutely certain: Whatever those dreams may have meant to her consciously, whether she truly believed in them or not, they gave us points of contact for a relationship which might otherwise have faltered. She was a highly verbal and thoughtful person who could not initiate conversation. The dreams supplied a needed departure for our exchange, which as time passed grew into a deep involvement. For a dying person this kind of involvement is crucial; it breaks a dangerous isolation. Her dreams were a means of keeping her mind and her life's energy occupied with the effort toward serious accomplishment during the last six months of her life. They kept her focused on her individuation, which eased her positively into her death. These months may otherwise have been filled only with pain, boredom, anguish, and humiliation.

How can I best describe what this experience meant to me? Sally gave me the opportunity to participate in a deeply personal exchange with her about the most profound issues of life on a day-to-day basis. She was in the very midst of them and was willing to discuss them to her fullest ability. Her questions drove me more deeply into studies of mythology, religion, and history. The book of her first dream might have been my book as well. I witnessed her death as both a normal process and a goal that can be the grand summing up of anyone's life.

More important for me, my contact with Sally helped to dispel the exclusively destructive aspects of death so prevalent in our society. Right before my eyes was a suffering and courageous human being whose struggle confirmed Jung's belief that the shadow can only play a gruesome part in the process of dying if it is not recognized in one's life. I learned in my six months' work with Sally that one must accept one's fate, no matter what the hazards and hardships, and be willing to let go of earthly ties whenever death threatens. Most important, I discovered one must live as fully as possible, trusting, as I think Sally came to trust, the deep regenerative roots of life symbolized for her by the tree. The process of individuation places death in its most rewarding perspective. Death becomes a part of life, and insofar as one accepts its reality, one truly lives.

Active Imagination A technique developed by Jung in which the conscious mind suspends its critical faculty and interacts with unconscious content that arises spontaneously. The conscious mind allows the image, mood, obsessive thought, or feeling arising from the unconscious to elaborate itself autonomously — to live its own life — while actively engaging and interacting with it, thereby creating a scenario. The experience is often given concrete expression, usually in written or graphic form. Thus objectified, the unconscious content becomes more accessible to understanding and assimilation, and the individual is freed from its domination. Technically, active imagination must arise spontaneously and is to be distinguished from closely related techniques such as "guided daydream" or "guided fantasy."

Analysis (Jungian) A healing and learning process, within the context of a dynamic relationship between analysand and analyst, in which unconscious material — dreams, fantasies — is explored to uncover the source of and to resolve psychological conflicts. An understanding of the importance of maintaining contact with the unconscious is communicated, as well as techniques by which this contact may be accomplished, in order to promote a psychological balance and to progress toward individuation.

Anima The archetype in the male psyche that is the inherited pattern of potential experience of female instinct. This archetype underlies and is basic to a complex which is affected by the individual's early experiences of women, primarily his mother, female siblings, and the collective images of women provided by his cultural experience. The images and affects that attach to the complex express what is other than the individual's male body-ego identity, such as his own unconscious femaleness, the unconscious, the inferior function. The anima assumes a generalized image of the individual's female ideal, which strongly influences his selection of a mate. Consciously related to, the anima functions as inspiratrice or muse — a bridge to the creative wellspring of the unconscious and to unknown potentialities for development. The anima serves as a guide in relationships, particularly with those who have a different outlook. When not consciously related to, the anima causes a man to be moody, capricious, ruthless, and snide about others.

Animus The archetype in the female psyche that is the inherited pattern of potential experience of male instinct. This archetype underlies and is basic to a complex which is affected by the individual's early experiences of men, primarily her father, male siblings, and the collective images of men provided by her cultural experience. The images and affects that attach to the complex express what is other than her female body-ego identity, such as her own unconscious maleness, the unconscious, the inferior function. The animus assumes a generalized image of the individual's male ideal, which strongly influences her selection of a mate. Consciously related to, the animus — presented in dreams as a single figure or a group — functions as inspirator or bridge to the unconscious as source of creative, mental, or spiritual initiative and wellspring of potentiality for development. The animus functions as guide to and expedites the pursuit of impersonal endeavors. When not consciously related to, the animus causes a woman to be opinionated, argumentative, rigid, controlling, and excessively critical of herself or others.

Archetype The name Jung gave to inborn, affectively charged structures of the psyche — psychological aspects of biological instincts — which embody the essence of the most basic and profound human needs and experiences (major life transitions in physical, psychological, and spiritual growth). Archetypes underlie the universal motifs and images of societal myths as well as individual dreams, visions, and fantasies.

While archetypal motifs are common to all of humanity, their imagery is culturally differentiated. As elements of the collective unconscious, the archetypes' origins and precise nature are unknown and unknowable; but when archetypes are constellated by the appropriate outer or inner situation and their images are encountered in dream, fantasy, or projection, their existence can be inferred. The effects of archetypes are intense emotional reaction, unexpected impulses, compulsive thoughts and behavior, and fascination with their images. As with other unconscious contents, archetypes tend to be projected, and like other aspects of the psyche, they have both positive and negative potential; they are creative sources of new ideas and possibilities but are destructive if they overwhelm or immobilize the conscious ego.

Attitudes (Psychological Types)   Extroversion and introversion refer to an individual's predominant conscious attitude or response to life. An extroverted type is primarily oriented to and motivated by the outer environment, generally at ease with society and its conventions. An introverted type is more attuned to the environment within, acting and reacting in response to inner dictates. He or she tends to have an uneasy relationship with the world at large, functioning best alone or in intimate, familiar situations. To the extent that one attitude is consciously developed in an individual, the opposite attitude remains relatively unconscious, expressed indirectly by less-adapted behavior.

Chthonic Mother   The archetype of the earth mother, the chthonic mother is dark, demonic, and that aspect of the mother archetype that is most remote and inaccessible to the consciousness of contemporary women because it is identified with the values of patriarchal society. Mythological embodiments of the chthonic mother include Tiamat, goddess of primitive chaos, and Erishkigal, queen of the underworld. Many other goddesses, among them Nut, Ishtar, Hathor, Bast, Kali, Freyja, Hecate, Persephone, and the Virgin Mary in her association with the moon and as the Pieta, possess chthonic aspects through their connections with earth, blood, blackness, death, the underworld, night, the night sky, moon, and ocean. ("Chthonic," from the Greek *chthon*, meaning "earth," is commonly used in a more limited sense to denote the underworld nature or aspect of deities.)

Complex   A network of affectively charged ideas and images rooted in an archetype. Composed largely of repressed psychic contents in conflict with conscious attitudes, a complex may become partially conscious, but to the extent that a complex remains unconscious, its underlying archetype infuses it with a powerful affective charge, and it tends to erupt spontaneously into behavior, operating as if it were an autonomous personality. Memory lapses, slips of the tongue, emotional outbursts, and compulsive behavior are some ways in which complexes manifest themselves. They are harmful only to the degree that they seriously disrupt or impair ego functioning. Jung wrote, "Everyone knows nowadays that people *have complexes*. What is not so well known, though far more important theoretically, is that complexes can *have us.*"

Coniunctio   The archetype of the union (conjunction) of opposites. Borrowed from alchemy, the term refers to a stage in the process that is usually symbolized by a mystical marriage. In analytical psychology, coniunctio frequently refers to a fourfold marriage configuration of woman-man, animus-anima, or to a more developed image of wholeness in which the outer union is complemented by an inner union between animus and great mother in a woman, or anima and wise old man in a man.

Consciousness   That psychic awareness made up of all thoughts, feelings, perceptions, behaviors known to the individual at any given time and which he or she can control or act upon at will. External stimuli and content from the unconscious enter and depart consciousness as they become associated with or disconnected from the ego, which is the organizing center of consciousness. Phylogenetically, modalities of consciousness have developed slowly with the evolution of the human psyche, and, in what appears to be an ontogenetic recapitulation, consciousness emerges gradually in the childhood of each individual.

Constellate   A term adapted by Jung to denote the activation by an outer circumstance of a corresponding inner archetype or complex which is then projected onto the outer situation. The word is also used to denote the apparent attraction to the individual of an outer circumstance which synchronistically complements, compensates, or expresses an activated complex.

Counter-Transference A reactive phenomenon that can occur during analysis, whereby the patient's transference (i.e., projection) of unconscious material onto the analyst constellates in the analyst corresponding unconscious contents characteristically manifested through projection and exaggerated emotional involvement. Jung describes an "unconscious identity with the patient," a "sphere of mutual unconsciousness," which until assimilated to consciousness by the analyst will obstruct the analytic process.

Ego A complex of bodily awareness, perceptual and cognitive function, attitudes, and memories which function as the central organizer of consciousness, as the "I" which knows and wills. It is the instrument of conscious identity, of adaptation to inner and outer worlds, and of the integration of experience.

Functions (Psychological Types) The four psychological functions are processes of conscious orientation and adaptation, developing in each individual to varying degrees and in various combinations, and modified by the attitude-type. *Feeling* and *thinking*, modes of judging by valuation or intellect, respectively, are paired as rational functions; *sensation* and *intuition*, modes of perception by concrete observations or subliminal impressions, respectively, are irrational (nonreasoning) functions. The functions in each pair are opposites: if feeling is the *superior* (most developed) function operating in consciousness within the predominant conscious attitude, thinking will be the *inferior* (least developed) function, existing in the unconscious with the opposite unconscious attitude. The other pair (in this instance, sensation and intuition) are the *auxiliary* functions, which, to the extent they are assimilated into consciousness, operate as adjuncts to the superior function and bridges to the inferior function. The eight type designations are based on the combination of the predominant conscious attitude with the superior function, for example, introverted feeling type.

Hierosgamos In antiquity the mythological sacred union, or marriage, of a female divinity, usually a moon goddess, and her brother/son/lover (for example, Isis and Osiris). Traditionally associated with the hierosgamos are the themes of fertility, death, and resurrection (as well as incest), for typically the lover dies after impregnating the goddess who then bears a divine child, a symbol of wholeness produced by the union of opposites. Thus, the hierosgamos became a central rite in the fertility mystery religions of antiquity, was later represented in Gnosticism by the union of Sophia and Yaweh, and still later in alchemy as the final stage of the work, the union of king and queen, or the conjunction of sun and moon. In Christianity the hierosgamos is represented in the cycle of Mary's impregnation by the Holy Ghost, followed by the birth, death, and resurrection of Christ (more recently in history by the Assumption of Mary), and in the relation of Christ as bridegroom to the Church as bride. Jung has called the hierosgamos an image of "the earthing of the spirit and the spiritualizing of the earth."

Identification An unconscious process in which an individual's identity becomes confused in some degree with that of another person, group, cause, institution, business, profession, or with a structural element of the psyche. When prolonged or extreme, it obstructs the development or expression of innate individuality. When reasonably proportioned, it is a process of experiencing models of potential identity, which is a part of normal identity formation.

Individuation A process of psychological growth and transformation toward the realization of one's true individuality and psychological potential in the context of increased awareness of the collective aspect of the unconscious and one's own community with all of mankind. Jung regarded individuation as a task belonging primarily to the second half of life and as essentially a preparation for death in the sense of growing to perceive and approach death as a normal, integral completion of life.

Mandala A two- or three-dimensional, circular or square composition — in graphic, poetic, or dance form — having a concentric, symmetrical pattern based upon the number four or its multiples. Purely geometric in form, or in the form of flower, cross, wheel, clock, a mandala presents an image of harmony and totality, as well as of a magical or sacred enclosure which affords containment and protection. Used in certain Eastern religions as a meditative device, mandalas were frequently observed by Jung to arise spontaneously from the unconscious in dreams or fantasy as compensatory and healing symbols of order and wholeness at times of psychic confusion and fragmentation.

Mother Archetype (*Great Mother, Earth Mother*) The archetype that is the inherited pattern of potential experience of mothering and being mothered. As the fundamental archetype, endemic to all species, it embodies the impersonal, inexorable, dual standpoint of "mother nature"; in the great-round of nature, it happens that destruction, barrenness, death, and decay inevitably and necessarily alternate with creation, fertility, birth, and flowering. The mother archetype includes the negative, death-dealing, devouring mother, and devilish witch together with the positive, life-giving, nurturing mother, and spiritually exalted wise old woman. An identification with the archetype will lead to too much or too little mothering. While the personal mother is the primary awakener and early carrier of projection of the mother archetype, it can be expressed in many forms. It may be associated with elements of nature, with hollow, concave vessels, protective magic circles or mandalas, and with many animals, helpful or menacing. Because it encompasses all of nature, it corresponds to the collective unconscious, and, in its most pristine representation, it is matter itself. Bast, Isis, Aphrodite, and Kali are four of the numerous representations of the mother archetype as mother goddess.

Negative Mother (*Terrible Mother*) The evil aspect of the mother archetype. Figuratively, it is the overwhelming, destructive, threatening, and regressive power of the collective unconscious. The negative mother is represented in mythology and folklore by female figures who wreak havoc on their victims, devour them, or lure them to destruction through seduction or enchantment — Lilith, the Gorgons, Calypso, the Lorelei, sirens, harpies, Frau Holle, the Baba Yaga, wicked witches and stepmothers, and such goddesses as Ishtar, Isis, Aphrodite, Kali, Hecate, and Hel in their terrible or evil aspects. Other representations may be devouring or entwining monsters, animals, and plants — serpents, dragons, whales, spiders, bittersweet, and coffins, graves, deep water, witches' familiars and paraphernalia.

Numinous   That affective property of an activated archetype that is evoked by its image or outer manifestation and experienced directly as ineffable, mysterious, terrifying, or awesome. The numinous effect exerts upon the individual in whom it is constellated an overwhelming, obsessive, emotional fascination of sufficient force to cause an alteration of consciousness.

Persona   The mask or facade of social adaptation that an individual presents to the outer world. A complex, the core of which is the archetype of conformity, the persona is a necessary, protective part-personality that masks individuality while reflecting the person's perception of collective expectations with regard to social role and social mores. When flexible and relatively conscious, the persona is a helpful mediator between individual and society. It is dangerous psychologically only when the individual is uncritically identified with it.

Projection   The process by which an unconscious aspect of oneself is perceived in exaggerated or distorted form as an attribute of some other person, group, or object. Projection occurs when the object exhibits some degree of correspondence with the unconscious content and exerts sufficient negative or positive fascination to activate the content. Projection is always characterized by compulsion and intense emotion and will continue or recur until the projected content is recognized and accepted as belonging to oneself.

Psyche   The totality of all psychological components and processes, conscious and unconscious. The psyche is a self-regulatory dynamic system based on the flow of energy between opposites and is knowable only through its manifestations, such as ideas, attitudes, feelings, impulses, fantasies, behavior, and moods.

Self   Archetype of wholeness and order, at once the center and the container of the totality of the psyche. The self is a function, uniting all pairs of opposites, of a source of energy which is the instigator and

284

director of the individuation process. It is manifested by way of projection, by means of symbols (notably geometric forms, especially the square and the circle, savior and hero figures, the child, various animals, insects and plants, precious stones, and images of a fourfold nature), and by the conflict of opposites, a conscious confrontation which is an essential precondition to an experience of this archetype. Jung has referred to the self as "the God within us."

Shadow The dark, unconscious underside of the ego personality. Its collective and personal aspects contain the repressed, primitive, inferior, discarded, and despised qualities, as well as the unrealized potentials of a group or individual. When the personal shadow is unacknowledged and unintegrated, the conscious personality tends to be two-dimensional and inauthentic; that is, the greater the degree of identification with the persona, the darker and more autonomous the personal shadow tends to be. In dreams and daily life the personal shadow appears as or is projected onto a person of the same sex as the individual, who frequently experiences the object of the projection as particularly irritating or intolerable. The collective shadow is projected onto an individual or an alien group — the scapegoat phenomenon. The archetypal shadow is symbolically represented by such figures as the devil, tempter, trickster, or witch.

Symbol An image by which a complex of ideas, feelings, and experience can be most efficiently and economically represented. A symbol can be only partially assimilated into consciousness and remains an inexhaustible source of potential transformation of consciousness.

Synchronicity The meaningful coincidence of two or more unrelated psychic or physical states or events which can be explained by their common connection with an activated archetype, for example, the simultaneous appearance to different individuals of identical thoughts, dreams, or the occurrence of a psychic state or product with a parallel physical state or outer event.

Transcendent Function A pivotal, symbol-forming function, comprising elements of both the conscious and unconscious areas of the psyche.

The transcendent function mediates between the conscious and unconscious and transforms their relationship from one of destructive opposition to that of constructive reciprocity and synthesis. Activated by a psychological impasse arising from conflict between opposing attitudes or demands of conscious and unconscious — extroversion/introversion, thinking/feeling, sensation/intuition, masculinity/femininity, spirituality/sensuality, individual/collective — the transcendent function constellates a uniting symbol which synthesizes and transcends the opposites. When assimilated into consciousness, the symbol reveals new possibilities of release from the deadlock and renewal of energy.

Trickster   Image of the archetype of mischievousness, unexpectedness, disorder, amorality, the trickster is an archetypal shadow figure that represents a primordial, dawning consciousness. Compensating rigid or overly righteous collective attitudes, it functions collectively as a cathartic safety valve for pent-up social pressures, a reminder of humankind's primitive origins and the fallibility of its institutions. Frequently uniting the opposites in itself, the trickster can have transformative powers as a transcendent symbol. Constellation of the archetype in an individual bogged down in the sterility of an excessively entrenched, well-ordered, or one-sided consciousness can provide access to creative possibilities in the collective unconscious, helping to restore psychic balance. Thwarting of conscious intentions, inner upheavals, outer mishaps, disrupted plans are likely indicators that the trickster has been constellated.

(The) Unconscious   The unknown region of the psyche, comprised of two levels: the personal and the collective. The unconscious can be characterized only in terms of the psychological phenomena apparently generated by it (and variously referred to as unconscious "products," "contents," "material," or "activity"), such as dreams or fantasies, projections, mental blocks, memory lapses, inappropriate reactions, involuntary behavior, unexpected thoughts, feelings, wishes, impulses. It is regarded as a source of consciousness that is progressively enriched by the assimilation of unconscious contents. Unconscious content appears to compensate any one-sided attitude or view held in consciousness, thereby maintaining or restoring psychic equilibrium and advancing the progress of psychic growth or individuation.

Wise Old Woman Image of a positive aspect of the mother archetype as transformative, spiritual, feminine wisdom, informed by the heart and instincts, down to earth, concrete, organic, pertaining to psychological growth, to personal relatedness, and to material expression of spiritual ideas. In a woman's psyche, the wise old woman is a mistress of initiation, or psychopomp, imposing suffering and sacrifice, guiding the woman toward psychological transformation while she remains rooted in her female nature. The wise old woman is closely related to the archetype of the self and is sometimes referred to as the feminine self or feminine aspect of the self. Some representations in mythology, folklore, and dreams include Sophia, Wisdom or Sapientia, priestess, sibyl, prophetess, good witch, city, flower, and transformative vessels — baptismal font, chemical retort, pressure cooker.